D1060330

TOP 50

MILITARY AIRCRAFT

Thomas Newdick

CHARTWELL
BOOKS

This edition published in 2017 by Chartwell Books, an imprint of The Quarto Group,
142 West 36th Street, 4th Floor, New York, NY 10018, USA
T (212) 779-4972 F (212) 779-6058 www.QuartoKnows.com

Copyright © 2017 Amber Books Ltd.
74–77 White Lion Street
London N1 9PF, United Kingdom
www.amberbooks.co.uk

10 9 8 7 6 5 4 3 2 1

ISBN: 978-0-7858-3562-2

Project Editor: Michael Spilling
Design: Colin Fielder
Picture Research: Terry Forshaw
Additional text: Martin J. Dougherty

Printed in China

CONTENTS

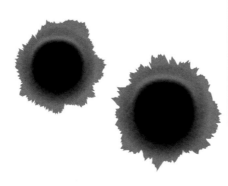

Introduction

Counting from 50 down to the greatest at number 1, this book rates the 50 best aircraft in history. Each type is selected based on what made it superior to other airplanes of the same period.

How to go about selecting the 50 greatest military aircraft? There is no shortage of contenders when it comes to making a choice, and a range of criteria can be used. However subjective, the aircraft that appear in the following pages all fulfil certain key requirements.

Selecting the 50 greatest fixed-wing military aircraft began with identifying those warplanes that are best remembered for their significant impact on entry to service. The fact that only fixed-wing types were considered made the job somewhat easier, ruling out some of the greatest military helicopter designs that would have otherwise held their own in such a list.

BATTLE TESTED

Most of those aircraft featured made their impact once thrown into battle. Success in combat is, after all, the true benchmark of a great military aircraft. On the other hand, the pace of aircraft development – especially during wartime – means that many aircraft that saw a successful combat debut were rendered obsolescent relatively quickly. Prime examples of this are the Fokker E series and the Junkers Ju 87. These two German designs both heralded a major change in the way air combat was fought – the former in World War I, the second in World War II. However, the Eindecker's dominance – the so-called 'Fokker scourge' – had come to an end by early 1916. The Stuka, meanwhile, became an enduring symbol of the early successes of the Nazi German war machine, but had been rendered obsolescent in its original role by 1941.

It is perhaps worth considering some of the types that almost made the list, and the reasons why they fell short. In the World War I era, perhaps the most obvious omission, for English-speaking readers, at least, is the Sopwith Camel. The Camel was highly manoeuvrable, and its pilots shot down over 1,200 enemy aircraft. However, it was outclassed relatively quickly, and was increasingly used for ground support. Overall, the rival SE5a proved a more enduring and revolutionary design.

Perhaps the finest World War II aircraft to miss out is the Petlyakov Pe-2, a Soviet equivalent to the British Mosquito and German Ju 88. Although it was the Allies' most prolific twin-engined tactical aircraft of the war, it lacked the step-change in performance heralded by the Mosquito, and was never quite as adaptable as the Ju 88. The Junkers 52/3m, the *Luftwaffe*'s classic World War II transport workhorse, was arguably more influential on commercial aviation, and its post-war exploits were certainly bettered by the Douglas C-47, which is included here.

From the Cold War era, a case could be made for including the Douglas A-1 Skyraider, a hard-hitting

An F-4E Phantom II from the 81st Tactical Fighter Squadron releases a stick of Mark 82 227kg (500lb) bombs over a practice range. The Phantom can carry more than 8,400kg (18,000lbs) of weapons on nine external hardpoints, including air-to-air missiles, air-to-ground missiles and bombs.

A flight of Junkers Ju 87D Stukas en route to a target on the Leninfgrad Front in Soviet Russia during the Eastern Front campaign of 1942. The German dive-bomber was a revoutionary aircraft for its time, providing tactical support for the German Army in the early years of World War II.

if antiquated close-support aircraft that served with distinction in Southeast Asia. On the other hand, the fact it served so well for so long was less a result of the excellence of its design, but the emergence of a new type of warfare for which more modern designs proved ill suited.

The Fairchild Republic A-10 Thunderbolt II may well be the modern type most deserving of a place in the list, not least for its stubborn refusal to bow out of service, despite repeated attempts by the US Air Force to discard it. However, it has achieved greatness in what is arguably a niche role – fixed-wing close air support conducted at low level – while many of its contemporaries are true multi-role masters.

While the vast majority of the 50 aircraft have been tested in large-scale conflicts, there are a handful of exceptions: aircraft that have proven genuinely successful without major battle honours. Chief among these are the Breguet XIX, an outstanding interwar design that was still useful enough to fly on anti-partisan operations in World War II, despite first flying in 1922. The Sukhoi Su-27 family has seen some action in small-scale conflicts, but its excellence lies in the fact that it has been one of the most successful modern fighters in terms of sales, as well as serving as the basis for a multitude of further developments.

Above all, I hope this list will encourage discussion and debate among those that read this book.

Douglas SBD-3 Dauntless

The Douglas Dauntless SBD (Scout Bomber, Douglas) was the standard US Navy attack aircraft at the outbreak of World War II. Although obsolescent, it gave good service and contributed to some of the most important victories of the conflict.

The dive bomber was a low-tech solution to the problem of delivering unguided bombs with any degree of accuracy. Diving steeply towards the target, the dive bomber reduced the margin of error compared to a conventional level approach. This was especially important when attacking fast-moving ships at sea.

Developed for the US Navy, the Dauntless SBD-1 model proved to have too short a range for naval operations. This was rectified on the SBD-2 model. The US Navy took delivery of both models, transferring the SBD-1s to the Marine Corps. However, the Dauntless was very vulnerable due to a lack of armour, and when the fall of France prevented a delivery of the improved SBD-3 model to its intended users, the navy took those and ordered more. The SBD-3 was designed to take punishment, and did not have the folding wings then

SBD-3 DAUNTLESS

This Dauntless was assigned to USS *Ranger* during the Operation Torch landings in North Africa during November 1942. Air power protected the fleet in addition to striking targets inland.

MARKINGS

Originally, US aircraft had a red 'meatball' in the centre of their white star, but this could cause identification issues when confused with the Rising Sun emblem of Japanese aircraft.

SPECIFICATIONS: SBD-3

Crew: 2

Length: 10.09m (33ft 1.5in)

Wingspan: 12.66m (41ft 6.5in)

Loaded weight: 4717kg (10,400lb)

Powerplant: Wright R1820-52

Maximum speed: 402km/h (250mph)

Armament: 2 x 12.7mm (0.50in) machine gun fixed forward, 2 x 7.62mm (0.30in) machine guns in rear defensive mount, 1 x 453kg (1000lb) or 227kg (500lb) bomb on centre pylon, 1 x 45kg (100lb) under each wing

A flight of 'Slow but Deadly' Dauntless SBDs shortly before the outbreak of World War II. The aircraft wear typical naval camouflage for the era.

common on carrier aircraft. It was also armoured, and mounted a pair of forward-firing 12.7mm (0.50in) machine guns in addition to a defensive 7.62mm (0.30in) machine gun in a traversing rear mount. This weapon was later upgraded to a twin mount. The SBD-3 could carry a

453kg (1000lb) bomb on the centreline and a light bomb or other munition under each wing. The SBD-3 was the current version at the critical battles of Midway and Guadalcanal.

LATER VARIANTS

Despite the obsolescence of the basic design, SBD-4, 5 and 6 variants were produced. The SBD-4 was equipped with airborne radar, which necessitated an upgraded electrical system. The SBD-5 version was the most numerous of all, with a more powerful engine, but was heavier, resulting in overall similar performance and shorter range. This was offset with 'plumbed' pylons allowing external fuel tanks to be carried at the expense of ordnance. It also featured improved sights that enhanced bombing accuracy. The final version, SBD-6, arrived in 1944 but never went to front-line combat units. Instead it was used for training and patrol work. A variant was produced for the US Army Air Force, designated A-24 banshee, but was not a success and was soon withdrawn from service.

COMBAT SERVICE

The Dauntless got off to a bad start when numerous Marine Corps aircraft were destroyed on the ground during the 7 December 1941 attack on Pearl Harbor.

The SBD was the mainstay of US carrier-borne strike forces in the months that followed, taking part in raids against Japanese-held islands. SBDs sank one carrier and damaged another at the Battle of the Coral Sea in May 1942, and arguably turned the tide of the Pacific War at Midway in June. In part due to the sacrifice of the Devastator torpedo bombers that attacked before them, SBDs sank three carriers at Midway and damaged another so badly it had to be scuttled.

LONG SERVICE

The Dauntless was overdue for replacement in service well before it won its laurels at Midway, but the development process for its successor – the Curtiss Helldiver – did not go smoothly, and so the Dauntless soldiered on. It saw action at Guadalcanal in 1942–43 and took part in the Allied landings in North Africa in 1942. In addition to

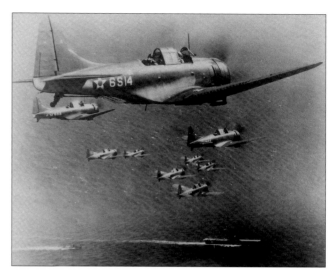

Squadrons operating from USS Enterprise *(CV-6) were assigned call signs based on their role and home carrier. VB-6 and VS-6 both operated Dauntlesses, with VS-6 (pictured here) specializing in the scouting role.*

DIVE BOMBER

Centreline bombs were held on a lever device that swung them clear of the aircraft when released. This prevented the bomb from striking the aircraft's propeller when dropped in a steep dive.

SBD-5 DAUNTLESS

This machine served with the US Marine Corps scout squadron in the Caribbean in 1944. It wears a typical 1944 Atlantic theatre colour scheme.

LATER INSIGNIA

In mid-1943, red bars were added to the insignia of US combat aircraft to aid recognition at a distance. The practice was not universally followed.

sinking more enemy warships than any other aircraft in the Pacific theatre, Dauntless aircraft also attacked land targets in Norway in 1943. Examples continued to serve as an anti-submarine platform after the SBD had been withdrawn from the strike role.

The SBD was withdrawn from combat operations after the end of the war, but a force in French hands served until 1949, and in a training role until the mid-1950s.

MiG-15

The Mikoyan-Gurevich MiG-15 was developed to intercept bombers, but proved a highly effective dogfighter. It was widely exported, with examples serving in the Chinese air force as well as the forces of Warsaw Pact nations.

Experience in World War II indicated that a powerful cannon armament was required to shoot down bombers; machine guns simply did not do enough damage to cripple a large aircraft. An interceptor also had to be fast enough to reach the bombers' altitude before they could penetrate far into friendly airspace.

NEW DESIGN

In response to an official requirement for such an aircraft, design work began in 1946 on what would become the MiG-15. The engine was copied from a Rolls-Royce unit sold to Russia, and other aspects of the design drew on expertise obtained from Germany at the end of World War II. The result was the Soviet Union's first aircraft with a pressurized cockpit containing an ejection seat. The MiG-15's first flight was in December 1947.

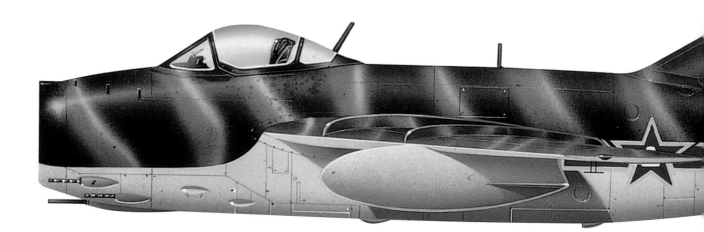

MIG-15BIS

A MiG-15bis wearing the colours of the Hungarian Air Force. The stubby MiG-15 with its large air intake was becoming dated by the mid-1960s, but remained an effective air-to-air platform.

CHINESE MIG-15

This aircraft fought during the Korean War for the People's Liberation Army (PLA) in 1950. Note the prominent wing fences, which reduce the tendency of swept-wing aircraft to stall due to spanwise (rather than front-to-back) airflow over the wings.

SPECIFICATIONS (MIG-15BIS)

Crew: 1

Length: 10.86m (35ft 7.5in)

Wingspan: 10.8m (33ft 0.75in)

Loaded weight: 6045kg (13,327lb)

Powerplant: Kilmov VK-1 Turbojet

Maximum speed: 1075km/h (668mph)

Armament: 1 x 37mm (1.45in) cannon, 2 x 23mm (0.9in) cannon

SERVICE IN KOREA

The Western powers became aware of the MiG-15 during the Korean War, when six MiGs clashed with a force of piston-engined P-51 Mustangs. Although the MiG-15 performed well, an upgraded version designated MiG-15bis was quickly put into service. This variant had a more powerful engine and lighter weight, improving range and performance.

MiGs flew out of Chinese bases, and could only be engaged once they crossed the Yalu River into Korea. Their presence changed the nature of the air war in Korea; up to that time the UN forces had air superiority and could operate against ground targets more or less at will. Losses of B-29 bombers mounted, forcing the move to less effective night missions, and air-to-air clashes became deadly for UN pilots.

The first jet-vs-jet air combat took place on 8 November 1950, when a US F-80 Shooting Star shot down a MiG-15. The F-80 was outclassed by the MiG, however, with the superior experience of US pilots offsetting this disadvantage to some degree. The F-86 Sabre replaced the F-80 in the fighter role, but its armament of six machine guns was still inferior to the cannon of the MiG-15. Claims of large numbers of air-to-air kills on both sides seem inflated, but overall the more experienced US pilots came out on top over the course of the conflict.

MIG-15UTI 'MIDGET'
'Midget' is the NATO reporting name for the MiG-15 UTI two-seat trainer. This example is in Iraqi service circa 1991.

ENGINE
The MiG-15bis used an engine developed from a copy of the Rolls-Royce Nene engine, which powered several contemporary fighters.

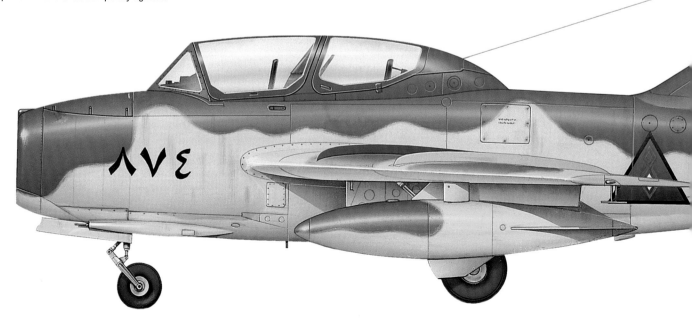

A surviving two-seat MiG-15 on display at a modern air show. Some air forces are known to have retained their MiG-15s almost up to the end of the 1990s.

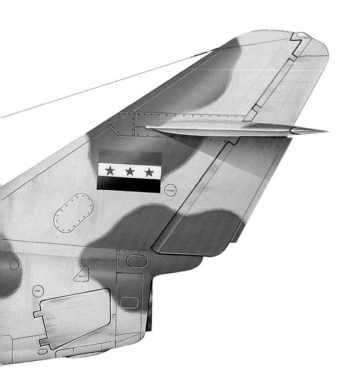

WORLDWIDE SUCCESS

The MiG-15 was primarily built in the Soviet Union, but also in Czechoslovakia and Poland. It served with air forces of various Warsaw Pact nations until the late 1960s, with some remaining in service as trainers after this. The MiG-15 was also adopted by the Chinese air force and by Egypt, where it saw action during the Suez Crisis. A MiG-15 shot down a British-designed Gloster Meteor that was in Israeli service, demonstrating once again the superiority of faster swept-wing fighters over first-generation straight-wing jets.

In 1958, a MiG-15 achieved the rather dubious distinction of being the first victim of the Sidewinder air-to-air missile, but overall the design proved highly effective. It was developed into the MiG-17, which saw action in Vietnam against US fighters. Other variants of the MiG-15 included a two-seater interceptor, a strike variant, several reconnaissance aircraft and trainers. Chinese-built versions (named Jianjiji F2 or J2) were further exported, with Russian and Chinese examples flying in the air forces of minor nations long after being withdrawn from service elsewhere.

Gotha bombers

The Gotha carried out raids on London and other targets in England, contributing to the belief that 'the bomber will always get through', which shaped inter-war doctrine and the development of more advanced bombers.

Air attacks against targets in England began in June 1915 using Zeppelins, which initially proved very difficult to counter. The bombload carried by these expensive, slow airships was quite small and the raids, although very frightening, did little material damage. Indeed, it has been estimated that the cost of the Zeppelin campaign against England was far higher than the damage caused. However, there is more to strategy than dollar values of

targets destroyed. The raids damaged British morale and necessitated the withdrawal of some fighter squadrons from the fighting over the Western Front, weakening the British effort there.

Zeppelin raids continued throughout the war, but from late 1916 onward a viable alternative existed in the form of the twin-engined Gotha bomber. The Gotha was challenging to fly and land, and tended to catch fire if a hard landing

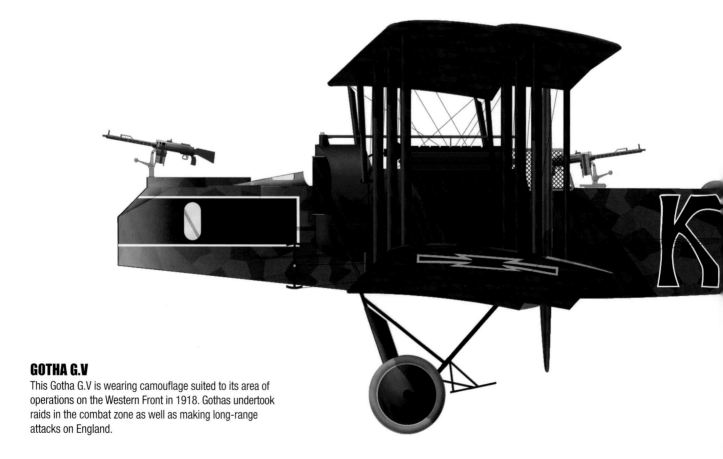

GOTHA G.V
This Gotha G.V is wearing camouflage suited to its area of operations on the Western Front in 1918. Gothas undertook raids in the combat zone as well as making long-range attacks on England.

Removing a section of the trailing wing edge created clearance for the 'pusher' configuration engines. Some ordnance was carried under the wing, but most was in an internal bay.

WEAPONS

The limited field of fire available to the Gotha's defensive machine guns is obvious. A firing tunnel through the rear fuselage provided a novel solution to the problem.

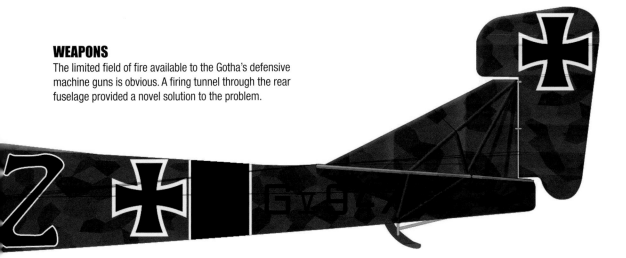

FUSELAGE

The Gotha's fuselage was of plywood and fabric over a frame of wood and steel. Although it was a large target, many hits would go straight through the aircraft without damaging anything important.

GOTHA G.IV

A Gotha G.IV operating over Flanders in 1917. The aircraft's design created very significant drag, contributing to its low speed and general clumsiness.

spilled fuel onto hot engine components, but it was capable of delivering a reasonable payload over a long distance. Fewer than 20 Gothas were in service by the end of 1916, but they made a big impression on those they attacked. The first major raid on England was made in May 1917 and involved 21 Gothas. Raids continued, many made at altitudes that prevented an effective response. However, by 1918, the fighter response was far more effective and losses were significant.

IMPROVED HEAVY BOMBERS

The initial Gotha G.I was developed into the G.II, which served on the Eastern Front. Engine troubles were cured by creating the G.III version, which was followed in 1917 by the Gotha G.IV. Development of this aircraft may have been assisted by the capture of a downed Handley Page O/400.

The Gotha V arrived in August 1917, featuring improved aerodynamics achieved mainly by streamlining the engine nacelles. The G.Va variant gained a biplane tail and the final G.Vb was given a nosewheel to improve safety on landing. A reconnaissance variant, designated Gotha G.VII, had a redesigned fuselage and the 'pusher' engines of the bomber reversed.

GOTHA G.IV

A Gotha G.IV in the colours of Kaghol (bombing unit) 3, which made the first daylight raid on London in June 1917.

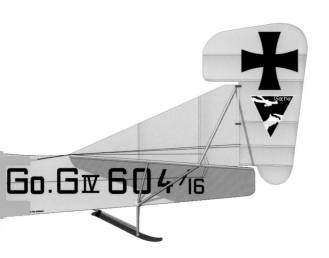

SPECIFICATIONS (G.IV)

SPECIFICATIONS (G.IV)

Crew: 3

Length: 12.2m (40ft 0in)

Wingspan: 23.7m (77ft 9in)

Loaded weight: 3648kg (8042lb)

Powerplant: 2 × Mercedes D.IVa, 193kW (260hp) each

Maximum speed: 135km/h (83mph)

Armament: 2 or 3 × 7.92mm (0.312in) Parabellum LMG 14 machine guns; up to 500kg (1100lb) of bombs

THE GOTHA IN COMBAT

Although it was a slow, unmanoeuvrable and large target, the Gotha could defend itself with two machine guns – one mounted in the nose and one at the rear of the crew compartment. Fighter pilots quickly learned that the best approach was to attack from behind and underneath, where the bomber had no defensive armament. As a counter, a novel 'firing tunnel' was incorporated on some examples, enabling the rear gunner to see and fire downwards.

Gothas also protected one another by flying in close formation, engaging an attacking fighter with fire from several machine guns. This was the forerunner of the 'combat box' tactic used during World War II, and proved effective against the fighters of the day. Although the damage inflicted by Gotha raids was small by the standards of World War II, the destruction wrought on cities that had previously been considered safe from attack caused a change in military thinking. The bomber, it was reasoned, would always get through and could level the cities of any combatant. The possession of a powerful bomber fleet was thus an essential requirement for any major power. This thinking persisted almost until the beginning of World War II, resulting in an over-emphasis on bombers at the expense of defensive fighters.

English Electric Canberra

47

The Canberra was developed to defeat interception by flying too high and too fast to be caught by fighters. After a long career as a strike platform, the Canberra continued to fly as a reconnaissance platform.

By the middle of World War II, the adage that 'the bomber will always get through' had been challenged. Crippling losses to air defences and fighter interception made long-range strategic air warfare a dubious proposition. Even heavily armed bombers flying in mutually supporting 'boxes' could be successfully intercepted. A different solution was required.

The Canberra was the first British jet bomber. Bearing a visual resemblance to the Gloster Meteor fighter, it carried no defensive armament. Instead, the Canberra was designed to operate at altitudes where fighters and

flak could not reach it. The guided missile was at that time in its infancy, so even if a fighter could reach a high enough altitude to make an interception, it had to do so during the limited time available. Missiles widened the envelope somewhat, but the Canberra still had a good chance to carry out its mission and withdraw without coming under attack.

THE CANBERRA IN SERVICE

The first Canberras went into British service in 1951, with an improved version appearing in 1954. The first

CANBERRA PR.MK 9

The PR.9 photo-reconnaissance variant of the Canberra was still in RAF service until 2006, serving in numerous conflicts during the second half of the 20th century.

SPECIFICATIONS (CANBERRA B.6)

Crew: 3

Length: 19.96m (65ft 6in)

Wingspan: 19.51m (64ft)

Loaded weight: 20,865kg (46,000lb)

Powerplant: 2 x Rolls-Royce Avon 109 Turbojet

Maximum speed: 973km/h (605mph)

Armament: 2724kg (6000lb) internal bomb load; gun pods or additional ordnance on wings

The Canberra proved easy to fly and had few vices, requiring a minimal conversion time from other aircraft.

operational use was during the Malayan Emergency and the Suez Crisis, where the Canberra was sufficiently impressive that the US air force adopted it.

The arrival of the Valiant, which was the first of the 'V-Bombers' and capable of delivering a larger payload over a longer range, allowed the Canberra to move from a high-altitude bombing role to low-level strike operations. This included tactical strikes but also delivery of nuclear weapons from low level. The Canberra's high

WOODEN TAIL

The wooden tail of the Canberra belonged to an earlier era, but it was still flying as late as Operation Iraqi Freedom in 2003.

speed enabled it to escape the blast from its weapon. As a result, although the Canberra was phased out of the conventional bombing role in the mid-1960s, some squadrons were retained in the nuclear strike role.

Other users found the Canberra highly effective. Australian Canberras took part in strikes in Malaya in the late 1950s and later served in the Vietnam War, where they flew almost 12,000 sorties for the loss of just two aircraft. US-operated Canberras also saw action in Vietnam.

The widely exported Canberra was sometimes encountered on both sides of a conflict, such as the Indo–Pakistani war of 1971. Argentine Canberras flew against British forces during the 1982 Falklands War, with one lost to an air-to-air missile and one to a ship-launched surface-to-air missile.

BAC CANBERRA T.MK.17

The Canberra T.Mk17 was a specialist electronic warfare training variant, housing its EW suite in a redesigned nose section.

THE ENDURING CANBERRA

The Canberra was retired from bombing operations by the RAF in 1972, but reconnaissance versions remained in service for many years afterwards. RAF Canberras were deployed as recently as the early 2000s, conducting reconnaissance over Iraq and Afghanistan. Earlier missions were not exclusively military; the Canberra was extensively used for map-making, notably over parts of Africa.

NASA continues to operate three modified Canberras as high-altitude research platforms. Although other aircraft can fly higher, the Canberra can carry a considerable weight of equipment to a high altitude, and provides a stable platform from which to conduct delicate scientific work. There are currently no plans to retire these aircraft as there is quite simply no better platform for the kind of work they do.

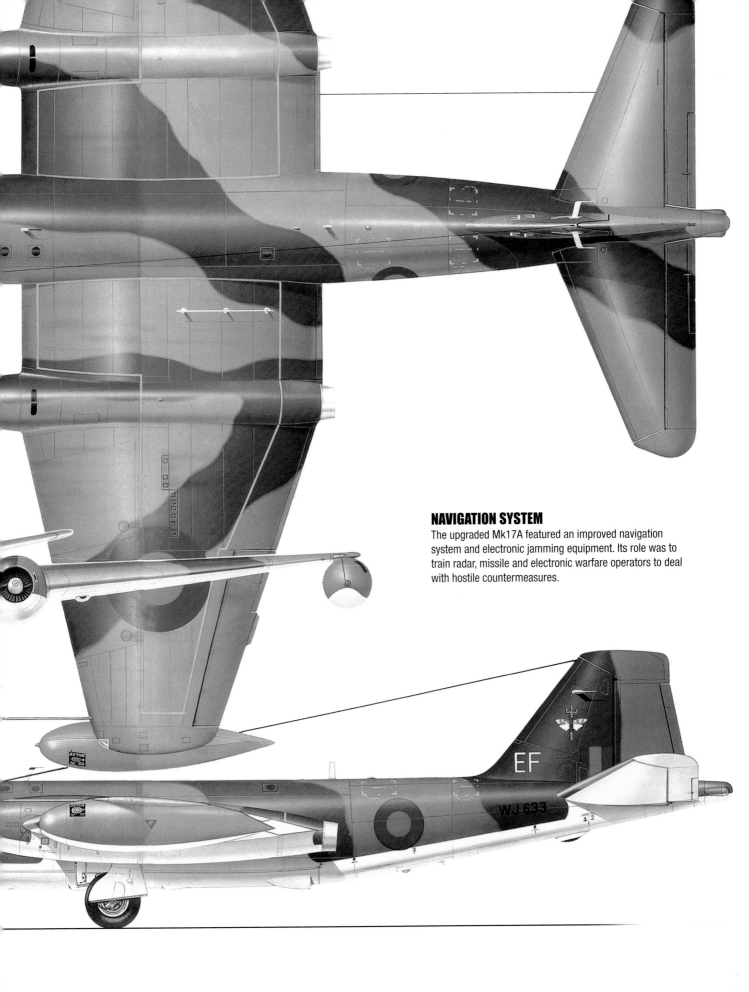

NAVIGATION SYSTEM

The upgraded Mk17A featured an improved navigation system and electronic jamming equipment. Its role was to train radar, missile and electronic warfare operators to deal with hostile countermeasures.

EF

WJ 633

Yak-3

The Yak-3 was a highly manoeuvrable fighter equipped with a powerful armament for its day. Its climbing and turning characteristics made it superior to any opponent it was likely to face.

The aircraft that went into service as the Yak-1 had other designations during its development, but served as the Yak-1 against the German invasion of Russia in 1941. Like many Russian designs, it was intended to be as simple as possible in order to facilitate mass production. This resulted in a small and lightweight aircraft that was available in sufficient numbers to contest airspace with the Luftwaffe.

The Yak-1 was inferior to the German Bf-109, but not enormously so. In the hands of a good pilot it was a deadly opponent, and the appearance of the improved Yak-3 in 1943 tipped the balance the other way. The Yak-3 was developed from a Yak-1 variant designated Yak-1M, with plywood used for much of the fuselage.

The wings were also of wood.

DOGFIGHTING WITH THE LUFTWAFFE

The Yak-3 first flew in 1943, but was not available for combat operations in any numbers until July 1944. Kill ratios were high, with aggressively handled Yak-3s routinely taking on superior numbers of German fighters and winning. Indeed, so effective was this aircraft that instructions were issued to German pilots not to get involved in a dogfight at low altitude with it if at all possible.

The Luftwaffe countered by changing tactics, attempting to 'bounce' Russian fighters by diving from above. Speed gained in the dive would take the German

YAKOVLEV YAK-1M

A Yak-1M, circa 1943, painted in white winter camouflage. The Yak-1M was designed to support and protect ground-attack aircraft, and was best suited to combat at relatively low altitudes.

pilots rapidly out of reach once their first pass was made, making it impossible for the Yaks to draw their opponents into a turning fight.

The key to the Yak-3's success was its light weight, most of which was positioned close to the centreline. The 20mm (0.78in) cannon was directly on the centreline and fired through the propeller hub, with two 12.7mm (0.5in) machine guns on the engine cowling. Many contemporary fighters had guns in the wings, increasing the amount of effort required to roll the aircraft and therefore reducing its turning capabilities.

The Yak-3 proved capable of out-turning the fighters of other wartime powers, and remained effective even when it came up against the upgraded Bf-109G. It was not perfect, however. The plywood construction was fragile and could be damaged by high-g manoeuvres, and both the engines and the control systems suffered

A row of Yak-3s of the Normandie-Niemen regiment stand idle shortly after the squadron was equipped with the type in July 1944. The Normandie-Niemen regiment was made up of Free-French pilots who fought as part of the Red Army on the Eastern Front.

YAK-3

The Yak-3 mounted very similar armament to the Messerschmitt Bf-109, with a cannon and two heavy machine guns grouped close to the centreline of the aircraft.

PNEUMATIC CONTROLS

The Yak-3 used a pneumatic system to move its control surfaces rather than a hydraulic one as with many other aircraft.

An early production Yak-3. Luftwaffe pilots were warned to avoid the fast, lightweight, super-manoeuvrable fighter in combat if possible.

YAKOVLEV YAK-1M
A Yak-3 in Free Polish colours. The Yak-3 was supplied to Poland and Yugoslavia, where it served into the 1950s.

from mechanical issues. Operational range was also quite limited.

VARIANTS

Numerous variants of the Yak-3 were produced, some of them testing different construction materials and methods. Some Yak-3s were given an uprated engine, resulting in very high top speed and rate of climb. Other experiments were less of a success; a tankbuster version was produced in small numbers but the light Yak-3 proved an unsuitable platform for the 45mm (1.7in) cannon that was this variant's main armament.

The Yak-3 was eventually supplanted by other fighters in the same series. The Yak-7, originally intended as a trainer, was put into production as a single-seat fighter and proved highly effective. The Yak-9 was superior to all German piston-engined fighters and was produced for a short while after the end of the war. The Yak-9P version armed the North Korean air force at the outbreak of the Korean conflict.

SPECIFICATIONS (YAK-3)

Crew: 1

Length: 8.5m (27ft 10in)

Wingspan: 9.2m (30ft 2in)

Loaded weight: 2692kg (5864lb)

Powerplant: Klimov VK-105PF-2 V-12 piston engine

Maximum speed: 646km/h (401mph)

Armament: 1 x Sh-VAK 20mm (0.78in) cannon on centreline, 2 x Beresin 12.7mm (0.50in) machine guns on engine cowling

Breguet XIX

The widely exported Breguet XIX set a record for the first non-stop Paris to New York flight in September 1930. As a warplane, it enjoyed a long and successful career in France, Spain, Greece, Yugoslavia and Poland.

The Breguet XIX was developed from a World War I light bomber, the Breguet XIV. A metal-framed biplane, the Breguet XIX used metal covering on the front of the fuselage and fabric on the rear. The wings were also covered in fabric. The design entered production in 1924. About 2000 were built in France, with another 700 or so licence-built in Spain.

In addition to these major users, the XIX was exported to Yugoslavia, Romania and Poland, where it formed the backbone of the air force in the 1920s, and to China. It was intended for the light strike and reconnaissance role, which required a good operating radius. This provided useful in peacetime, with several long-distance records set by users worldwide.

MANY VARIANTS

The commonest military variants of the Breguet XIX were the A2 (reconnaissance) and B2 (bomber) versions. A night

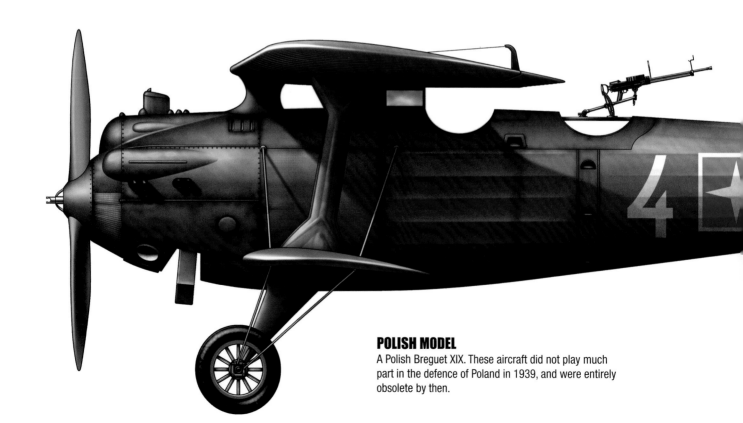

POLISH MODEL
A Polish Breguet XIX. These aircraft did not play much part in the defence of Poland in 1939, and were entirely obsolete by then.

Flying a Breguet XIX, Maurice Bellonte and Dieudonné Costes performed the first westbound crossing of the North Atlantic, from Paris to New York, in 1930.

ARMAMENT
The twin-Lewis-gun defensive mount was common on many World War I and early inter-war designs, but was ineffective against fast, armoured World War II fighters.

fighter, designated CN2, was produced with additional forward-firing armament. Other minor variants were produced for export customers, typically using different engines.

The bomber version of the Breguet XIX was capable of carrying a small bombload in an internal bay or larger ordnance externally, while the reconnaissance variant carried a camera instead. Both primary versions were equipped with a fixed machine gun for the pilot and a twin machine gun mount for use by the observer. An additional downward-facing weapon was fitted for the ground attack role.

Numerous specialist versions of the Breguet XIX were created for record-setting purposes, achieving a number of remarkable exploits. Flights from one continent to another were a very difficult undertaking in the 1920s, but the XIX was one of the aircraft that demonstrated what could be done with flights from Japan to Paris then London, and from Brussels to Leopoldville. Most famous of these

45

RECORD BREAKER

At the time of its introduction, the XIX was faster than many fighters, as well as possessing a much greater operating radius. This made it attractive to record-setting pioneers. The first non-stop flight from France to the USA took more than 37 hours – a remarkable feat of endurance for the crew.

BREGUET BRE.19 A.2

The record-breaking Point d'Interrogation ('Question Mark') was a unique aircraft with an enclosed cockpit, based on a civilian sport variant designated Breguet XIX GR.

SPECIFICATIONS (BREGUET XIX A.2)

Crew: 2

Length: 9.5m (31ft 3in)

Wingspan: 14.8m (48ft 8in)

Loaded weight: 2347kg (5175lb)

Powerplant: Renault 12KD V12 engine

Maximum speed: 234km/h (146mph)

Armament: 1 x Vickers 7.7mm (0.303in) machine gun fixed forward, 2 x Lewis 7.7mm (0.303in) machine guns on observer's mount, 1 x Lewis 7.7mm (0.303in) machine gun on ventral mount

record-setting aircraft was the Point d'Interrogation, which made the first non-stop East-to-West Transatlantic flight in 1929, flying from Paris to New York.

THE BREGUET XIX IN SERVICE

Essentially an advanced World War I-era design, the Breguet XIX was obsolete by the outbreak of World War II. However, the design gave good service in the 1920s and 1930s, during various colonial incidents, rebellions and 'brushfire wars'. Strike aircraft were useful for 'colonial policing' and were at times used to make punitive raids against distant targets. Previously, such a raid would have required a hazardous operation by a 'flying column' of fast-moving ground forces, which still gave no guarantee of reaching the target before rebels or insurgents moved on. Aircraft provided a rapid response to which most colonial opponents had no reply.

The Breguet XIX served in the Spanish Civil War and was an effective strike aircraft, but suffered badly at the hands of more modern fighter aircraft. The same fate was met by Yugoslav aircraft during the German invasion of 1941. Capable of only 234km/h (146mph), it was an aircraft from an earlier time and simply could not survive in a changed air-warfare environment. Greek XIXs did undertake some useful reconnaissance work during the Axis invasion of 1940, but again were too slow and cumbersome to operate freely within range of hostile fighters.

WING CONFIGURATION

The Breguet XIX was a sesquiplane design; that is, it had one large wing and a smaller one. Among other advantages, this permitted better downward visibility than identical upper and lower wings.

Su-27 family

The Sukhoi Su-27m, given the NATO reporting name 'Flanker', is very large for a fighter aircraft. Numerous variants and developed versions have appeared since its introduction in 1982.

The Su-27 was developed as a high-end air superiority fighter, comparable to (and intended to contend with) the US F-15 Eagle. It is visually very similar to the MiG-29 'Fulcrum' but is larger and more capable, with a greater missile capability and much longer range. The partnership between the two is similar to that of the US F-15 and F-16; an expensive air superiority platform complemented by a cheaper short-range fighter that can be deployed in greater numbers for the same cost.

Despite its size, the Su-27's power-to-weight ratio is greater than one, i.e. it can accelerate in a vertical climb. This has enabled pilots to develop a range of spectacular manoeuvres involving bringing the aircraft almost to

a stop then accelerating hard. While mainly serving to demonstrate the capabilities of the aircraft at air shows, these manoeuvres translate into impressive air-to-air dogfighting capabilities.

VARIANTS

The Su-27S and P variants are often simply designated Su-27. The S variant was built with air-to-ground capability, while the P is a pure air-to-air machine. The Flanker's primary role is air superiority, with the capability to escort strike aircraft deep into enemy territory. Armed with a 30mm (1.1in) cannon and ten hardpoints for external ordnance, the Su-27 normally carries a mix of

SU-27UB 'FLANKER-C'
An Su-27UB, two-seat trainer version. These aircraft carry exactly the same systems as a single-seater and can be switched to a combat role if necessary.

'RUSSIAN KNIGHTS'

The Su-27s of the Russian Knights aerobatic display team became a popular attraction at air shows after the end of the Cold War.

SPECIFICATIONS (SU-29P)

Crew: 1

Length: 21.94m (72ft)

Wingspan: 14.7m (48ft 3in)

Loaded weight: 33,000kg (72,750lb)

Powerplant: 2 x Saturn/Lyulka AL-31F turbofans

Maximum speed: 2500km/h (1553mph)

Armament: 1 x 30mm (1.18in) cannon, 10 hardpoints for external ordnance

medium and short range missiles in the air-to-air role. The Su-27SK version was produced for the export market, featuring an increased payload, and was followed by the modernized Su-27MSK. The Su-27SM is a modernized version of the standard aircraft in Russian service. Later members of the Su-27 family are often designated Su-30 and include several sub-types constructed for different roles or intended clients.

A navalized version, sometimes designated Su-27K and sometimes Su-33, features folding wings and fuselage canards, plus an arrestor hook and other equipment for carrier operations. Numerous variants of this aircraft also exist or have been planned, including specialist electronic warfare platforms, reconnaissance aircraft and a multi-role version.

The Su-27M series is a multi-role platform built on a version of the airframe fitted with canards, while the Su-27IB series is a two-seat strike version with a considerably modified airframe. The family continues with the Su-35 series, which is based on an improved version of the same airframe, and the advanced Su-37.

ENGINES
The twin engines of the Su-27 produce 12,500kg (27,557lb) of thrust, enabling the aircraft to accelerate in a steep climb.

SU-27K 'FLANKER-D'
This aircraft served with the 1st Squadron, Severomorsk Regiment, Russian Naval Aviation. The Su-27K 'Flanker D' (also designated Su-33) is designed for carrier operations, and has folding wings and an arrestor hook.

The combination of controllable canards and powerful thrust enables later members of the Su-27 family to make very high angle-of-attack manoeuvres.

THE SU-27 IN SERVICE

The Su-27 has a range of users, some resulting from export sales and others from the breakup of the Soviet Union. As a result, Flankers have been used by both sides in some conflicts. The Flanker, predictably perhaps, proved superior to the MiG-29 'Fulcrum' in the 1998–2000 conflict between Ethiopia and Eritrea.

The Su-27 family also caused friction between Russia and China. Designating the aircraft J-11, the Chinese government bought a quantity of Su-27s and acquired a licence to build more, but ended up in dispute with Russia over licence terms for both the J-11 and the navalized J-16 version.

With so many versions of this aircraft in service, and significant numbers of the original Su-27 still flying, it seems likely that the Flanker will continue to serve as a front-line air superiority platform for some years to come.

Nieuport 17

43

With a lineage going back to a racing design, the Nieuport 'fighting scouts' were fast and highly manoeuvrable, if rather fragile. They were instrumental in restoring the balance of air power over the Western Front.

The Nieuport 10 was developed as a racer before the outbreak of war, and was a natural candidate for adaptation as a military aircraft. The original two-seat design was modified to carry a single pilot after the two-seater (crewed by a pilot and an observer) proved to be underpowered.

SINGLE-SEATER FIGHTER

The Nieuport 11 was developed from the 10, as a single-seater from the outset. It proved superior to German aircraft of the time and was adopted for service in various nations. Indeed, it outlived the larger and more powerful two-seat Nieuport 12 in front-line combat squadrons.

GUN
An engine cowling mounting not only made aiming the gun simpler, but also allowed the pilot to more readily clear jams.

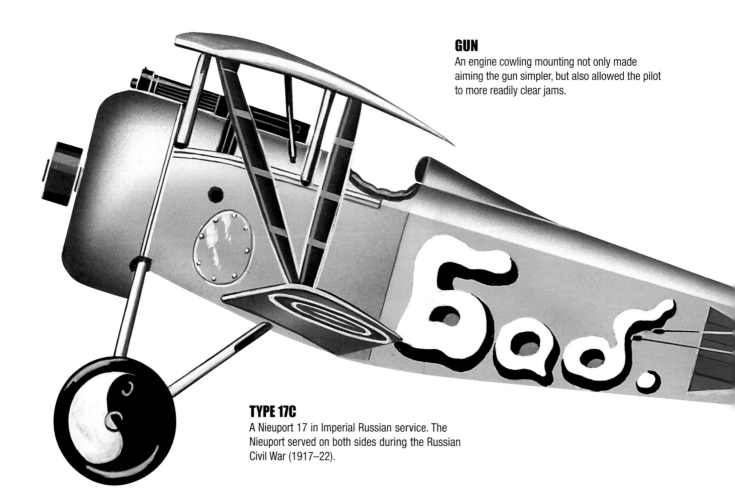

TYPE 17C
A Nieuport 17 in Imperial Russian service. The Nieuport served on both sides during the Russian Civil War (1917–22).

SPECIFICATIONS

Crew: 1

Length: 5.74m (18ft 10in)

Wingspan: 8.22m (26ft 11in)

Loaded weight: 565kg (1246lb)

Powerplant: Le Rhone 9J 9-cylinder rotary engine

Maximum speed: 177km/h (110mph)

Armament: 1 x 7.7mm (0.303in) Lewis or Vickers machine gun

The narrow lower wing of the Nieuport 17 contributed to its agility and rate of climb, but was fragile. It was replaced by a larger wing on the Nieuport 28.

WING SURFACES

One design flaw of the Nieuport fighting scouts was a tendency to shed fabric from the upper wing surface, sometimes with catastrophic consequences.

A series of variants on the 12 followed, with the Nieuport 16 being an improved and more powerful aircraft based on the Nieuport 11. The 16 was followed by the further improved 17, which became one of the most important aircraft of the war.

The Nieuport 17 had larger wings and a more robust structure compared to the 11, and also a more powerful engine. Most importantly, later 17s (designated 17bis) replaced the wing-top mounted machine gun with a weapon synchronized to fire through the propeller. Further developed machines followed, but the 17 was the definitive Nieuport fighter.

FIGHTING SCOUTS

When the first Nieuports were developed, the concept of fighters had not yet become prevalent; single-seaters were considered to be useful mainly as scouts. It was not long before the scouts began fighting one another to deny the enemy air reconnaissance, however, and within a short time combat became the single-seater's primary role.

Early Nieuport fighting scouts were important in countering what became known as the 'Fokker Scourge' of 1915; a period of dominance by German aircraft. The agile Nieuport was far more effective than earlier designs, and was well liked for its speed and rate of climb. New aircraft appeared at an incredible rate, and any

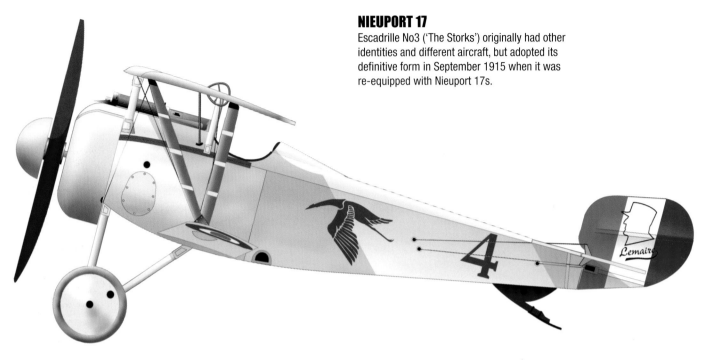

NIEUPORT 17

Escadrille No3 ('The Storks') originally had other identities and different aircraft, but adopted its definitive form in September 1915 when it was re-equipped with Nieuport 17s.

NIEUPORT 23

This Belgian Nieuport 23 differs only slightly from the 17, notably in the upper wing design and the offset positioning of the Vickers machine gun.

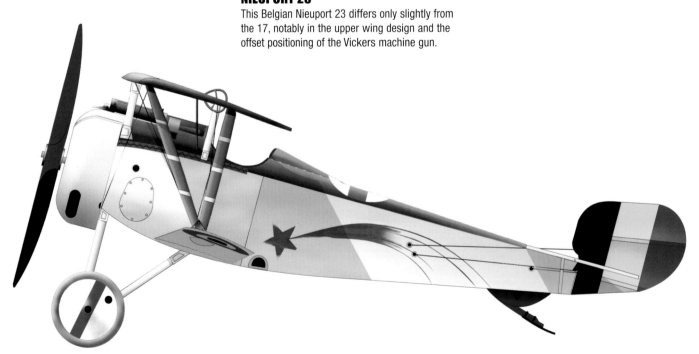

technical advantage was likely to be quickly offset by an improvement in enemy capabilities. Thus a larger and more powerful Nieuport was a necessity almost as soon as the 11 had entered service.

The Nieuport 17 was a worthy successor, and was especially important in the air battles over the Verdun and the Somme in 1916. It was highly effective for a time, but eventually had to be replaced with more advanced aircraft. In the meantime, however, 17s were flown by many notable fighter aces including Albert Ball, William Bishop and Georges Guynemer.

THE NIEUPORT IN SERVICE

In addition to the French military, Nieuports were supplied to the Royal Naval Air Service and later to the Royal Flying Corps, largely due to a shortage of other machines.

A pilot from the famous Lafayette Escadrille stands by a Nieuport 17. This French World War I squadron was composed largely of American volunteer pilots who signed up before the United States' entry into the war.

Spain, Russia and the Netherlands produced licence-built versions, while several other countries bought the Nieuport to equip their own air arms. German designers also copied the Nieuport design, making modifications to the tail section.

Almost every French fighter squadron flew the Nieuport 17 at one point, and some American units arriving in 1917 were initially equipped with them. Nieuport 17s were still flying in British squadrons into 1918, by which time the design was outdated. Many survived as trainers after the war, with significant numbers exported worldwide.

E-3 Sentry

Essentially a giant flying radar, the E-3 Sentry greatly enhances the capabilities of air combat assets by detecting and tracking targets, and by guiding pilots to where they need to be.

An E-3 Sentry assigned to the 961st AWACS Squadron at Kadena Air Force Base, Japan, takes off during exercises held at Cope Tiger 2002 at Wing 1 Air Base Korat, Thailand.

The E-3 is based on the Boeing 707 airliner, modified to carry a large radome on dorsal struts. An extensive suite of other instrumentation is carried within the fuselage, along with processing and communications equipment to analyze the raw sensor data and provide it to pilots in a useful format.

Variously referred to as Airborne Warning and Control (AWACS) and Airborne Early Warning (AEW), this capability requires a mission crew of up to 19 personnel in addition to four flight crew. The E-3's radar provides coverage up to the stratosphere and out to a range of 375km (250 miles). When flying at high altitude, the radar is less limited by the curvature of the Earth's surface and the aircraft is able to 'look down' to identify air and maritime targets that might otherwise be lost in surface clutter.

E-3A AWACS SENTRY
Introduced into USAF service in 1977, this Sentry was selected to equip a multinational NATO unit based in Germany.

E-3A Sentry
An E-3A, dating from the early 1980s. Most E-3As were later converted to E-3B standard, increasing the AWACS crew from 13 to 17–19.

CREW SPACE
The AWACS has a flight crew of four: pilot, co-pilot, navigator and flight engineer. The use of a civilian airframe eliminated the costs required to develop a dedicated platform, and provided plenty of space for crew and electronic systems.

ELECTRONIC EQUIPMENT
Electronic equipment is arranged in bays within the fuselage, grouping equipment used for communications, signal and data processing, command and control, and navigation.

REFUELLING PROBE
A refuelling probe was situated above the flight deck, in the nose of the aircraft.

RADAR ANTENNA
The most obvious feature of the E-3 is its large radome. The antenna revolves six times per minute when in use and once every four minutes when not.

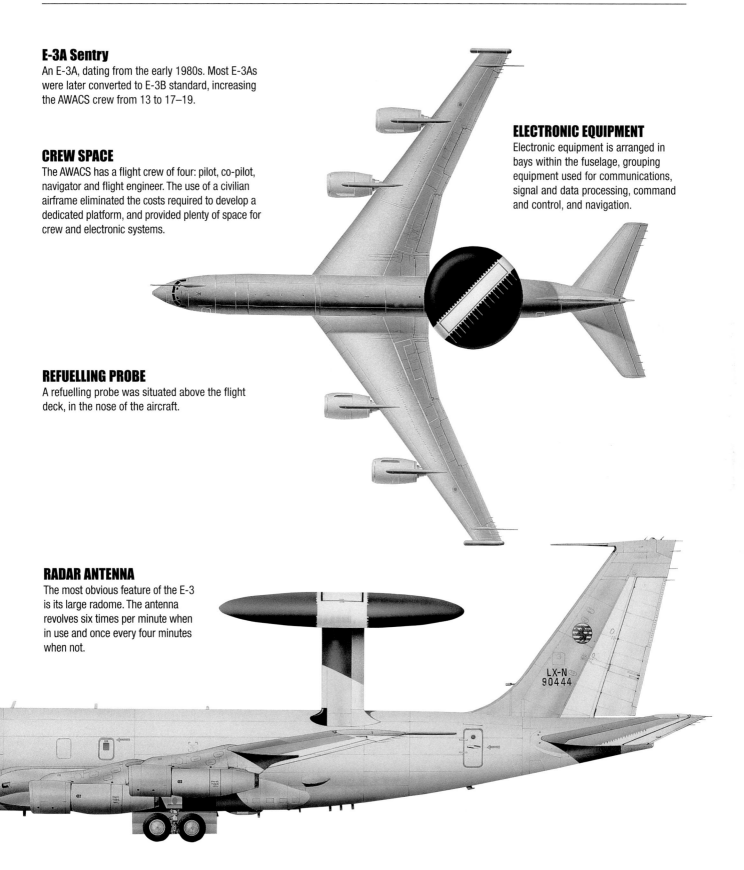

An E-3A Sentry lands at Incirlik Air Base, Turkey. The aircraft and crew was assigned to the 970th Expeditionary Aerospace Air Control Squadron in support of Combined Task Force, Operation Northern Watch (ONW). ONW enforced the no-fly zone over northern Iraq from 1997 to 2003.

Mission duration on internal fuel stores is around 11 hours, which can be extended with in-flight refuelling. A rest area is provided for the crew, enabling very long-duration missions to be flown at need.

Upgrades during the service life of the aircraft have enhanced its capabilities and ensured that information is distributed in an effective and timely manner. Situational awareness has always been important in all forms of combat, but in the modern environment is has become absolutely critical. Gone are the days when hostiles could be identified by their insignia or the design of their aircraft; today's military situation is far more complex.

Aircraft and naval assets may be operating in a cluttered environment, with neutral and civilian traffic nearby and often no clear threat until an attack is made. The ability to identify friendly and non-hostile contacts and to keep track of them is as essential as detecting and tracking potential hostiles or deducing hostile intent from the actions of a given aircraft.

THE E-3 IN SERVICE

The E-3 Sentry is operated by the US Air Force and the RAF under the designation AWACS and AEW respectively. Other users include France and Saudi Arabia. The E-3 entered service in 1977, during the Cold War, and initially was expected to provide early warning and interception of air strikes in a major conflict if one occurred. It has seen service in several smaller conflicts since.

A British Royal Air Force E-3C (AWACS) heads back to Afghanistan after being refueled over Pakistan by a KC-135 Stratotanker, during Operation Enduring Freedom , 2002. The E-3C provided air traffic control for coalition aircraft over Afghanistan.

The E-3 was highly useful in enforcing the no-fly zone over the Balkans in the 1990s, not least since it could often track aircraft from their point of origin and back to base, providing information not available with shorter-ranged radar equipment that only covered the nearby area. Operations over Iraq in 1990–91 and 2003 were closer to the E-3's intended role, with E-3s providing information on enemy movements to aircrews and commanders in the combat area.

The E-3 has also seen service in disaster-relief operations, acting as a communications and command platform for personnel from military and civilian agencies in the wake of destructive hurricanes. Further upgrades are scheduled for the 2020s, ensuring that the E-3 remains in service for many years to come.

SPECIFICATIONS (EC-3C)

Crew: 4 + 17 AWACS specialists

Length: 46.62m (152ft 11in)

Wingspan: 44.43m (145ft 9in)

Loaded weight: 147,418kg (325,000lb)

Powerplant: 4 x Pratt & Whitney TF-33 turbofan

Maximum speed: 855km/h (530mph)

Armament: None

Fokker E series

The Fokker Eindecker was the first aircraft to be fitted with an interruptor apparatus, which allowed firing of a machine gun through the propeller. It quickly came to dominate the airspace over the Western Front.

The Eindecker ('monoplane') was developed from an unarmed reconnaissance aircraft designated M.5. It was introduced early in World War I, at a time when most armed aircraft used guns on a movable mount. This made accuracy difficult for pilots who had to fly and shoot in different directions, and even for a dedicated gunner the problem of anticipating the pilot's manoeuvres as well as those of an enemy aircraft was a tough one.

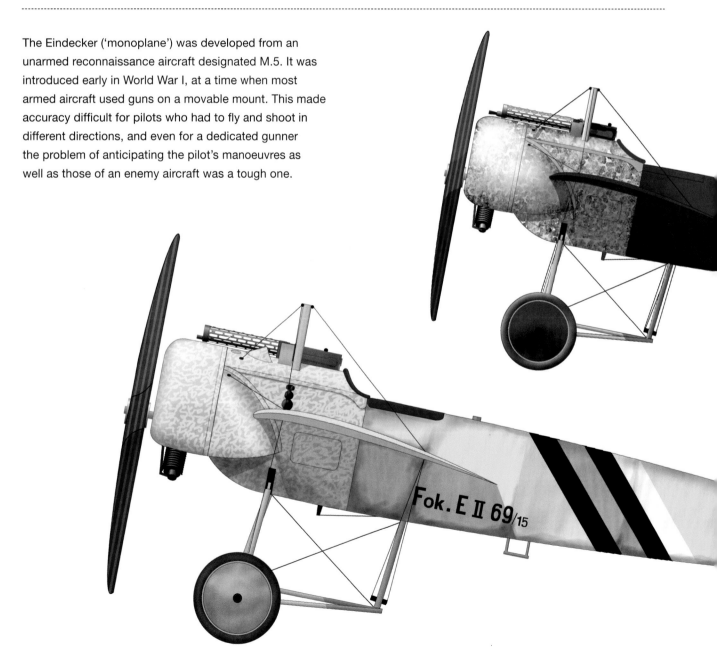

SPECIFICATIONS (FOKKER EINDECKER)

Crew: 1

Length: 7.2m (23ft 7.5in)

Wingspan: 9.5m (31ft 2.75in)

Loaded weight: 610kg (1345lb)

Powerplant: Oberursel 9-cylinder rotary engine

Maximum speed: 140km/h (87mph)

Armament: 1 x 7.92mm (0.312in) machine gun firing through propeller

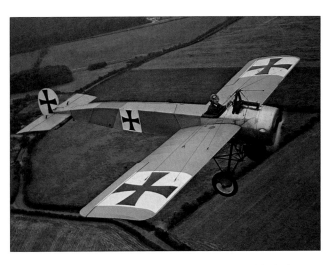

Even with a fixed forward-firing gun, hitting a target was a tricky business. Opening fire from as close as possible was one solution, resulting in near-collisions whether the target was hit or not.

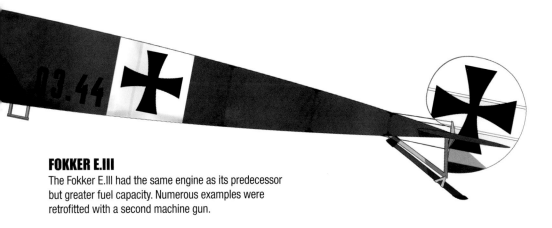

FOKKER E.III

The Fokker E.III had the same engine as its predecessor but greater fuel capacity. Numerous examples were retrofitted with a second machine gun.

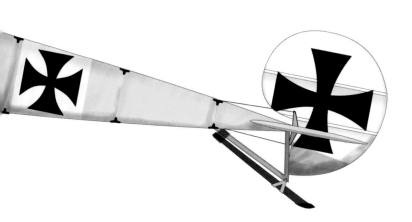

FOKKER E.II

The Fokker E.II was designed from the outset as a fighter, where the E.I was a converted reconnaissance aircraft with a retrofitted machine gun.

German ace Max Immelmann sits in the cockpit of a Fokker E.III. The Fokker E series were introduced primarily to counter Allied observation aircraft, which proved to be extremely vulnerable to the German scouts with their forward-firing armament.

Two-seaters were also heavier and more cumbersome than single-seat scouts.

The Eindecker used an interruptor mechanism to prevent its fixed machine gun from firing at a time when bullets would strike the propeller, reducing the potential rate of fire a little but enabling the pilot to line up his aircraft and shoot when he thought best. The advantages over offset guns were significant, and the Eindecker began an impressive career when Max Immelmann scored his (and the Eindecker's) first kill in August 1915.

'FOKKER SCOURGE'

The Eindecker was superior to all the aircraft it faced at that time, and inflicted such heavy losses that the period was later dubbed the 'Fokker Scourge'. However, operations were limited by a need to prevent the interruptor mechanism from being copied by the enemy; Eindeckers were not permitted to fly over hostile territory in case one was shot down. The interruptor was not flawless; Immelmann shot part of his own propeller off when the synchronization gear malfunctioned.

German air combat tactics also developed during this period. Eindeckers were originally assigned as escorts for reconnaissance formations, but experience indicated the value of allowing fighters to seek out and engage the

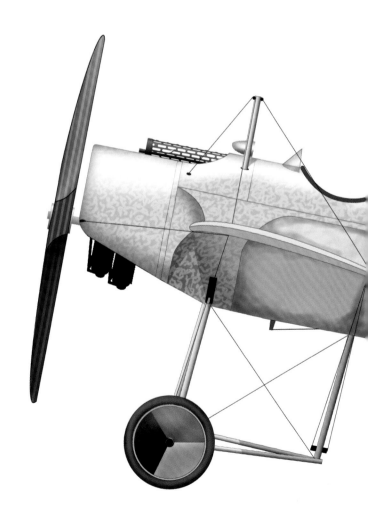

enemy rather than always acting defensively. Eindeckers typically operated in groups of four, which were directed towards areas where enemy aircraft were known or likely to be operating. This basic concept of fighter control proved effective and became standard in the years that followed.

THE EINDECKER IN SERVICE

In the hands of 'aces' like Immelmann and Oswald Boelke, the Eindecker was extremely effective despite its small numbers. Fewer than 100 were operational on the Western Front at the end of 1915, but they had an effect out of all proportion to the number of aircraft. A handful were sent to the Eastern Front, where they proved just as devastating to the Russian air force.

Improved versions appeared over time, with more powerful engines and a second machine gun. The Eindecker always suffered from a lack of engine power, however, which was offset by its agility. This weakness was not recognized by those who faced the Fokker Scourge, and it was not until the improved Nieuport fighters appeared that an Eindecker could be engaged with any confidence.

Overall, the Eindecker's dominance was short-lived, with the advantage in air combat going this way and that as new designs appeared on an almost weekly basis. By mid-1916 there were better aircraft on both sides and the world-beater of 1915 was overdue for replacement. By the time the Eindecker was phased out it had been credited with shooting down more than 1000 enemy aircraft.

FOKKER E.IV

The Fokker E.IV was given a more powerful engine and either one or two additional guns, but was outdated by the time of its introduction and did not repeat the success of the earlier models.

ENGINE

The larger engine of the E.IV was not an improvement. Much of the design's previously good manoeuvrability was lost, and the engine was troubled by mechanical issues.

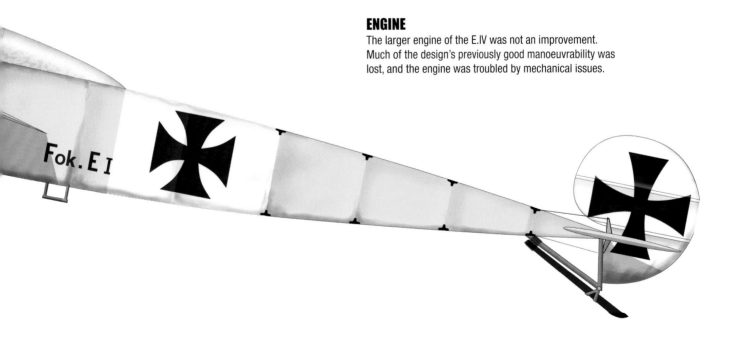

Dassault Mirage III

Undertaken as a private venture, the delta-wing Mirage III became an enormous export success as well as arming the air force of France. It fought in several conflicts of the mid to late 20th century.

DELTA WING

The high sweep of the Mirage III's delta wing resulted in reduced drag at high speeds, while enabling the aircraft to dispense with a conventional tail surface.

First flying in 1956, the Mirage III was less manoeuvrable than some of its competitors due to the delta wing configuration, but it was fast, breaking Mach 2 in 1958 – the first European design to do so in level flight. High speed and a good rate of climb made the Mirage attractive as an interceptor, especaily in an era where nuclear weapons could only be delivered by bombers.

Armament was limited by modern standards but entirely adequate for the era, consisting of a pair of 30mm (1.1in) cannon plus two heat-seeking Magic missiles for close-range combat and a larger radar-guided Matra missile.

SPECIFICATIONS

Crew: 1

Length: 14.75m (48ft 5in)

Wingspan: 8.22m (27ft)

Loaded weight: 12,700kg (27,998lb)

Powerplant: SNECMA Atar 9C afterburning turbojet

Maximum speed: 2112km/h (1320mph)

Armament: 2 x 30mm (1.1in) cannon plus external stores; typically 2 x Sidewinder or Magic heat-seeking missile plus 1 x Matra R.530 radar-guided missile

ISRAELI MIRAGE
A Mirage IIICJ in Israeli colours, at the time of the 1967 Six-Day War. Although not an outstanding strike aircraft, the Mirage proved to be an excellent air-to-air platform.

TURBOJET ENGINE
The Atar turbojet engine of the Mirage III was used in a variety of Mirage variants and also in the Etendard and Super Etendard naval strike aircraft.

Two Mirage III aircraft of the Royal Australian Air Force take off on a mission during the joint Australian, New Zealand and US (ANZUS) Exercise TRIAD '84.

EARLY MIRAGES

Mirage I and II were essentially development platforms, with the Mirage IIIA as a preproduction series. The first production version of the Mirage was the IIIC, with the slightly enlarged IIIB configured as a two-seat trainer. By 1961 the air superiority/interceptor version was joined by the Mirage IIIE, a multi-role platform that could undertake strike missions as well as functioning as a fighter. The IIIE had an enlarged fuselage and was complemented by the

MIRAGE IIICJ

The Mirage IIICJ was primarily an interceptor, designed to climb fast and travel at high speeds in a straight line. The ability to get into missile range of incoming bombers was of extreme importance in the early Cold War years.

Mirage IIID trainer. A reconnaissance version designated Mirage IIIR followed.

THE MIRAGE III IN SERVICE

The Mirage III was bought by a number of export clients and built under licence in several nations. A major user was Israel, whose pilots contributed to the Mirage's export success by demonstrating its effectiveness in the Six-Day of 1967. More than 80 per cent of Arab aircraft downed in the conflict were at the hands of Mirages, although ground-attack performance was less impressive.

Renewed Arab–Israeli conflict in 1973 saw the Mirage used only in the air-to-air role, where again it was highly successful. Although slow to turn, the Mirage possessed excellent speed and acceleration, and could out-climb its opponents.

Performance in South African hands against insurgent forces in Angola was not so impressive, largely due to a lack of strike range and poor rough-field capability. Argentine Mirages similarly lacked the range to effectively attack the British task force off the Falkland Islands in 1982.

VARIANTS

The Mirage 5 was developed in response to an Israeli request for a version suited to its needs. The expensive and technologically sophisticated radar of the IIIC model was not required, so a simplified version was developed. However, politics intervened and sale of the Mirage 5 to Israel became impossible. The Mirage 5 thus went into French service while the Israelis developed their own aircraft, designated Kfir, from the Mirage III. South Africa also developed its own multi-role fighter, designated Cheetah, from the Mirage III.

Mirage 5s were bought by a number of overseas clients, and were licence-built in Belgium. These aircraft were upgraded with improved electronics, and a range of variants appeared in service to clients worldwide. Israel flew the Mirage 5 under the designation of Nesher, many of which were sold to Argentina.

The Mirage 50 was developed from the Mirage 5, gaining improved electronics and a more powerful engine. Some existing Mirage IIIs have also been upgraded to Mirage 50 standards, serving as a multi-role strike/fighter platform.

WEAPONS
In addition to its two 30mm (1.1in) cannon, the Mirage III could carry around 4000kg (8818lb) of external stores, including missiles, bombs, rocket pods or long-range fuel tanks.

Polikarpov I-16

Given the pace of fighter development in the 1930s, it is all the more remarkable that the Soviet-designed I-16 was essentially the best fighter in the world for a period of six years. It only met its match once pitted against the Luftwaffe's Messerschmitt Bf 109E.

Design of this single-seat fighter began in spring 1933 by Polikarpov's team at the Central Design Bureau (TsKB). The initial prototype established the I-16's characteristic appearance: a cantilever low-wing monoplane with a stubby fuselage accommodating a radial powerplant. The fuselage was of mainly wooden construction and the metal wing was equipped with long-span split-type ailerons, which could also be used as landing flaps. The main landing gear units retracted inwards into the wing.

The first prototype, known as the TsKB-12, was powered by an M-22 engine that produced 358kW (480hp). A maiden flight was achieved on 31 December 1933.

This was followed by the TsKB-12S, which introduced an imported Wright SR-1820-F3 Cyclone radial that produced 529kW (710hp). A first flight of the re-engined prototype took place on 18 February 1934.

With the original M-22 engine, the new fighter displayed a maximum speed of 359km/h (223mph) at sea level. However, the American powerplant yielded improved results: a top speed of 43km/h (272mph) at 3000m (9845ft). In the event, the aircraft was ordered into production with the indigenous M-22 engine, under the designation I-16.

TRICKY HANDLING

From the beginning, the I-16 developed a reputation as a very demanding aircraft for its pilots. However, it offered impressive speed and excellent rate of climb. It was these attributes that led to official support for the aircraft, and an order being placed for 30 I-16s with the M-22 engine. Of this initial batch, intended for evaluation, 10 aircraft took part in the May Day flypast over Moscow in 1935.

With more advanced fighters on the drawing board, it was always intended that I-16 production would be

GUN ARMAMENT

Gun armament comprised four 7.62mm (0.3in) ShKAS machine guns, two synchronized in the forward fuselage and two in the wings; the wing machine guns were replaced on some aircraft by two 20mm (0.78in) ShVAK cannon; a 12.7mm (0.5in) UB machine gun was sometimes added to the fuselage-mounted armament.

FUEL LOAD

Fuel was housed in a single tank located in the central fuselage between the cockpit and engine installation. Total capacity was 255 litres (56 gallons). No fuel gauge was fitted in the cockpit; the pilot had to listen to the engine note to determine when fuel was low while keeping a close eye on his watch.

Even though it was thoroughly outclassed by German fighters, the I-16 continued in front-line service until late in 1943. The 29th IAP (Istrebitel'nyi Aviatsionnyi Polk or Fighter Air Regiment) was one of the most heavily engaged units in the early months of the war, using its I-16s to attack German ground forces. It was the first air force unit to receive the Guards title, becoming the 1st Guards IAP during the defence of Moscow on 6 December 1941.

TAIL SURFACES
The tail surfaces were necessarily large to counter the lack of stability caused by the short rear fuselage. In spite of the designers' best efforts, the I-16 had only limited stability longitudinally, and needed concentration from the pilot at all times. However, this instability brought great dividends in manoeuvrability at high speeds, where the rod-actuated elevators were noticeably effective.

terminated in 1939. By this time, a number of improvements had been made to the basic I-16, including changes to the armament and engine. However, the basic design proved so good that the I-16 was returned to production to make up for the shortage of more modern equipment after the Axis invasion of the Soviet Union. As a result, additional batches of I-16s rolled off the production line during 1941–42.

In its definitive form, the 1-16 was fitted with a more powerful 820kW (1100hp) M-63 engine. Total production of all versions amounted to 7005, including dual-control trainers.

From 1935, series-production 1-16 Type 4 (imported Cyclone) and Type 5 (M-25 engine) fighters were delivered to the Soviet air force. Supply of the Type 5 to the Spanish Republican air arm began in October 1936, and this model was followed by the Type 6 (M-25A) and Type 10 (M-25V).

Soviet I-16s flew in China against the invading Japanese in 1937. Early in 1938, the I-16 Type 10 began to equip Chinese units; in 1939, Soviet I-16s were engaged in furious air battles with Japanese army fighters at Nomonhan on the Manchurian border. The I-16 took a prominent part in the Winter War, but was obsolescent (even in its latest Type 24

The I-16's predecessor was the Polikarpov I-153 biplane fighter. This example of the 'Chaika' (seagull) was the first of three restored examples to take to the air in a programme sponsored by the Alpine Fighter Collection at Wanaka in New Zealand in the mid-1990s. It is seen during flight testing in Russia in September 1997.

COCKPIT

The cramped cockpit was equipped with only rudimentary instruments. No radio or oxygen equipment was fitted, and there was no indicator for the undercarriage. The pilot was provided with a control column with a yoke-type grip, and a cable-cutter for severing the undercarriage retraction cables if they became stuck open.

SPECIFICATIONS

Crew: 1

Length: 6.04m (19ft 9.75in)

Wingspan: 8.88m (29ft 1.5in)

Equipped weight: 1475kg (3252lb)

Powerplant: 1 × M-62 radial piston engine

Maximum speed: 490km/h (304mph) at 3000m (9845ft)

Armament: Typically 4 x 7.62mm (0.3in) machine guns; plus a bombload of up to 200kg (441lb) on underwing racks, with the alternative of 6 x RS-82 rockets

version) when Germany and its Axis counterparts invaded the Soviet Union in June 1941. At that time, nearly two-thirds of the Soviet air force fighter arm comprised I-16s. The type bore the brunt of the invasion and suffered heavy losses on the ground and in the air during 1941. In Soviet propaganda, the type became renowned for Taran ramming attacks on German bombers and fighters, in which the Soviet pilot risked his aircraft and himself in order to defeat the enemy.

Only in late 1943 was the 1-16 finally withdrawn, the type having achieved a worldwide 'first', being the precursor of all the cantilever low-wing monoplane fighters with retractable landing gear to go into large-scale service.

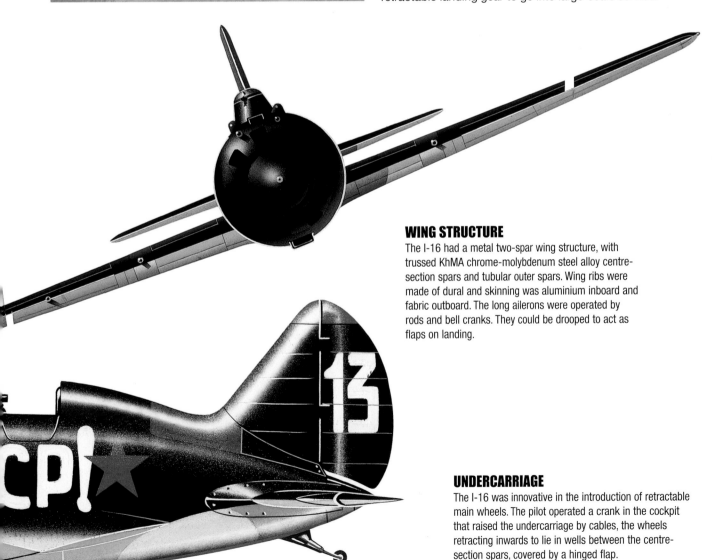

WING STRUCTURE

The I-16 had a metal two-spar wing structure, with trussed KhMA chrome-molybdenum steel alloy centre-section spars and tubular outer spars. Wing ribs were made of dural and skinning was aluminium inboard and fabric outboard. The long ailerons were operated by rods and bell cranks. They could be drooped to act as flaps on landing.

UNDERCARRIAGE

The I-16 was innovative in the introduction of retractable main wheels. The pilot operated a crank in the cockpit that raised the undercarriage by cables, the wheels retracting inwards to lie in wells between the centre-section spars, covered by a hinged flap.

B-25 Mitchell

The North American B-25 became the ubiquitous medium bomber in US Army Air Force service during World War II, serving in all theatres where the air arm found itself at war and being delivered to a number of export operators, including the Royal Air Force. By the end of the war, the Mitchell had probably served on more fronts than any other combat type.

The B-25 Mitchell was the most widely used USAAF light/medium bomber of World War II. It also turned its hand to a variety of specialist roles and saw service with the US Navy and Marine Corps.

North American developed the NA-40 attack bomber design in response to a US Army Air Corps specification that was issued in January 1938. A first NA-40 prototype made its maiden flight in March 1939. After incorporating various modifications recommended by the Army, North American produced the definitive B-25 model, which made its first flight from Wright Field on 19 August 1940.

This was followed by the B-25A, which had additional armour and self-sealing fuel tanks. The first unit of the USAAC to be equipped with the B-25 and B-25A was the 17th Bombardment Group.

B-25J 'BETTY'S DREAM'
This aircraft flew in the southwest Pacific with the United States Air Force 499th Bomb Squadron, otherwise known as the 'Bats Outa Hell'. The front end of the aircraft was painted with a huge bat figure with teeth and wings.

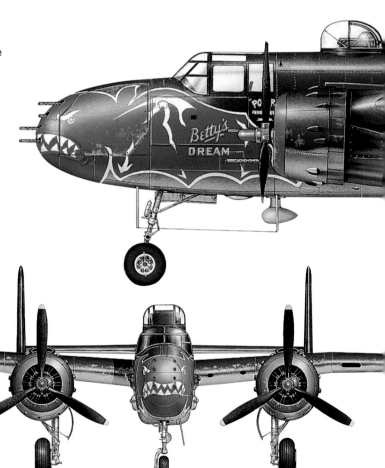

WINGS
The Mitchell bomber had a characteristic inverted gull wing, which made the aircraft much more manoeuvrable.

BOMBS
The Mitchell bomber could carry 1361kg (3000lb) of bombs in its two vertical bomb bays.

SPECIFICATIONS

Crew: 5

Length: 16.12m (52ft 11in)

Wingspan: 20.60m (67ft 7in)

Empty weight: 9208kg (20,300lb)

Powerplant: 2 × Wright R-2600-13 radial piston engines

Maximum speed: 457km/h (284mph) at 4570m (15,000ft)

Armament: 6 x 12.7mm (0.5in) machine guns (2 each in nose, Bendix dorsal turret and ventral station), plus a maximum bombload of 1361kg (3000lb)

The B-25B introduced a Bendix power-operated dorsal turret and a ventral turret, and dispensed with the tail guns: the B-25C was similar but had 1268kW (1700hp) Wright R-2600-13 engines in place of the earlier R-2600-9s. B-25C production totalled 1619, this version also introducing an autopilot and additional underwing bomb racks. It was followed by 2290 examples of the generally similar B-25D.

With the outbreak of war, the 3rd BG began a long tour of the Southwest Pacific region. The 17th BG meanwhile was groomed to take part in a daring attack on Tokyo. On 18 April 1942, the first of 16 B-25Bs led by Lieutenant Colonel James H. Doolittle took off from the deck of the

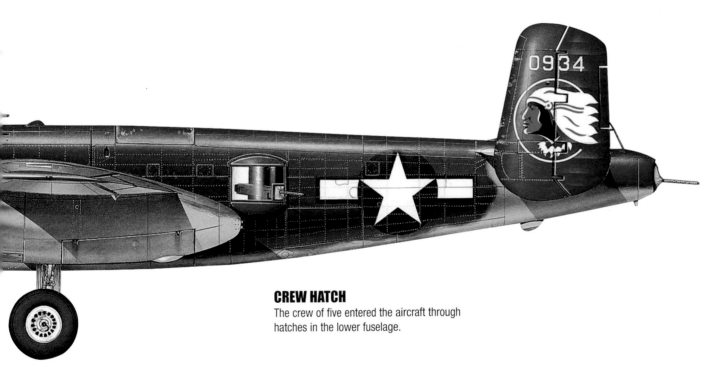

CREW HATCH
The crew of five entered the aircraft through hatches in the lower fuselage.

aircraft carrier USS Hornet for a 1184-km (714-mile) flight to the Japanese capital, and to other objectives at Nagoya, Kobe and Yokohama. The raid achieved immense morale and propaganda value for the Americans, although the damage inflicted was minimal.

While the B-25 was operating over New Guinea, it was also introduced into action with the US 12th Air Force in North Africa, the 10th Air Force in India, the 11th Air Force in the Aleutians, and with the RAF as the Mitchell Mk I

One of around 45 examples of the Mitchell that are still airworthy, 'Briefing Time' is operated by the Mid-Atlantic Air Museum in Reading, Pennsylvania. This B-25J features a Norden bombsight and original radio equipment as well as a working bomb bay loaded with six genuine 113kg (250lb) bombs.

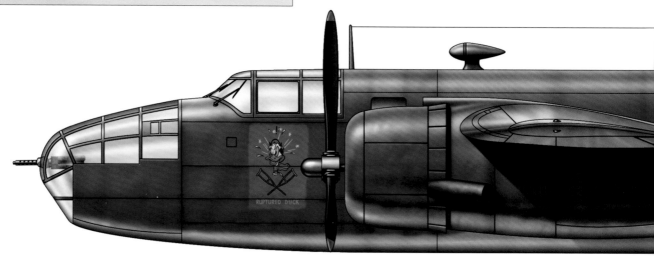

and Mitchell Mk II with No. 2 (Bomber) Group. As early as March 1942, the first of 850 B-25s was en route to the Soviet Union, where the type saw extensive service with the Soviet armed forces.

LOW-LEVEL RAIDERS

It was in New Guinea that the B-25 became one of the most terrifying weapons of the war in the Pacific. Here the US 5th Air Force adopted low-level strike tactics with B-25s and Martin B-26s against Japanese airfields and shipping. Under the guidance of Major Paul I. ('Pappy') Gunn, the B-25C and subsequent marks were fitted with up to eight forward-firing 12.7mm (0.5in) Browning M2 machine guns, and carried a load of fragmentation bombs. The operations of B-25s in this theatre became legendary,

Built in Kansas City in 1944–45 as a B-25J, 'Executive Sweet' saw service throughout the war as a crew trainer in the United States. In 1948, the aircraft was converted as a VB-25J VIP transport for the USAF. In December 1954, it was upgraded by Hayes Aircraft for civilian use as a VB-25N. It is now kept airworthy by the American Aeronautical Foundation.

'RUPTURED DUCK'

Flown by Lieutenant Ted W. Lawson, 'Ruptured Duck' was one of 16 B-25Bs used in the Tokyo raid on 18 April 1942. After the raid, this bomber ditched in the China Sea west of Shangchow, China. The five crew were badly injured, but were all rescued.

DORSAL TURRET

The dorsal turret was used as protection against fighters attacking from above, but could be locked forwards to provide extra weight of fire at the nose end.

the most devastating employment of the B-25 being in the Battle of the Bismarck Sea in March 1943.

1943 saw the introduction of the North American B-25G and B-25H, which were fitted with differing types of 75mm (2.9in) cannon: these did not prove to be entirely successful. The anti-shipping B-25G (405 built) featured the M4 75mm (2.9in) cannon and six machine guns, and was used against Japanese targets by the US air forces in the Far East. Even more heavily armed was the B-25H (1000 built) with a 75mm (2.9in) cannon and 14 (or in late versions 18) 12.7mm (0.5in) machine guns.

The most widely employed mark was the B-25J, with either a glazed or a solid nose: this was passed to the RAF as the Mitchell Mk III. A total of 4390 B-25Js were built from a contract for 4805, with Wright R-2600-92

engines and 12 12.7mm (0.5in) machine guns. The US Navy and Marine Corps used the PBJ-1C (50), PBJ-1D (152), PBJ1-G (1), PBJ-1H (248), and PBJ-1J (255) sub-types. Ten examples of an F-10 reconnaissance version were converted from B-25Ds. During 1943–44, 60 B-25D, B-25G, B-25C and B-25J aircraft were modified as advanced trainers with the respective designations AT-25A, AT-258, AT-25C and AT-25D; these were subsequently redesignated as TB-25D, TB-25G, TB-25C and TB-25J.

Some 9816 B-25s of all marks were produced. Mitchells continued in use for many years after the war, particularly in the air arms of smaller nations. The US Air Force's last B-25 staff transport was retired on 21 May 1960. Other post-war modifications included TB-25L and TB-25N trainers.

Lockheed U-2

The U-2 is today best remembered for the central role it played in the dramatic Cold War incident of 1960 to which it lent its name. Despite the appearance of more advanced platforms, the U-2 has continued to excel in service, and today's U-2S provides decision-makers with critical imagery and signals intelligence.

The U-2 was a product of the rejection of President Eisenhower's proposed 'Open Skies' policy for mutual US and Soviet reconnaissance over-flights of each other's territory, which was rejected by the Soviet Union. In August 1955, Lockheed flew a first example of the U-2 reconnaissance aircraft, built by the company's secretive 'Skunk Works'. Powered by a Pratt & Whitney J57 engine, it was characterized by glider-like wings permitting extended range and operations at altitudes that would put it out of reach of interceptors.

On 1 May 1960, during an over-flight of the Soviet Union, a Central Intelligence Agency (CIA)-operated U-2 flown by Francis Gary Powers was shot down by a surface-to-air missile. However, the U-2 remained a key intelligence-gathering platform of the Cold War, including in the Cuban Missile Crisis of 1962.

U-2C
This aircraft was built in the late 1950s as a U2-A. Converted to a U-C, it was involved in the Pave Onyx Advanced Location and Strike System trials in 1975.

EJECTOR SEAT
To save weight, the first U-2s were not fitted with an ejection seat, though they were added later. The type had a reputation for being difficult to handle on landing.

A U-2 in flight. The key to the U-2's altitude and range performance was its long wing span. It was effectively a powered glider, with its lightweight structure and high aspect ratio wing.

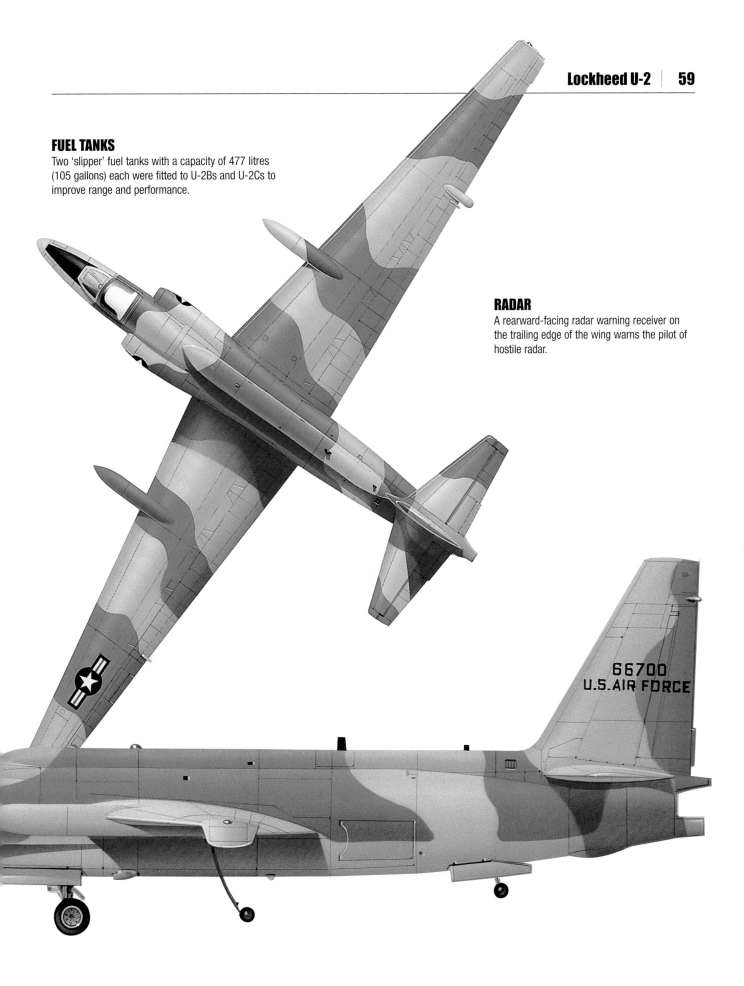

FUEL TANKS
Two 'slipper' fuel tanks with a capacity of 477 litres (105 gallons) each were fitted to U-2Bs and U-2Cs to improve range and performance.

RADAR
A rearward-facing radar warning receiver on the trailing edge of the wing warns the pilot of hostile radar.

66700
U.S. AIR FORCE

The U-2 Dragon Lady is considered the leader among manned intelligence, surveillance and reconnaissance systems. An aircraft such as this collected images over the Gulf Coast region in 2005 after Hurricanes Katrina and Rita devastated the area.

While the initial version U-2A version was powered by a 46.70kN (10,500lb) J57-P-37 or 49.80kN (11,200lb) J57-P-37A turbojet, the U-2B was an improved production version with strengthened airframe, J75-P-13 or J75-P-13B turbojet of 70.27kN (15,800lb) or 75.60kN (17,000lb) thrust respectively, and increased fuel capacity. The U-2C covered both new builds and conversions with enlarged inlets for the J75-P-13B and an extended nose and dorsal 'canoe' for sensor carriage.

The U-2CT was the two-seat conversion trainer version, two of which were produced with separate stepped cockpits. Next in line was the U-2D, converted from the U-2A and with the sensor-filled 'Q-bay' behind the cockpit modified to accommodate either a second seat or more systems. The U-2E was produced via conversion of existing U-2A and U-2B aircraft with advanced electronic countermeasures fit for CIA work. The U-2F was another

U-2A conversion, this time with an aerial refuelling receptacle. Perhaps most unusual was the U-2G: two U-2Cs fitted with arrester hook and other modifications for carrier trials.

NEW ENLARGED VERSION

Meanwhile, Lockheed had begun work on an enlarged version able to carry additional sensors. This was the U-2R, first flown on 28 August 1967. It was 40 per cent larger and considerably more capable than the original aircraft. Initial examples were delivered to both the US Air Force and the CIA. In November 1979, the U-2 production line reopened to provide 37 new airframes. A total of 25 of these aircraft were initially designated as the TR-1A and were designed to carry the ASARS-2 battlefield surveillance radar. With the end of the Cold War, the TR-1A designation was dropped in favour of U-2R, reflecting their basic commonality.

SPECIFICATIONS (U-2B)

Crew: 1

Length: 15.14m (49ft 8in)

Wingspan: 24.38m (80ft)

Loaded weight: 10,478kg (23,100lb)

Powerplant: 1 x non-afterburning 75.65kN (17,000lb) thrust J75-P-13B turbojet

Maximum speed: 853km/h (530mph)

Armament: None

BODY
Communication, navigation and mission equipment was housed in the long dorsal spine of the aircraft.

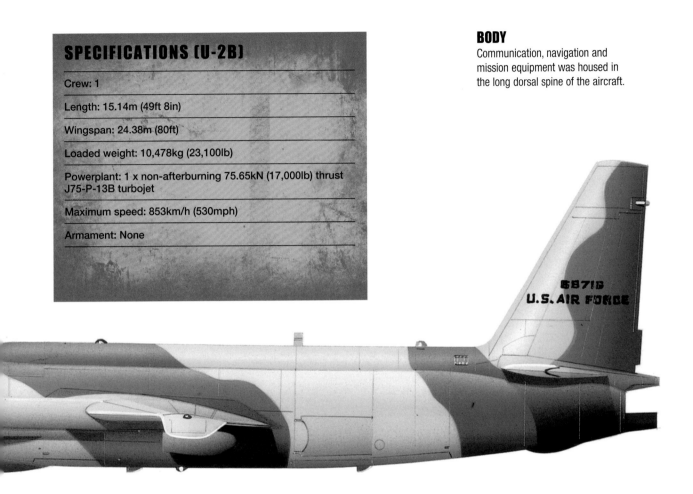

TWO-TONE CAMOUFLAGE
This aircraft was designed for high-altitude atmospheric sampling as a WU-2A. This two-tone grey camouflage was designed for operations in Europe in the 1970s.

As well as seven U-2Rs, the new batch included three two-seat TR-1B and U-2RT trainers; ultimately, the latter shared the U-2RT designation. Finally, NASA was recipient of two aircraft equipped to ER-2 standard for use as earth resources monitoring platforms.

While new sensors are continually being added to the U-2 fleet, airframe modifications were limited until 1992, when Lockheed began to replace the J75 turbojet with the General Electric F118-GE-101 turbofan, first flown in a TR-1A in March 1989. Since 1994, $1.7 billion has been invested to modernize the U-2 airframe and sensors. These upgrades included the fleet-wide transition to the F118 engine, which resulted in the redesignation of all USAF single-seat aircraft to the U-2S. Two-seaters are designated TU-2S, and both versions are in service with the 9th Reconnaissance Wing at Beale Air Force Base, California, which maintains operational detachments worldwide.

Avro Vulcan

Although only employed in anger during the twilight of its career, the delta-winged Vulcan was the best of the Royal Air Force's 'V-bombers' and one of the most enduring designs of the United Kingdom's post-war aircraft industry. The bombing missions it flew to the Falklands in 1982 were for many years the longest ever staged.

Following World War II, the United Kingdom set about establishing an airborne nuclear deterrent. This led to Specification B.14/46, which called for an aircraft with performance including the ability to strike a target at a range of 2735km (1700 miles) with a 4536kg (10,000lb) 'special bomb'.

The next step was Specification B.35/46, which saw design and development of three 'V-bombers' for the RAF: the Vickers Valiant, Avro Vulcan, and Handley Page Victor. The second to enter service was the Vulcan, but not before its delta planform had been tested using the company's Type 707 one-third-scale research aircraft.

The first of two Vulcan prototypes made its maiden flight on 30 August 1952 powered by four 28.91kN (6500lb st) Rolls-Royce Avon turbojets, although these were later

replaced by 35.59kN (8000lb st) Armstrong Siddeley Sapphire turbojets and then 66.72kN (15,000lb st) Rolls-Royce Conway turbofans. The second prototype was flown on 3 September 1953, and the first production Vulcan B.Mk 1 took to the air on 4 February 1955.

WING MODIFICATIONS

Early trials led to a modification of the wing, to mitigate the effect of buffeting that could lead to fatigue failure. Before the type entered service, therefore, the wing was modified with a kinked, rather than straight, leading edge. First flown as such in October 1955, previous B.Mk 1s were modified to the same standard.

Vulcans flew on the power of a variety of different engines, early B.Mk 1s having 48.93kN (11,000lb st) Bristol

VULCAN B.MK 2
This Vulcan was used for long-range bombing raids during the Falklands War of 1982.

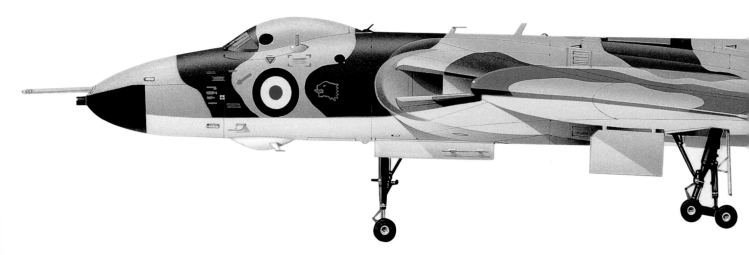

SPECIFICATIONS

Crew: 5

Length: 30.5m (100ft 1in)

Wingspan: 33.83m (111ft)

Loaded weight: 90,720kg (200,000lb)

Powerplant: 4 x 88.97kN (20,001lb st) Bristol Olympus turbojet engines

Maximum speed: 1038km/h (645mph)

Armament: Blue Danube hydrogen bomb; Blue Steel nuclear missile; or 21,454kg (47,300lb) of conventional bombs

DELTA WING
The delta wing was the Vulcan's most outstanding feature; it helped to eliminate buffeting and high-g manoeuvring at altitude.

ENGINES
The Vulcan's Rolls-Royce Olympus engines were embedded in the wings.

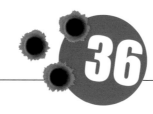

Siddeley Olympus Mk 101 turbojets; later machines had Olympus Mk 102 or 104 engines, each rated at 53.38kN (12,000lb st) or 60.05kN (13,500lb st) respectively. In 1961, the B.Mk 1 was modified with a tailcone carrying electronic countermeasures (ECM) equipment, becoming the Vulcan B.Mk 1A.

A prototype for the B.Mk 2 was first flown on 31 August 1957. As well as more powerful engines and a modified wing of increased area with a cranked leading edge, the B.Mk 2 added an inflight-refuelling capability. The production Vulcan B.Mk 2 entered service during 1960, and its primary weapon was initially the Blue Steel standoff bomb.

VULCAN B.MK 2A

During 1962–4, all in-service B.Mk 2s were re-engined with 88.96kN (20,000lb st) Olympus 301 engines. The definitive version was the Vulcan B.Mk 2A, produced as a new-build aircraft and, via conversion, with Blue Steel capability, terrain-following radar for the low-level penetration role, and yet more advanced ECM capability.

In 1973, some aircraft were adapted to Vulcan B.Mk 2MRR standard for the maritime strategic reconnaissance role, with additional electronic, optical and other sensors. By the early 1980s, it had been decided that the cost of extending the fatigue life of the surviving aircraft was too high to be acceptable, and it was decided to withdraw all Vulcan aircraft between June 1981 and June 1982.

Retirement of the RAF's Vulcans was underway at the time of the Argentine invasion of the Falkland Islands in April 1982. In response, several aircraft were pooled from three squadrons to constitute a force that could attack the Falklands from a base on Ascension Island. Another six aircraft were modified as Vulcan K.Mk 2 inflight-refuelling tankers. The tankers were the last Vulcans to remain in service, and were retired in March 1984.

Production of the Vulcan amounted to 134 in the form of 45 B.Mk 1 and 89 B.Mk 2 aircraft.

BLUE STEEL BOMB

This Vulcan B.Mk 2 is armed with a Blue Steel missile, a rocket-propelled nuclear missile with an operational range of 926km (575 miles). This aircraft is painted in anti-flash white and served with 617 Squadron.

Ground crewmen prepare a Royal Air Force
Vulcan Display Team Vulcan B. Mk 2 aircraft
for a demonstration during Air Fete '85, soon
after the model was retired from service.

FALKLAND ISLANDS RAIDER

XM607 was the first Vulcan to raid the airfield at Port
Stanley during the Falklands War, to deny access to the
Argentinians. The Vulcan had to fly a 16-hour round
trip from Ascension Island, more than 12,600km (7829
miles) away.

B-24 Liberator

Although overshadowed in popular history by the Boeing B-17 Flying Fortress, and latterly by the B-29 Superfortress, the Consolidated B-24 was built in larger numbers than any other US military aircraft of World War II, and is the most prolific four-engined aircraft in history.

In response to a January 1939 request from the US Army Air Corps (USAAC), Consolidated began a design study for a heavy bomber with performance superior to that of the B-17. The design proposal received the company designation Model 32 and the prototype XB-24 was flown on 29 December of the same year.

EARLY MODELS

The completion of a small-scale development batch of seven of the service test YB-24s kept Consolidated busy in 1940, while initial orders comprised 36 of the initial production B-24A for the USAAC, and 120 aircraft for France. By the time that the first production aircraft began to come off the line at San Diego, France had already capitulated, and the aircraft of the French order were completed to British requirements, as specified in an order for 164 that had been placed soon after that of France. The Royal Air Force introduced the Liberator name, later adopted by the US Army Air Force, and the first of these machines flew on 17 January 1941.

B-24D LIBERATOR 'TEGGIE ANN'

'Teggie Ann' was the command aircraft of the 'Liberandos', the 376th Bomber Group. This unit suffered heavy losses following the attacks on the Romanian oil fields at Ploesti in 1944.

The B-24 was produced in very large numbers – almost 19,000 units. It is the most produced heavy bomber in history, and the most produced American military aircraft.

SPECIFICATIONS (B-24J)

Crew: 11

Length: 20.6m (67ft 8in)

Wingspan: 33.5m (110ft)

Loaded weight: 25,000kg (55,000lb)

Powerplant: 4 × Pratt & Whitney R-1830-35 or -41 turbosupercharged radial engines, 900kW (1200hp)

Maximum speed: 488km/h (290mph)

Armament: Guns: 10 × 12.7mm (0.5in) M2 Browning machine guns in 4 turrets and 2 waist positions; bombs: short-range (640km/400 miles); 3600kg/8000lb

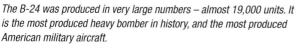

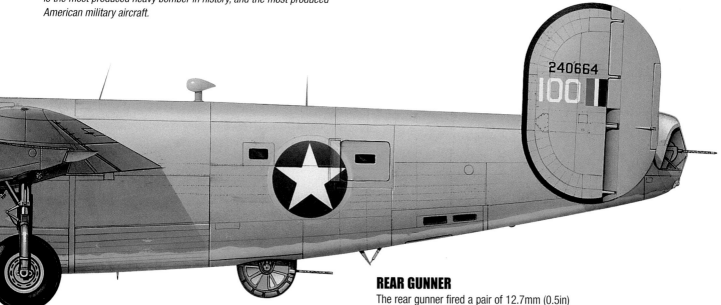

REAR GUNNER
The rear gunner fired a pair of 12.7mm (0.5in) machine guns from a powered turret.

LONG WING SPAN
The very long wing span of the USAF B-24s gave the aircraft excellent long range and good performance at high altitude.

The original XB-24 prototype had meanwhile been modified to XB-24B standard with self-sealing fuel tanks and armour, as well as R-1830-41 turbocharged engines. Nine aircraft were produced for the USAAF with the designation B-24C.

PLOESTI RAID

The first major production version, the B-24D with R-1830-43 engines, appeared late in 1941. A policy decision to concentrate B-24s primarily in the Pacific theatre (where the type's long range was used to good effect) resulted in most of the 2738 B-24Ds being deployed against Japan. However, the Eighth and Ninth Air Forces in Europe and North Africa also received the aircraft, one of their outstanding raids being the attack on the Ploesti oil refineries on 1 August 1943.

The first production model to come from the Ford production line was the B-24E with revised propellers. Consolidated and Douglas also built the B-24E version, some with R-1830-65 engines; total production was 801 aircraft. Production then switched to the B-24G, of which 430 were built. This version introduced a two-gun nose turret to counter head-on Luftwaffe fighter attacks. It

was followed by 3100 B-24H aircraft with various makes of nose turret. This model came from a new production line operated by North American. Similar aircraft were produced by Consolidated, and also by Douglas and Ford.

The major production version was the B-24J, of which 6678 were built, incorporating a Motor Products nose turret, new-type autopilot and bombsight.

The B-24L (1667 built) was similar to the B-24D, with the tail turret replaced by two manually controlled 12.7mm (0.5in) machine guns, of which Consolidated built 417 and Ford 1250, while the B-24M (2593 built) introduced a Motor Products two-gun tail turret.

RAF SERVICE

In RAF service, the initial Liberator Mk I and Mk II lacked direct US equivalents, while the B-24D was designated as the Liberator Mk III. The Liberator GR.Mk VI was a B-24J equipped for Coastal Command work, while the Liberator B.Mk VI was the same, but used as a heavy bomber in the Middle and Far East.

This huge manufacturing effort (which produced a total of 18,313 aircraft in five and a half years) involved the Consolidated, Douglas, Ford and North American plants,

the total including many aircraft for the Royal Air Force (in which Liberators served with 42 squadrons) and US Navy (with whom Liberators served under the designation PB4Y) and also the 25-passenger C-87 version, of which 282 were produced.

The first Liberator to be built in great numbers, the B-24D had a Plexiglas nose.

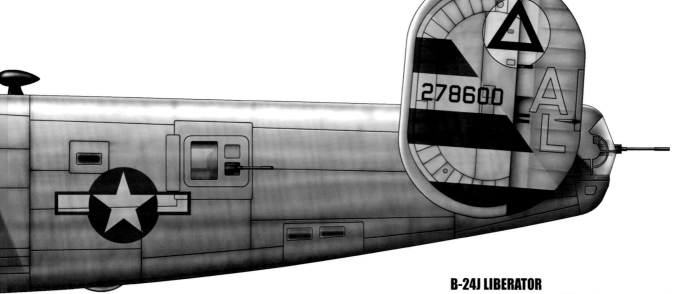

B-24J LIBERATOR

The B-24J included a new kind of nose turret, and two machine guns in the beam of the aircraft.

Fokker D.VII

Generally considered the best of the German fighting scout aircraft of World War I, the Fokker D.VII enjoyed a production run of around 3300 in the second half of 1918. In service with the Luftstreitkräfte, it soon proved to be a formidable opponent.

The Fokker D.VII was designed by Reinhold Platz as the successor to the same company's D.VI, but it had a number of improvements. In the event, both the D.VI and D.VII were subject to a service evaluation at Adlershof in January 1918. The operational pilots involved in these trials were unanimous in their verdict in favour of the D.VII. Despite this, both types entered service, but only 59 examples of the D.VI were ever completed.

Although the D.VII did not immediately defeat its stablemate, it did serve to confirm Fokker as the pre-eminent

builder of German fighting scouts. Albatros Werke, which had been Fokker's arch-rival for production contracts, saw its own scouts phased out of production after the Adlershof trials. Instead, the rival firm was ordered to manufacture the D.VII in its own factories.

Early-production D.VIIs were powered by the 119kW (160hp) Mercedes D.III water-cooled engine with car-type frontal radiator, but later in 1918 the 138kW (185hp) BMW was introduced and provided much improved performance.

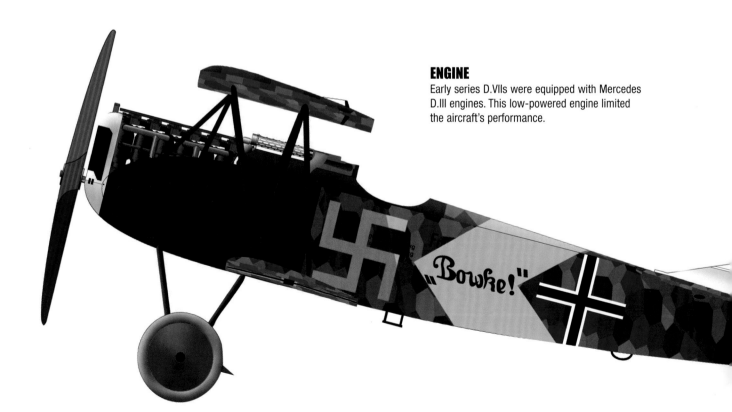

ENGINE
Early series D.VIIs were equipped with Mercedes D.III engines. This low-powered engine limited the aircraft's performance.

The D.VII became the fighter of choice for Hollywood movies during the industry's heyday of the 1920s. Here, a pilot looks over his shoulder in anticipation of beginning another dogfight for the cameras.

STRONG CONSTRUCTION
The huge strength of the aircraft's wings and fuselage meant it could be vigorously manoeuvred in combat.

COLOUR SCHEMES
Fokker D.VII aces wore a succession of elaborate colour schemes during World War I.

SIMPLE CONSTRUCTION

The success enjoyed by the D.VII stemmed not only from its straightforward flying characteristics, which were maintained right up to its ceiling and included a docile stall with no sudden wing drop, but also because of simple construction and ease of repair. The wings were of wooden construction covered with fabric, and the fuselage was a braced steel-tube box girder; the nose was metal-clad forward of the lower wing, and plywood-covered aft of this, stretched fabric being applied on top. The lower wing was fabricated as a single unit, the lower fuselage longerons being interrupted to allow the wing spars to pass right through the fuselage – an arrangement that gave considerable strength. All interplane and centre-section struts were of streamline-section steel tube.

SPECIFICATIONS

Crew: 1

Length: 6.954m (22ft 10in)

Wingspan: 8.9m (29ft 2in)

Loaded weight: 906kg (1997lb)

Powerplant: 1 × BMW III 6-cylinder piston engine, 138kW (185hp)

Maximum speed: 189km/h (117mph)

Armament: 2 × 7.92mm (0.312in) LMG 08/15 Spandau machine guns

FOKKER D.VII

This D.VII was flown by Leutnant Carl Degelow, commander of Jasta 40. He was an ace with 30 victories and received the Pour le Mérite on 9 November 1918, just two days before the war's end.

CLIMBING POWER

When powered by the over-compressed BMW.III engine the D.VII could outclimb all opponents and had a higher ceiling, giving it a competitive advantage over the Allied SE.5a and SPAD XIII.

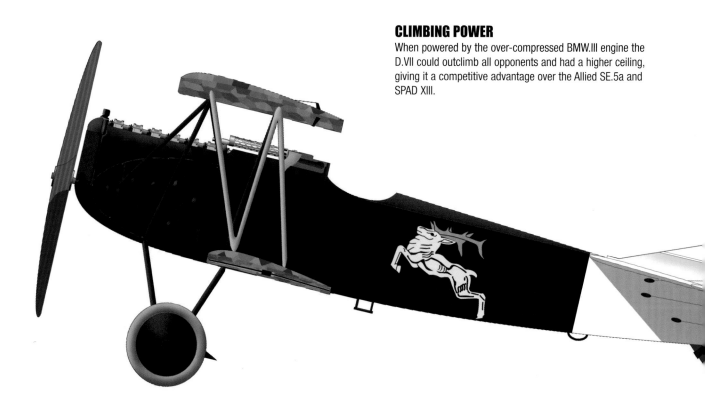

Among the aircraft's few faults were incidents of rib failure and fabric shedding on the upper wing. Another problem was heat from the engine that occasionally ignited phosphorus ammunition, and fuel tanks that sometimes broke at the seams.

INTO SERVICE

The first Geschwader to receive the D.VII was Geschwader Nr 1, deliveries being made to its Jasta 4, 6, 10 and 11 late in April 1918, only days after the death of its illustrious commander, Manfred von Richthofen, in a Fokker Dr.I triplane. JG 1 was followed by Jastas 12, 13, 15 and 19 of Geschwader Nr 2 and Jastas 2, 26, 27 and 36 of Geschwader Nr 3. In due course, a total of 46 Jastas were flying D.VIIs on the Western and Southern Fronts, roughly 65 per cent of the German fighting scout strength. There is no doubt that, notwithstanding the excellent quality of

Allied scouts that entered service in 1918, such as the SE5a and Snipe, the French and British squadrons held a healthy respect for the D.VII, with its austere-looking angular wings and rectangular boxlike fuselage. This respect was evidenced by a clause in the Armistice agreement that specifically required the handing over of all first-line D.VIIs to the Allies. Indeed, the D.VII saw further combat service after World War I, being taken into combat by Poland during the Polish–Soviet War, mainly for ground attack, and by the Hungarian Soviet Republic during the Hungarian–Romanian War of 1919.

Among the well-known pilots and aces whose high scores were achieved in D.VII cockpits were men such as Ernst Udet, Erich Löwenhardt, Rudolf Berthold, Olivier Freiherr von Beaulieu-Marconnay and Georg von Hantelmann, not forgetting Hermann Goering, who flew an all-white D.VII.

Fokker D.VII 'U.10' of Jasta 65 on display at the National Air and Space Museum, Washington, DC.

Avro Lancaster

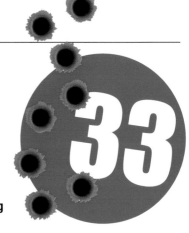

The United Kingdom's best heavy bomber of World War II, the four-engined Avro Lancaster is famed for its role in the 'Dambusters' raid of 1943 and for other high-profile missions. Above all, it bore the brunt of Royal Air Force Bomber Command's relentless night-bombing offensive against Nazi Germany.

Considering its later success, it is somewhat surprising that the Lancaster's path to operational service was a fairly difficult one. Its roots lay in the Avro Manchester, an unsuccessful twin-engine bomber. Even before deliveries of the Manchester to the RAF had begun, studies were underway that envisaged a four-engine version of the same basic airframe.

The first prototype Lancaster was a converted Manchester fitted with enlarged outer wing panels and powered by four 854kW (1145hp) Rolls-Royce Merlin X engines. In its initial form, the prototype retained the Manchester's triple tail assembly, but was later modified to the twin fin and rudder assembly that became standard on production Lancasters. The prototype flew on 9 January 1941.

The new bomber was an immediate success, and major production orders were placed. Such was the speed of development during the war that the first production Lancaster was flown in October 1941, a number of partially completed Manchester airframes being converted on the

CREW
The Lancaster had a crew of seven: pilot, navigator, flight engineer, bomb aimer/nose gunner, mid-upper gunner, radio operator, and rear gunner.

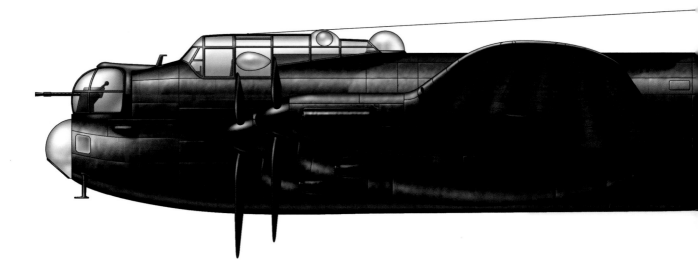

An Avro Lancaster that is part of the Royal Air Force Battle of Britain
Memorial Flight takes part in a display.

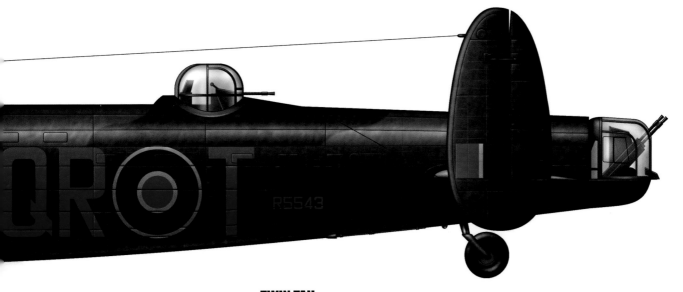

TWIN TAIL
The twin tail layout gave the Lancaster great stability.
Many parts of the airplane could be damaged and the
bomber would still be flyable enough to get home.

line to emerge as Lancaster Mk I (from 1942 designated as Lancaster B.Mk I) aircraft.

Lancasters soon began to replace Manchesters, and such was the demand for production that a shortage of Merlin engines was threatened. This was countered by licence production by Packard in the United States of the Merlin not only for Lancasters but also for other types. A further insurance was provided in another way: the use of 1294kW (1735hp) Bristol Hercules VI or XVI radial engines.

Meanwhile, the Merlin Lancasters were going from strength to strength. The prototype's engines gave way to 954kW (1280hp) Merlin XXs and 22s, or 1208kW (1620hp) Merlin 24s in later production aircraft.

PRODIGIOUS WEAPONS LOAD

The Lancaster's bomb bay was originally designed to carry 1814kg (4000lb) of bombs, but was progressively enlarged to carry bigger and bigger bombs: up to 3629 and 5443kg (8000 and 12,000lb) and eventually to Barnes Wallis' enormous 9979kg (22,000lb) 'Grand Slam', which was the heaviest bomb carried by any aircraft in World War II.

The Lancaster was first revealed to the public after the 17 August 1943 raid on Augsburg by 12 aircraft from Nos. 44 and 97 Squadrons. Flown at low level, unescorted and in daylight, the raid inflicted considerable damage on a factory producing U-boat engines, but the cost was high, seven aircraft being lost. The raid perhaps confirmed to the Air Staff that unescorted daylight raids by heavy bombers were not a practicable proposition.

The German battleship *Tirpitz* was attacked on several occasions by Lancasters until, on 12 November 1944, a combined force from Nos. 9 and 617 Squadrons found the battleship in Tromso Fjord, Norway, and sank her with 5443kg (12,000lb) 'Tallboy' bombs, also designed by Barnes Wallis. Meanwhile, No. 617 Squadron first used the 'Grand Slam' against the Bielefeld Viaduct on 14 March 1945, causing considerable destruction.

The Lancaster B.Mk I remained in production throughout the war, and Armstrong Whitworth delivered the last in February 1946. Production encompassed two Mk I prototypes, 3425 Mk Is, 301 Mk IIs, 3039 Mk IIIs, 180 Mk VIIs and 430 Mk Xs, for a grand total of 7377. These were built by Avro (3673), Armstrong Whitworth (1329), Austin Motors (330), Metropolitan Vickers (1080), VickersArmstrong (535) and Victory Aircraft (430). At least 59 Bomber Command squadrons operated Lancasters, which flew more than 156,000 sorties and dropped, in addition to 618,350 tonnes (608,612 tons) of high-explosive bombs, more than 51 million incendiaries.

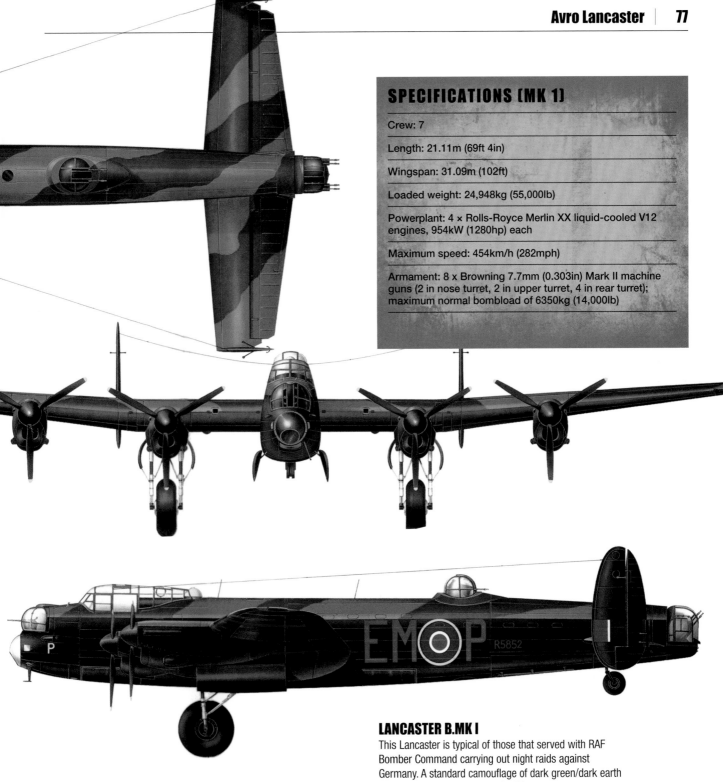

SPECIFICATIONS (MK 1)

Crew: 7

Length: 21.11m (69ft 4in)

Wingspan: 31.09m (102ft)

Loaded weight: 24,948kg (55,000lb)

Powerplant: 4 × Rolls-Royce Merlin XX liquid-cooled V12 engines, 954kW (1280hp) each

Maximum speed: 454km/h (282mph)

Armament: 8 x Browning 7.7mm (0.303in) Mark II machine guns (2 in nose turret, 2 in upper turret, 4 in rear turret); maximum normal bombload of 6350kg (14,000lb)

LANCASTER B.MK I

This Lancaster is typical of those that served with RAF Bomber Command carrying out night raids against Germany. A standard camouflage of dark green/dark earth upper surfaces and black undersides was common across the entire fleet.

BOMB BAY

The key to the Lancaster's success was its huge bomb bay, which could carry up to 7.11 tonnes (7 tons) of bombs. With modification, it could carry the massive 10.16-tonne (10-ton) 'Grand Slam' bomb.

Junkers Ju 87

Symbolic of the initial effectiveness of Hitler's military conquests in Western Europe, the Ju 87 'Stuka' gained notoriety for its early use as a terror weapon. However, its fortunes changed with the Battle of Britain in 1940, after which it was used increasingly as an anti-tank aircraft.

The Junkers Ju 87 is now best known as the Stuka, a contraction of the German word *Sturzkampfflugzeug*, or 'dive-bomber'. The Ju 87 was initially designed as a form of airborne artillery to support the German military's evolving tactics, which would later be dubbed 'Blitzkrieg'. In this role it was capable of delivering weapons with great accuracy, but without aerial supremacy it proved very vulnerable to enemy fighters.

The Ju 87 was first flown in in 1935, and the first of three prototypes featured twin vertical tail surfaces and a Rolls-Royce Kestrel engine. After the loss of the first prototype when it suffered a tail collapse during dive

tests, the second prototype introduced a single fin and rudder and was powered by a 455kW (610hp) Junkers Jumo 210A engine. Official evaluation of this aircraft and a further improved third prototype led to a pre-production batch of 10 Ju 87A-0 aircraft with the 477kW (640hp) Jumo 210Ca engine.

The initial Ju 87A-1 production version began to enter service in spring 1937, and the Legion Condor tested three examples under operational conditions during the Spanish Civil War in 1938–9.

To support the invasion of Poland in September 1939, the Luftwaffe fielded all five Stukageschwader

JU 87B-1
This Ju-87B-1 was involved in the campaign against France in May 1940. The Ju 87B was the first mass-produced model.

Parked on a Greek airfield during the Balkans campaign of spring 1941,
this Ju 87B Stuka is flanked by a 500kg (1102lb) bomb.

JU 87R-2/TROP

Some air crews would personalize their
aircraft markings, as with this graphic
image of a snake. This Stuka served in
North Africa as part of the Africa Corps.

thus far equipped with Ju 87s. It was in this campaign that, with little effective opposition in the air, the Stuka's legend was born. With sirens screaming, the cranked-wing dive-bombers wrought havoc among Polish troops and civilians, effectively destroying the country's lines of communications, bridges, railways and airfields.

LONG-RANGE VERSION

During the difficult Norwegian campaign, the Ju 87R was introduced, with underwing fuel tanks for long-range missions. Based on the Ju 87B, the R-model had extra fuel and provision for one 250kg (551lb) bomb.

During the Battle of Britain, the Ju 87R and the Ju 87B were heavily committed until withdrawn temporarily as a result of losses suffered at the hands of Royal Air Force fighters. The Ju 87B-1 featured a redesigned fuselage,

streamlined wheel spats, a 895kW (1200hp) Jumo 211Da engine and maximum bombload of 500kg (1102lb), increased to 1000kg (2202lb) in the Ju 87B-2.

At the end of 1941, the Ju 87D, a much refined version with a 1051kW (1410hp) Jumo 211J-1 and increased armour protection for the crew, entered service on the Russian front, and appeared in North Africa the following year. Notable sub-variants of the D-series included the Ju 87D-2, which was strengthened and fitted with a glider-tow hook; the Ju 87D-3 for ground attack with increased armour protection; the Ju 87D-5 dedicated close-support version with jettisonable landing gear and no dive brakes; the Ju 87D-7 night ground-attack model converted from Ju 87D-3s and Ju 87D-5s, with 1119kW (1500hp) Jumo 211P and wing-mounted machine guns replaced by 20mm (0.78in) MG 151/20 cannon; and the Ju 87D-

Ju 87G 'STUKA'

This Stuka was flown by Major Theo Nordmann over Soviet Russia in 1944. The Ju 87G included two 37mm (1.4in) Flak 18 guns designed for knocking out tanks and armoured fighting vehicles.

8, a day version of the Ju 87D-7 without night-flying equipment or flame-dampers.

Last of the line, the Ju 87G was a specialist anti-tank conversion of the Ju 87D-5 with a 37mm (1.4in) cannon beneath each wing. It achieved notable success, particularly in the East. Unquestionably the greatest exponent of the Stuka was Hans-Ulrich Rudel, whose personal tally of a battleship, cruiser and a destroyer sunk, and 519 tanks destroyed, far exceeded any other.

Total Ju 87 production was said to be 5709 and the aircraft also served with Bulgaria, Hungary, Italy and Romania. Surprisingly, the bulk of this impressive production total was completed after 1940, when the type's vulnerability without adequate fighter cover had been confirmed.

SPECIFICATIONS (87D-1)

Crew: 2

Length: 11.5m (38ft)

Wingspan: 13.8m (45ft)

Loaded weight: 6600kg (14,520lb)

Powerplant: 1 x 1051kW (1410hp) Junkers Jumo 211J-1 12 cylinder V piston engine

Maximum speed: 410km/h (254mph)

Armament: 2 × 7.92mm (0.312in) MG 17 machine guns forward, 1 × 7.92 mm (0.312in) MG 15 machine gun to rear; up to 1800kg (3960lb) underwing bombload

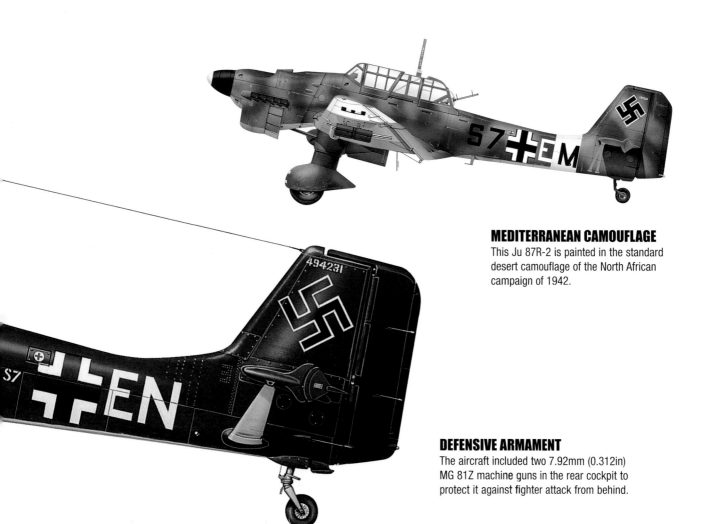

MEDITERRANEAN CAMOUFLAGE
This Ju 87R-2 is painted in the standard desert camouflage of the North African campaign of 1942.

DEFENSIVE ARMAMENT
The aircraft included two 7.92mm (0.312in) MG 81Z machine guns in the rear cockpit to protect it against fighter attack from behind.

de Havilland Mosquito

Originating in 1938 as a de Havilland private venture, the D.H.98 Mosquito was initially intended for use as an unarmed bomber or reconnaissance aircraft – one that would fly so fast and high that defensive armament would not be required.

The D.H.98 was based around a powerplant of two Rolls-Royce Merlin engines, and all-wood construction was selected from the outset to preserve strategic materials. So advanced was de Havilland's design that it did not find Air Ministry favour until the outbreak of World War II. With the real possibility of a shortage of light alloys, an all-wood aircraft now became a useful alternative to more conventional aircraft.

In December 1939, de Havilland began detail design work, leading to an order for 50 aircraft in March 1940. At this stage, in-production aircraft remained the clear priority, and it was not until 25 November 1940 that the prototype Mosquito Mk I was flown for the first time. The new bomber immediately demonstrated performance well in excess of that included in the specification, including a 'dash' speed of almost 644km/h (400mph).

PRIORITY STATUS

After official trials beginning in February 1941, the Mosquito was assigned priority production status in July of that year. Three prototypes were built and the last of these to fly, on 10 June 1941, was of a photo-reconnaissance (PR) version. The PR version was the first of the Mosquitoes to enter operational service. This Mosquito PR.Mk I made an initial sortie over France on 20 September 1941.

Next into service was the bomber version, the first of these being designated Mosquito B.Mk IV. Deliveries to the Royal Air Force's No. 105 Squadron began in November 1941. All versions of the Mosquito had accommodation for a crew of two, seated side by side.

SPECIFICATIONS (B.MK.IV)

Crew: 2

Length: 13.57m (44ft 6in)

Wingspan: 16.5m (54ft 2in)

Loaded weight: 10,200kg (22,440lb)

Powerplant: 2 x Rolls-Royce Merlin 76 V-12 liquid-cooled inline piston engines developing 1257kW (1710hp)

Maximum speed: 655km/h (407mph)

Armament: Maximum internal bombload 4 x 227kg (500lb) bombs

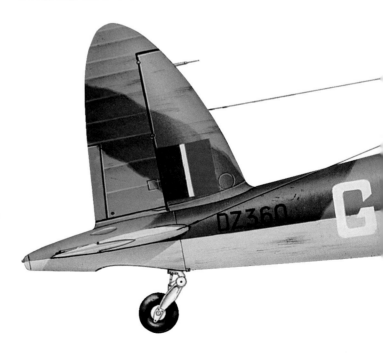

MOSQUITO B.MK IV

No. 105 Squadron was the first unit to operate the B.Mk IV.
The squadron carried out many daytime attack missions
on targets over Europe.

WOODEN WINGS

Like the fuselage, the wings were of a wooden
construction. The frame was glued, pinned and
screwed together, with a fabric covering. For this
reason, enemy gunfire would sometimes pass through
them without doing much damage.

MERLIN ENGINE

The Mosquito's Merlin engines were constantly
uprated to keep the aircraft ahead of its
competitors and opponents.

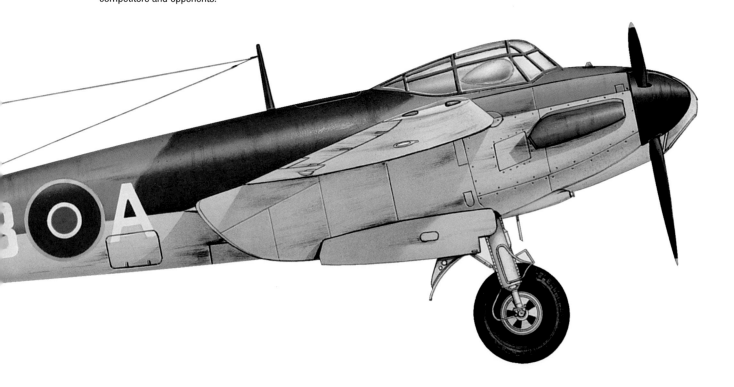

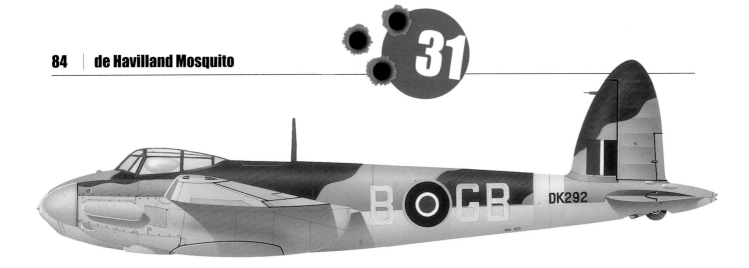

MOSQUITO B.MK IV SERIES 2

The B.Mk IV Series 2 was the first Mosquito to fly unescorted, high-speed attack missions over Germany. It could carry an internal bombload of 907kg (2000lb).

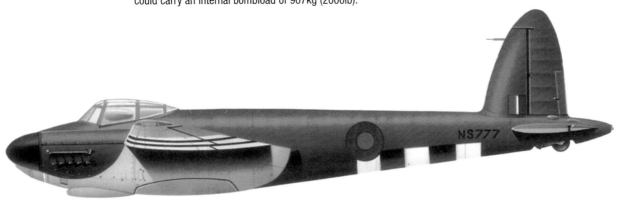

MOSQUITO PR.MK XVI

The Mosquito PR.Mk XVI was the photo-reconnaissance counterpart of the B.Mk XVI bomber. It was the RAF's standard high-altitude reconnaissance airplane in the later stages of World War II.

MOSQUITO NIGHT-FIGHTER

The second prototype, first flown on 15 May 1941, was configured as a night-fighter. It initially carried AI Mk IV radar and a nose armament of four 20mm (0.78in) cannon and four 7.7mm (0.303in) machine guns. Designated Mosquito NF.Mk II, the type began to enter service first with No. 157 Squadron, which made its initial operational sortie on the night of 27–28 April 1942. The type equipped No. 23 Squadron shortly afterwards, and this was the first unit to operate the type in the Mediterranean theatre when based at Luqa, Malta, from December 1942. These were deployed not only as night-fighters, but also in a day or night intruder role, making the first night intruder sortie on 30–31 December 1942.

The Mosquito T.Mk III was a dual-control trainer used for conversion to the type, and 343 were constructed.

The Mosquito was built not only in the UK, but also by the de Havilland factories in Australia and Canada; when production was finally terminated, a total of 7781 had been built. The most extensively built version was the Mosquito FB.Mk VI, an intruder or fighter-bomber developed from the F.Mk II fighter prototype: it had provision for internal and underwing bombs and, from 1944, for rocket projectiles.

Many examples of the Mosquito continued to give valuable service in the RAF during the immediate post-war years. PR Mosquitoes were used extensively in the Middle East and Far East; No. 81 Squadron in Malaya was the last unit to use the type operationally, in late 1955.

The bomber versions were displaced by English Electric Canberras in 1952–3, some then being used in a training role, with others converted for PR or target tug duties. In this latter role some examples remained in service as late as 1961.

Fighter versions, however, disappeared in the early 1950s, their role taken over by the new generation of jet fighters.

With its pressurized cockpit, the Mosquito B.Mk XVI could fly at an altitude of 12,192m (40,000ft). This aircraft was flown by No. 571 Squadron, which formed at Downham Market in April 1944 as a light bomber unit with No. 8 (Pathfinder) Group.

Consolidated Catalina

The exceptional flying boat of World War II, the 'Cat' was perhaps all the more remarkable since it had first been ordered for the US Navy back in 1933. It served with great success throughout World War II, and it became the most extensively built flying boat in aviation history.

Outstanding among parasol monoplane flying boats, Isaac Laddon's Consolidated PBY design was first flown with a pair of 615kW (825hp) Pratt & Whitney R-1830-58 radials on 28 March 1935. Among its distinctive features were the stabilizing floats that, when retracted, formed the wingtips. Production orders followed quickly and the PBY-1 entered service with 671kW (900hp) R-1830-64 engines with the US Navy's Patrol Squadron VP-11F in October 1936.

In 1937, the modified PBY-2 joined the US Navy, followed by the PBY-3. While the PBY-2 featured minor equipment changes only, the PBY-3 ordered in November 1936 had 746kW (1000hp) R-1830-66 engines.

The PBY-4, which appeared in 1938, featured the large midships 'blister' gun positions that were to become a well-known characteristic of the Catalina, as the boat came to be named (Consolidated, meanwhile, identified its design as the Model 28). The powerplant for the PBY-4 was a pair of 783kW (1050hp) R-1830-72 Twin Wasp engines.

The outbreak of World War II brought orders from the United Kingdom, Australia, Canada and the Dutch East Indies for a new version, the PBY-5 with 895kW (1200hp) R-1830-82 or -92 radials and greater fuel capacity. By the date of the United States's entry into the war, the US Navy possessed 16 PBY-5 squadrons, three of PBY-3s and two of PBY-4s.

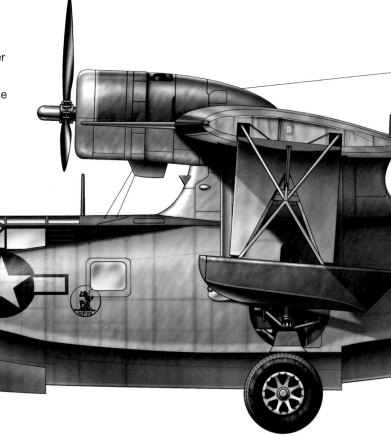

Consolidated first flew the XPBY-5A in November 1939. This was converted with a tricycle-type undercarriage from a PBY-4 and was the first amphibious variant.

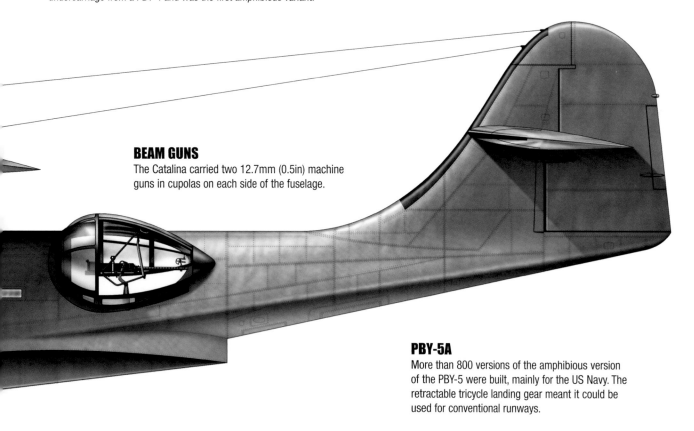

BEAM GUNS
The Catalina carried two 12.7mm (0.5in) machine guns in cupolas on each side of the fuselage.

PBY-5A
More than 800 versions of the amphibious version of the PBY-5 were built, mainly for the US Navy. The retractable tricycle landing gear meant it could be used for conventional runways.

AMPHIBIOUS DEVELOPMENTS

Following tests with a retractable tricycle wheel landing gear in the last PBY-4, the final 33 US Navy PBY-5s were completed in this amphibian form, as were 761 PBY-5A aircraft.

Following early successful use of the PBY-5 by the RAF's Coastal Command in 1941 as the Catalina Mk I, large orders continued to be placed for the US Navy, additional production being undertaken by Canadian Vickers and Boeing of Canada. A total of more than 500 examples eventually served with the RAF alone, while in Canadian service the PBY-5 was named the Canso.

Extensive service use of the PBY series suggested that the hull would benefit from hydrodynamic improvement. The Naval Aircraft Factory (NAF) carried out the necessary research and development work to achieve this end, receiving an order for these modified aircraft under the designation PBN-1 Nomad. This featured a taller fin and rudder, and 138 of the 156 built were supplied to the Soviet Union.

PBY-6A

When the final production version was built by Consolidated, to the extent of 235 PBY-6A machines between April 1944 and April 1945, the improvements of the NAF were among the package of changes incorporated. The PBY-6A amphibians had search radar mounted over the cockpit; 112 were delivered to the US Navy, 75 to the US Army Air Force (as the OA-10B) and 48 to the USSR.

Production of this classic aircraft, which ended in April 1945, included 2398 by Consolidated and 892 by NAF and the Canadian manufacturers, plus an unknown number built in the Soviet Union under the designation GST. Soviet production aircraft were powered by Mikulin M-62 radial engines, a developed version of the M-25 (licence-built Wright R-1820 Cyclone), which had a power rating of 671–746kW (900–1000hp).

Among the Catalina's memorable achievements were the successful shadowing of the German battleship *Bismarck*, which led ultimately to the warship's destruction, and the trailing of the Japanese fleets in the early stages of many of the naval battles in the Pacific.

SPECIFICATIONS (PBY-5A)

Crew: 8

Length: 19.47m (63ft 10in)

Wingspan: 31.7m (104ft)

Loaded weight: 16,066kg (35,420lb)

Powerplant: 2 × 895kW (1200hp) Pratt & Whitney R1830-92 twin Wasp radial piston engines

Maximum speed: 288km/h (175mph)

Armament: 2 x 7.62mm (0.3in) machine guns in bow, 1 x 7.62mm (0.3in) firing after from hull step, 2 x 12.7mm (0.5in) machine guns in beam position; up to 1814kg (4000lb) of bombs or depth chargers

The PBY series continued in service with a very large number of air arms after World War II, when machines surplus to American requirements were transferred to the Allies.

BOW CABIN

The nose section provided accommodation for one crew member who acted as an observer. The panel below the station was blind, but would have been used as a bomb-aiming window.

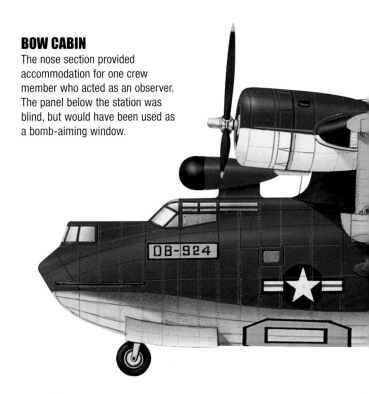

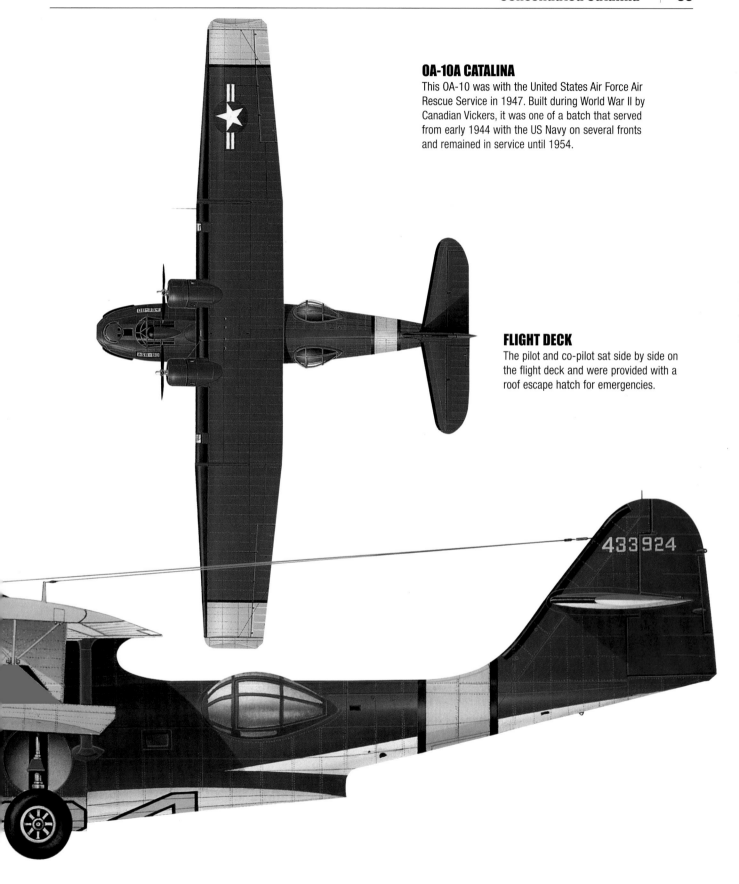

OA-10A CATALINA

This OA-10 was with the United States Air Force Air Rescue Service in 1947. Built during World War II by Canadian Vickers, it was one of a batch that served from early 1944 with the US Navy on several fronts and remained in service until 1954.

FLIGHT DECK

The pilot and co-pilot sat side by side on the flight deck and were provided with a roof escape hatch for emergencies.

F4U Corsair

The F4U had a troubled introduction to service in World War II, but by the end of the conflict it was challenging for a place among the best single-seat fighters of the war. It remained a viable ground-attack aircraft and night-fighter during the subsequent fighting in Korea.

Vought began to develop the Corsair in 1938, in response to a US Navy request for a new single-seat fighter to operate from its aircraft carriers. The approach taken by the design team was to combine the smallest possible fuselage with the most powerful engine then on offer: the Pratt & Whitney XR-2800 Double Wasp. Developed under the company designation V-166B, the fighter was characterized by its unusual inverted 'gull wing' configuration, which was a result of the need to accommodate the undercarriage. The landing gear would have had to incorporate very long oleos

PACIFIC WAR ACE
Flown by Lieutenant Ira C. 'Ike' Kepford, leading US Navy ace in the Pacific, during early 1944, this F4U-1A – perhaps the most famous of all the wartime Corsairs – carries Kepford's 16 kill markings in the form of Imperial Japanese rising suns.

The likely key to the Corsair's longevity was the combination of its superior air combat capabilities, a high top speed, the ability to absorb combat damage and a strong wing – all of which helped to produce a world-beating warplane.

CORSAIR CONSTRUCTION

Apart from the highly cranked wing – which could be folded for storage below the carrier deck – the fighter utilized a broadly conventional airframe of all-metal construction. The FG-1 version differed in having fixed rather than folding wings.

SPECIFICATIONS (F4U-1)

Crew: 1

Length: 10.17m (33ft 4.5in)

Wingspan: 12.5m (41ft)

Empty weight: 4074kg (8982lb)

Powerplant: 1 × Pratt & Whitney R-2800-8 radial engine

Maximum speed: 671km/h (417mph) at 6066m (19,900ft)

Armament: 6 x 12.7mm (0.5in) machine guns in the wings

to provide enough ground clearance for the large-diameter propeller. Since long undercarriage gear was not best suited to operations from a carrier deck, the solution was found in positioning the main gear units at the 'pinion point' of the wing, which allowed their length to be reduced.

After being ordered in June 1938, the first XF4U-1 prototype took to the air on 29 May 1940. However, it was soon decided that the planned armament would need to be upgraded in light of combat experience from the first years of World War II. It was not until February 1941, therefore, that the US Navy accepted the prototype, before placing an order for the 585 F4U-1 initial production aircraft in June 1941. After a first flight by a production aircraft in June

The Royal New Zealand Air Force received its first Corsairs in March 1944 under lend-lease. After the initial deliveries, New Zealand began to assemble its own aircraft and, by the time the country stopped building Corsairs in 1945, the RNZAF had acquired 424.

1942, the first examples of the F4U-1 were handed over to the US Navy the following month.

Initial carrier trials revealed a host of problems with the Corsair, and it was judged unsuitable for carrier service. In response, Vought developed a number of 'fixes', including revised landing gear and a raised cockpit to give the pilot a better view forward. After 688 F4U-1s had been built, subsequent aircraft incorporated the aforementioned changes and were designated F4U-1A.

COMBAT

The Corsair went into combat with land-based units, beginning with the US Marine Corps' VMF-124 at Guadalcanal in February 1943. An operational US Navy squadron, VF-17, was established in April 1943. Other wartime operators were the Royal Navy and Royal New Zealand Air Force, with which it initially served as the Corsair Mk I (F4U-1) and Corsair Mk II (F4U-1A).

GUY BORDELON

This Korean War F4U-5N, named 'Annie Mo', was flown by Lieutenant Bordelon of VC-3, who lived up to his nickname 'Lucky Pierre' when assigned ashore at K-6 under Detachment Dog in mid-1953. Tasked with hunting nocturnal 'Bedcheck Charlie' raiders, Bordelon became the only non-Sabre ace of the war, downing four Yaks and a Lavochkin.

JESSE FOLMAR (RIGHT)

Piloting a Goodyear-built FG-1D (F4U-4), Marine pilot Captain Folmar of VMA-312 was able to claim the only Corsair versus MiG kill in September 1952. Attacked by MiG-15s, Folmar downed one using his 20mm (0.78in) cannon before bailing out after being hit by another MiG-15.

Successive production variants included the F4U-1B for the UK and the F4U-1C with four 20mm (0.78in) cannon in place of the standard six machine-gun armament. The F4U-1D (also manufactured as the F3A-1D and FG-1D; known in the UK as the Corsair Mk III and Corsair Mk IV, respectively) had a R-2800-8W water-injection engine and revised armament, while the F4U-1P was a photo-reconnaissance variant. The next major development was the F4U-2 night-fighter, produced by conversion and with radar and reduced armament. More important numerically was the F4U-4, the significant difference of which was its R-2800-18W or R-2800-42W engine. Sub-variants were the F4U-4C with cannon armament, the F4U-4E and F4U-4N night-fighters, and the F4U-4P photo-reconnaissance variant. Development of the Corsair continued after the war with the F4U-5 fighter-bomber with R-2800-32W engine and its F4U-5N night-fighter and F4U-5P reconnaissance counterparts. The XF4U-6 prototype low-altitude variant featured a R-2800-83W engine, additional armour protection and increased weapon-carrying capability; it was built as the AU-1. Last of the line was the similar F4U-7 with R-2800-18W, which was operated by the French Navy.

Production of the Corsair involved not only Vought but also Brewster, under the designation F3A-1, and Goodyear, as the FG-1. Between them, the three manufacturers produced 12,571 examples of the fighter by 1952.

US Navy Corsairs were credited with 2140 victories against the Japanese in the Pacific for the loss of only 189 of their own number, and the type continued to score aerial kills during the Korean War.

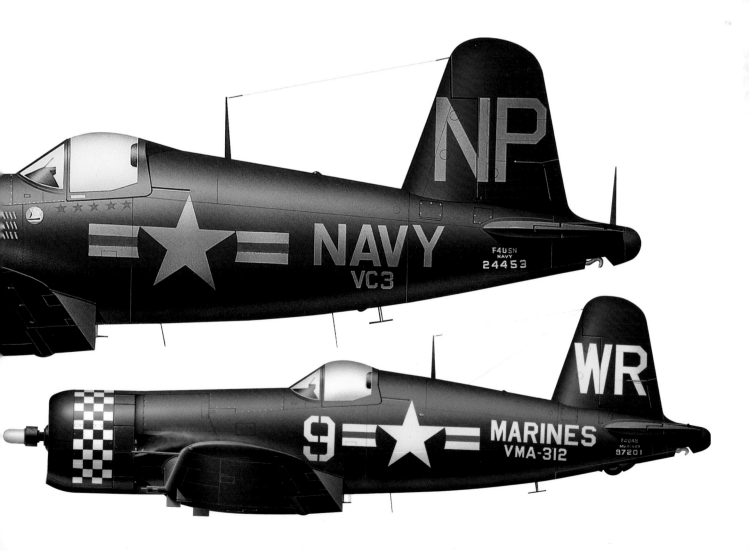

# F-15 Eagle

Despite its age, the F-15 remains the US Air Force's premier air superiority fighter, with a 105:0 kill ratio that is unequalled by any other warplane of its generation. As well as seeing extensive combat in US and Israeli hands, the F-15 has been a notable export success, and sales of Advanced Eagle versions continue.

Prompted by the poor showing of US Air Force fighters in combat over Vietnam, the air arm launched the Fighter Experimental (FX) programme in April 1965. So urgent was the requirement for a new air superiority fighter that McDonnell Douglas was ordered to develop the aircraft immediately, without a fly-off against competing designs.

The first F-15A prototype was completed at St Louis in June 1972 and airlifted to Edwards Air Force Base, California, for its maiden flight on 27 July 1972. After 10 single-seat development F-15A aircraft, two TF-15A development twin-seaters and 10 Category II development aircraft, the Eagle entered service with the 58th Tactical Training Wing at Luke AFB, Arizona, which received its first F-15A in November 1974.

A total of 355 production F-15As was eventually built, together with 57 fully mission-capable two-seat F-15B trainers. The operational career of the Eagle began with the first delivery of an F-15A to the 1st TFW at Langley AFB, Virginia, in January 1976.

NOMENCLATURE

When it first flew Eagles, the unit this aircraft belonged to was part of Tactical Air Command, and was known as the 58th Tactical Fighter Wing. With the USAF reorganization of the 1990s, it later became the 58th Fighter Squadron, 33rd Fighter Wing, Air Combat Command. As of 2017, the 58th FS was a joint graduate flying and maintenance training wing for the F-35 Lightning II.

ENGINE SPACING

To minimize asymmetric handling problems, the engines are mounted close together; to prevent damage to one engine causing reciprocal damage to the other, they are separated by a titanium keel.

SPECIFICATIONS (F-15E)

Crew: 2

Length: 19.43m (63ft 9in)

Wingspan: 13.05m (42ft 9.75in)

Empty weight: 14,379kg (31,700lb)

Powerplant: 2 × Pratt & Whitney F100-PW-220 turbofans

Maximum speed: More than 2655km/h (1650mph) at high altitude

Armament: 1 x 20mm (0.78in) M61A1 cannon and maximum of 11,000kg (24,250lb) of ordnance

MIG-KILLER

Seen in the markings it carried in the early 1990s, this aircraft accounted for four out of the 58th Tactical Fighter Squadron's 16 kills during the 1991 Gulf War. Among its pilots were Colonel Rick Parsons, Captain David G. Rose and Captain Anthony R. Murphy.

The F-15C was the next production version, complemented by the two-seat F-15D. The F-15C was first flown on 26 February 1979. The F-15C/D was completed with improved APG-63 radar and provision for conformal fuel tanks on the sides of the intakes. Initial F-15C deliveries were made to the 18th TFW at Kadena Air Base, Okinawa, in September 1979.

The F-15A/B was exported to Israel, while the F-15C/D was supplied to Israel, Japan and Saudi Arabia, the Japanese aircraft being built under licence by Mitsubishi as the F-15J (single seat) and F-15DJ. The first two F-15Js were built in the US, with eight more subsequently assembled by Mitsubishi. McDonnell Douglas also built the first 12 F-15DJs, before production switched entirely to Japan, where Mitsubishi built 163 F-15Js and 36 F-15DJs, bringing the overall total to 213 aircraft.

ADDITIONAL FUEL

Although the F-15C is externally similar to the preceding F-15A, internal space was found for an additional 907kg (2000lb) of fuel, while the F-15C/D was the first operational model to be able to carry conformal fuel tanks (CFTs).

NEW RADAR

From 1989 the F-15C/D incorporated the AN/APG-70 radar (a much-modified APG-63). Using the same antenna, the APG-70 had new signal processor systems nearly five times quicker than those of the APG-63, while able to handle much larger volumes.

In the 1990s, the USAF improved its F-15A-to-Ds through an ambitious Multi-Stage Improvement Program (MSIP) that replaced the original AN/APG-63 with the more advanced APG-70 radar, new avionics and digital central computers. More recently, surviving USAF F-15Cs have undergone the 'Golden Eagle' upgrade, providing them with new AN/APG-63(V)3 active electronically scanned array (AESA) radars and a new passive targeting capability. As of early 2017, only three active USAF squadrons operated the type, with the Air National Guard being the primary user.

STRIKE EAGLE

The F-15E Strike Eagle was developed in the late 1970s to replace the USAF's precision strike F-111F. Officially

A US Air Force F-15C, flown by Brigadier General David A. Deptula, Operation Northern Watch co-commander, over northern Iraq during routine patrols of the northern no-fly zone in December 1998.

launched in 1984 as F-15C/D production was winding up, the F-15E combined all the attributes of the basic air-defence fighter with cutting-edge strike-attack technology via the LANTIRN (Low-Altitude Navigation and Targeting Infrared for Night) system that added terrain avoidance/following radar and targeting forward-looking infrared — permitting round-the-clock, all-weather operations.

Trials of the Strike Eagle began in 1982 using a modified TF-15A two-seater. The first production F-15E took to the air on 11 December 1986. The USAF procured 236 F-15Es, all of which had been delivered by July 1994. The avionics of USAF Strike Eagles are also being upgraded, with the most significant current project being the Radar Modernization Program (RMP) now under way to introduce the AN/APG-82(V)1 AESA radar.

The Strike Eagle has formed the basis for a range of advanced, multi-role export F-15s, beginning with the F-15S for Saudi Arabia, deliveries of which began in September 1995. Israel ordered a similar variant, designated F-15I Ra'am (Thunder), 25 of which were procured.

The F-15K Slam Eagle is a highly advanced Strike Eagle derivative developed to meet a South Korean requirement. It has been followed by the F-15SA (Saudi Advanced) for Saudi Arabia, produced by Boeing and by local upgrade of earlier F-15S jets. Singapore received the F-15SG, while the latest export customer is Qatar, which signed up for the F-15QA version, similar to the Saudi Advanced model. Qatar's long-standing request for up to 36 F-15s was approved in September 2016, and these may be the most capable Eagles yet.

A6M Zero

Although it began to be outclassed midway through the war in the Pacific, few fighters have made such an impact in their first years of combat. Flying from carriers and land bases, the Imperial Japanese Navy's A6M Zero fighter swept away all opposition during combat operations against China and in the initial Japanese successes in World War II.

Best known as the Zero, the Mitsubishi A6M, which carried the Allied codename 'Zeke', derived its popular name from its official Navy designation of Type 0 Fighter. The Zero was the most famous Japanese single-seat fighter of World War II, and in its early years of service was one of the most capable aircraft of its class anywhere in the world.

Originally designed to meet an IJN specification calling for a carrier-based fighter to replace the Mitsubishi A5M, the new design was a cantilever low-wing monoplane. In its initial production A6M1 form it was powered by a 582kW (780hp) Mitsubishi MK2 Zuisei radial engine, and it

completed its maiden flight on 1 April 1939. Although the new fighter immediately exhibited formidable agility and generally excellent performance, its maximum speed was some way short of the specification required by the Navy.

The introduction of a 690kW (925hp) Nakajima NK1C Sakae engine was intended to address the deficiency of the A6M1 and led to the A6M2, the prototype of which flew for the first time on 18 January 1940. The A6M2 was a much more realistic proposition and was immediately ordered by the IJN, which in July 1940 placed a contract for 15 pre-production aircraft for combat evaluation in China.

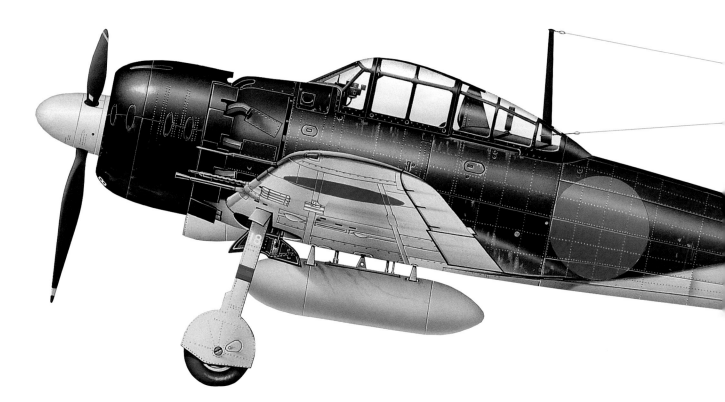

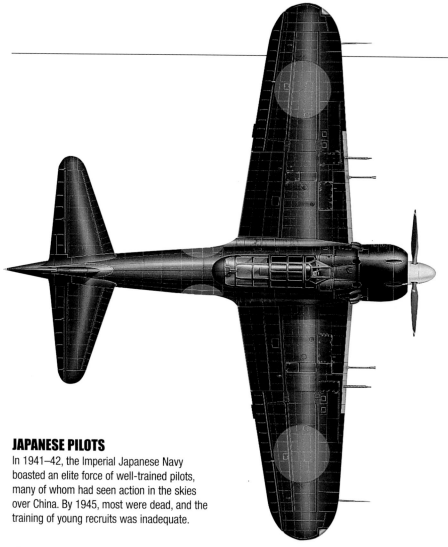

A6M5C

Externally similar to the standard A6M5, the A6M5c variant featured improved armament in the form of two 13.2mm (0.52in) machine guns outboard of the wing cannon. Only 93 A6M5c models were built.

ARMOUR

Throughout the war in the Pacific, a major shortcoming of the Zero was its inadequate armour. The A6M5 attempted to redress this by means of its self-sealing fuel tanks and improved pilot protection.

JAPANESE PILOTS

In 1941–42, the Imperial Japanese Navy boasted an elite force of well-trained pilots, many of whom had seen action in the skies over China. By 1945, most were dead, and the training of young recruits was inadequate.

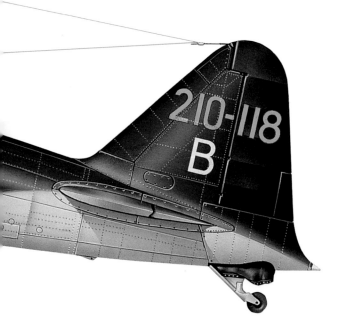

Most flying Zeroes have had their engines replaced with similar American units. Only one, the Planes of Fame Museum's A6M5, has the original Sakae engine. The A6M2 pictured was flown by the Confederate (today, Commemorative) Air Force in the 1990s, with a Pratt & Whitney R-1830 engine.

As the A6M2 began to reach service units, it gradually replaced the IJN's previous single-seat fighter, the ultra-manoeuvrable Mitsubishi A5M. The latter served on into the early war years, as is proved by this collection of A6M2s and A5Ms lined up on an airfield at the beginning of the war in the Pacific.

At the end of July 1940, the fighter was ordered into production as the Navy Type 0 Carrier Fighter Model 11 (A6M2 Model 11). Sub-variants included the A6M2 Model 21 that featured manually folded wingtips, and the A6M2-K two-seat trainer. A floatplane version of the Zero was built by Nakajima (a total of 327 aircraft) under the designation A6M2-N.

REVISED VERSIONS

A new powerplant in the form of the Nakajima NK1F Sakae 21 produced the A6M3 Model 22. The same unit was found in the A6M3, which featured clipped wings instead of the previous folding wingtips.

The major production version emerged as the A6M5 Model 52. This entered service in 1943 and was intended as a response to the rapidly improving Allied fighters that were now appearing in the Pacific theatre. Sub-variants included the A6M5a, A6M5b and A6M5c, which featured different armament arrangements, and the A6M5-S night-fighter, which was armed with a 20mm (0.78in) cannon mounted obliquely in the rear fuselage. This series also led to a two-seat training version, the A6M5-K. While the A6M5 had essentially exhausted the development potential of the

LATE-WAR ZERO

The first production variant was the A6M2. This example sports late-war camouflage, with dark green upper surfaces and grey undersides. It served with the 402nd Chutai (squadron) 341st Kokutai (naval air corps) at Clark Field in the Philippines in 1944.

A6M2 VARIANTS

Production A6M2 fighters with two wing-mounted 20mm (0.78in) cannon and two nose-mounted 7.7mm (0.303in) guns were fitted with the 708.4kW (950hp) Nakajima Sakae 12 radial. It was with this version that the Japanese Navy escorted the raiding force sent against Pearl Harbor, and gained air superiority over Malaya, the Philippines and Burma.

Zero fighter, the desperate situation that faced the Japanese by late 1944 led to the introduction of the A6M6, which was effectively an A6M5c re-engined. The first large-scale production version in this series was the A6M6c Model 53c, followed by the dual-role fighter/dive-bomber A6M7 Model 63 that featured a rack below the fuselage rack for one 250kg (551lb) bomb; the aircraft entered production in mid-1945.

The final variant of the Zero to enter flight testing was the A6M8c Model 64c, of which two prototypes were built with 1119kW (1500hp) Mitsubishi MK8K engines. However, no series aircraft were produced before the end of the war. The Zero fighter displayed its superiority over all opposition

EARLY SERVICE

One of the very first Reisens to reach the Imperial Navy, this pre-series A6M2 operated with brilliant success against the Chinese in the second half of 1940 with the 12th Rengo Kokutai (combined naval air corps) in the Hankow region. These aircraft lacked folding wingtips and numerous other small refinements.

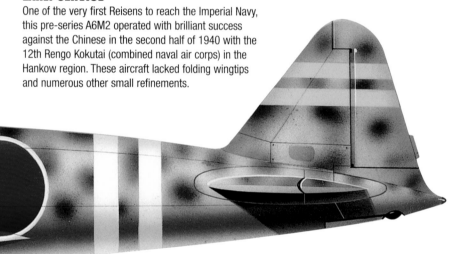

SPECIFICATIONS

Crew: 1

Length: 9.12m (29ft 11.1in)

Wingspan: 11m (36ft 1.1in)

Empty weight: 1876kg (4136lb)

Powerplant: 1 × Nakajima NK2F Sakae 21 radial engine

Maximum speed: 565km/h (351mph) at 6000m (19,685ft)

Armament: 1 x 7.7mm (0.303in) machine gun and 1 x 13.2mm (0.52in) machine gun in nose, 2 x 20mm (0.78in) cannon in wings, plus provision for 2 x 250kg (55lb) bombs

that it met in the Japanese War. Its success continued during the opening phases of the Pacific War during 1941 and early 1942. However, the Battle of Midway in June 1942 proved to be a turning point in the conflict and in the fortunes of the A6M. From now on, Allied fighters increasingly gained the upper hand and the A6M would never again enjoy wide-scale air superiority. In the absence of suitable replacement fighters in sufficient numbers, the Zero remained in service until the end of the war, including on kamikaze missions. Around 10,450 examples were built by Mitsubishi and Nakajima, while 515 A6M2-K and A6M5-K trainers were built by Hitachi and the 21st Naval Air Arsenal at Omura.

B-17 Flying Fortress

The classic four-engined heavy bomber in US Army Air Force service during World War II, the Boeing B-17 was the mainstay of the strategic daylight bombing campaign against German industrial and military targets. Although more B-24s were built, the B-17 ultimately dropped more bombs than any other US aircraft in World War II.

The Boeing Model 299 was designed to meet a May 1934 requirement of the US Army Air Corps, calling for an advanced day-flying strategic bomber that would be able to fly higher, and carry far heavier defensive armament, than other bombers of the time. The new bomber was required to carry a 907kg (2000lb) bombload over a distance of between 1640 and 3540km (1020–2200 miles) at speeds of between 322 and 402km/h (200–250mph).

The four-engine Model 299 Flying Fortress was first flown on 28 July 1935, powered by 559kW (750hp) Pratt & Whitney R-1680-E Hornet radial engines. A few weeks later, the prototype demonstrated its potential when it was flown 3380km (2100 miles) to Wright Field, Ohio, for official testing. The journey was completed at an average speed of 406km/h (252mph). The prototype set out the basic configuration of the aircraft: a low-wing cantilever monoplane, a circular-section fuselage with capacious bomb bay, fixed tailwheel landing gear and defensive armament that included five 7.62mm (0.3in) machine guns – a number that would increase progressively during the type's development. Beginning in August 1937, a total of 12 YB-17 (later Y1B-17) service test aircraft were taken

'LITTLE MISS MISCHIEF'

This B-17G-35-VE, 42-97880, served with the 91st Bomb Group, 324th Bomb Squadron and received 'Little Miss Mischief' nose art by Corporal Anthony L. Starcer while at Bassingbourn, England.

SPECIFICATIONS (B-17G)

Crew: 9–10

Length: 22.66m (74ft 4in)

Wingspan: 31.62m (103ft 9in)

Empty weight: 16,391kg (36,135lb)

Powerplant: 4 × Wright R-1820-97 radial engines

Maximum speed: 462km/h (287mph) at 7620m (25,000ft)

Armament: Twin 12.7mm (0.5in) machine guns in each of the chin, dorsal, ventral and tail turrets, 5 x trainable 12.7mm (0.5in) machine guns in other positions, plus up to 7983kg (17,600lb) of bombs

The vast armadas of the US 8th Air Force, equipped mainly with the Boeing B-17, ranged far and wide over Germany and occupied Europe from 1942 to 1945. Bombing individual factories and other precision targets, they also whittled away at the fighter strength of the Luftwaffe in some of the largest and bloodiest air battles in history.

AIRFRAME REBUILD

After being damaged by flak during a mission on 15 October 1944, 'Little Miss Mischief' recovered to Bassingbourn. The relatively undamaged forward part of the aircraft was mated with the rear portion of B-17G 'Wallaroo Mark II', which had previously crash-landed on a non-combat sortie.

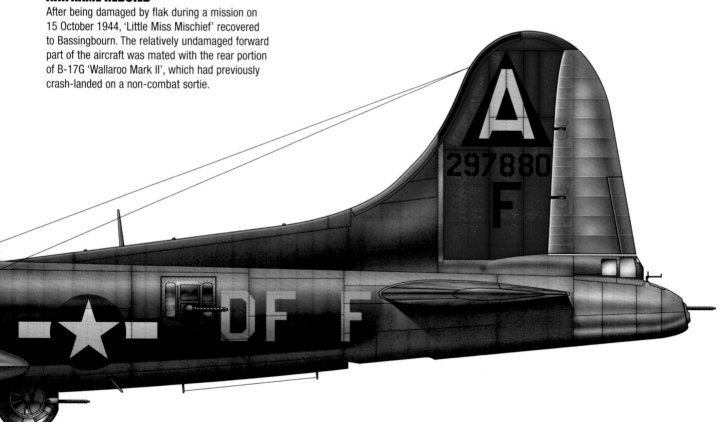

on hand by the USAAC for evaluation. Compared to the initial prototype, the Y1B-17 was powered by 694kW (930hp) Wright GR-1820-39 radial engines and included accommodation for a crew of nine.

The development aircraft were followed by small numbers of B-17B and B-17C bombers in 1940–1, and by the B-17D in 1941. The latter incorporated early combat lessons from World War II, adding self-sealing tanks and additional armour for protection for the crew.

The B-17E introduced the enlarged vertical tail surfaces and tail gun position characteristic of all subsequent B-17s, as well as power-operated twin-gun turrets aft of the cockpit and below the centre fuselage. A total of 512 B-17Es were produced, this version being the first US Army Air Force heavy bomber to see combat in Europe with the 8th Air Force.

DEFINITIVE VERSION

A total of 3400 B-17F bombers, with enlarged one-piece nose transparency, was produced during 1942–3. These were followed by the principal variant, the B-17G, which, in reply to calls for improved nose armament to counter

the Luftwaffe's head-on attacks, introduced the two-gun 'chin' turret; production totalled 8680 B-17G aircraft by Boeing, Douglas and Lockheed-Vega. To increase the type's operational ceiling, later production examples were equipped with improved turbochargers.

The Fortress was deployed principally in Europe during the war, with much smaller numbers operating in the Far East. The type carried out many epic raids, with large formations of bombers, each bristling with heavy machine guns and providing mutual protection against enemy fighters, pounding across the daylight skies over Hitler's Reich. In due course, heavy losses forced the Americans to introduce escort fighters – the P-38, P-47 and P-51.

One temporary expedient involved the use of a small number of B-17s modified as YB-40 'escort' aircraft, some aircraft carrying up to 30 machine guns.

Fortresses (B-17Cs, Fs and Gs) also served in small numbers with RAF Bomber and Coastal Commands.

Almost 13,000 examples of all versions of the B-17 were built, but only a few hundred B-17Gs remained in USAAF service after the end of World War II, and these were soon made redundant.

B-17D FLYING FORTRESS
The B-17D included extra armoured protection.
Only 42 mark Ds were built.

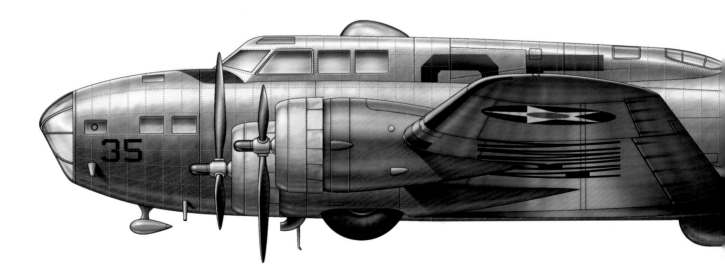

'Shoo Shoo Shoo Baby', a B-17G, is one of the most historic of the preserved
Flying Fortresses. The aircraft flew 24 combat missions from England with
the 91st Bombardment Group, before being interned in Sweden. It was later
restored for the National Museum of the United States Air Force in Ohio.

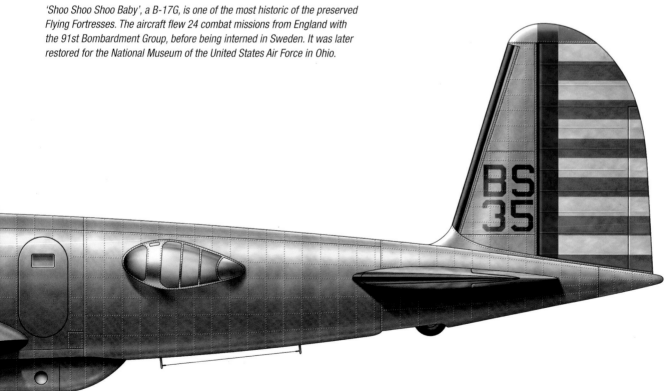

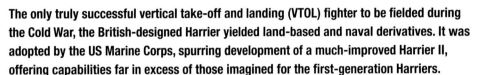

Harrier

The only truly successful vertical take-off and landing (VTOL) fighter to be fielded during the Cold War, the British-designed Harrier yielded land-based and naval derivatives. It was adopted by the US Marine Corps, spurring development of a much-improved Harrier II, offering capabilities far in excess of those imagined for the first-generation Harriers.

The history of the Harrier can be traced back to 1957 and an agreement between Hawker Aircraft and Bristol Aero-Engines to develop a tactical fighter based on the latter's BE-53 turbojet engine that provided direct jet-lift for vertical take-off. The key to the engine, and to the Harrier's revolutionary concept, was four exhaust nozzles in fore and aft pairs, swivelling to vector the thrust from directly backwards (for horizontal flight) to just forward of the vertical (for hovering flight). Stability in the hover and during low-speed manoeuvres was provided by reaction-control jets mounted in the nose, tail and each wingtip.

Six prototype Hawker P.1127 Kestrel prototypes were completed, and the first of these completed its initial hovering flight on 21 October 1960. There followed nine

pre-production aircraft Kestrel F(GA).Mk 1 aircraft for operational evaluation beginning in March 1964. Another six development aircraft were the first to carry the famous Harrier name and led to the single-seat Harrier GR.Mk 1 for ground-attack and reconnaissance aircraft. These entered service with the Royal Air Force in April 1969, followed soon after by the Harrier T.Mk 2 trainer. These initial models were powered by the Pegasus Mk 101 turbofan rated at 84.52kN (19,000lb st).

The addition of the 95.64kN (21,500lb st) Pegasus Mk 103 produced the Harrier GR.Mk 3 and T.Mk 4, which equipped four operational RAF squadrons. While these validated the concept of operations for a VTOL aircraft, they were succeeded in RAF service by the far more capable

FALKLANDS VETERAN
This Sea Harrier FRS.Mk 1 (X2457) is seen as it appeared immediately after the Falklands conflict, the drab scheme broken only by the roundels, a few warning marks and three kill markings on the nose, depicting two Daggers and an A-4 Skyhawk.

WEAPONS FIT
This Sea Harrier FRS.Mk 1 is armed with a pair of AIM-9L 'Nine-Lima' Sidewinders, and has two 30mm (1.1in) Aden cannon pods under the fuselage. The overall dark sea-grey colour led to the 'Shar' being nicknamed 'Muerte Negro' ('Black Death') by the Argentines.

SPECIFICATIONS (HARRIER GR.MK 3)

Crew: 1

Length: 14.27m (46ft 10in)

Wingspan: 7.7m (25ft 3in)

Empty weight: 5579kg (12,300lb)

Powerplant: 1 × Rolls-Royce Pegasus Mk 103 turbofan

Maximum speed: Over 1186km/h (737mph) at low altitude

Armament: Up to a normal load of 2268kg (5000lb) of stores on wing and fuselage pylons, normally including two 30mm (1.1in) Aden cannon pods, bombs and/or rockets

A radar-equipped US Marine Corps AV-8B Harrier II assigned to Marine Medium Helicopter Squadron 162 (Reinforced) makes a vertical take-off from a US Navy amphibious assault ship while en route to the Middle East in 2005.

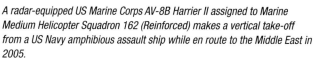

SEA-PROOFING

The dangers of salt water corrosion resulted in the naval Sea Harrier having additional protection, while the Rolls-Royce Pegasus Mk 104 was a parallel to the RAF's Mk 103 except for similar proofing.

Harrier GR.Mk 5, which was introduced to service in 1988. The US Marine Corps Harrier story began with an order for McDonnell Douglas AV-8A and TAV-8A aircraft that were produced in the UK. The USMC had one training and three operational squadrons equipped with the type; the only other operators of the first-generation Harrier were Spain (AV-8S and TAV-8S Matador) and Thailand, which acquired four Spanish jets when these were replaced in service by Harrier IIs.

The Harrier II began life as a joint McDonnell Douglas/ BAe project and was intended to carry a larger warload over a longer range. Envisaged as the 'Super Harrier' in the early 1980s, it was first flown on 9 November 1978, as the YAV-8B. This featured a new wing, new Rolls-Royce F402 series engine, and carbon-fibre structure. The USMC took delivery of a first AV-8B production aircraft in 1983. The TAV-8B was its two-seat counterpart.

The Harrier GR.Mk 5 for the RAF was broadly similar to the AV-8B. Once the USMC introduced a night-attack capability on its AV-8Bs, the RAF did the same via the Harrier GR.Mk 7 upgrade. The first production GR.Mk 7 was delivered in May 1990, and was complemented by a second-generation trainer, the Harrier T.Mk 10. The final RAF iterations were the Harrier GR.Mk 9 and T.Mk 12, which were retired from service in December 2010.

The 205th AV-8B off the production line was the first fully equipped example of the improved AV-8B Harrier II Plus, first flown on 22 September 1992, and equipped with AN/APG-65 radar. As of early 2017, the AV-8B remained in large-scale USMC service and in smaller numbers with the navies of Italy and Spain.

SEA HARRIER

The BAe Sea Harrier was developed for the Royal Navy as a radar-equipped version of the GR.Mk 3 for service from aircraft carriers. The initial Sea Harrier FRS.Mk 1 became operational in March 1980 and saw successful combat service in the Falklands War. It was later upgraded to Sea Harrier FA.Mk 2 standard with Blue Vixen radar and AIM-120 AMRAAM missile capability. These aircraft were withdrawn from Royal Navy service in 2006, when their place on carrier decks was taken by the Harrier GR.Mk 7. First-generation Sea Harriers survived in Indian service until 2016.

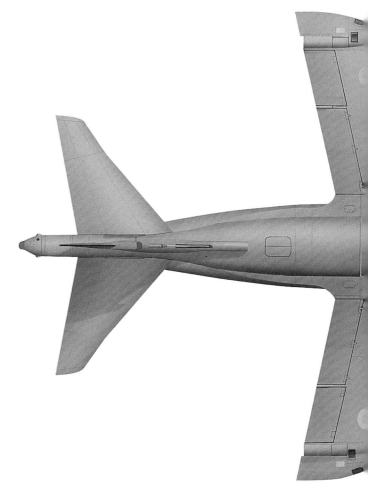

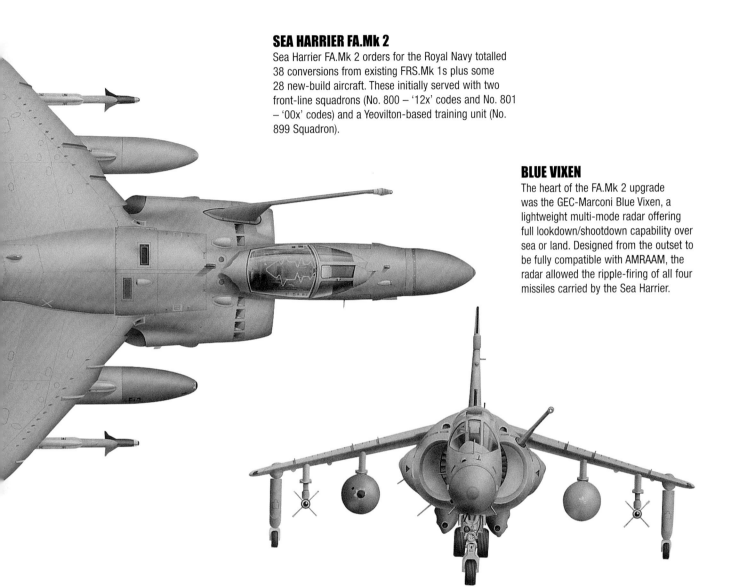

SEA HARRIER FA.Mk 2

Sea Harrier FA.Mk 2 orders for the Royal Navy totalled 38 conversions from existing FRS.Mk 1s plus some 28 new-build aircraft. These initially served with two front-line squadrons (No. 800 – '12x' codes and No. 801 – '00x' codes) and a Yeovilton-based training unit (No. 899 Squadron).

BLUE VIXEN

The heart of the FA.Mk 2 upgrade was the GEC-Marconi Blue Vixen, a lightweight multi-mode radar offering full lookdown/shootdown capability over sea or land. Designed from the outset to be fully compatible with AMRAAM, the radar allowed the ripple-firing of all four missiles carried by the Sea Harrier.

COCKPIT

Although it retained the original head-up display (HUD) from the FRS.Mk 1, the FA.Mk 2 cockpit was considerably redesigned to incorporate two multi-function head-down displays. All vital inputs were made via a 'hands-on throttle and stick' system or via an up-front controller.

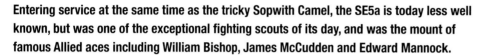 SE5a

Entering service at the same time as the tricky Sopwith Camel, the SE5a is today less well known, but was one of the exceptional fighting scouts of its day, and was the mount of famous Allied aces including William Bishop, James McCudden and Edward Mannock.

The Royal Aircraft Factory SE5a began life at the same time as the same company's SE5. It entered service only three months later than its predecessor, in June 1917. Design of the SE5a was undertaken by H.P. Folland, working at the Royal Aircraft Factory, Farnborough, in 1916.

The SE5a was a very well-proportioned single-seat fighting scout, with angular lines as a result of its semi-rectangular fuselage section. The wings and tailplane were of parallel chord, and power was provided by a 149kW (200hp) geared water-cooled Hispano-Suiza 8 (which

later became the Wolseley Viper). When first introduced to service, the SE5a suffered from engine problems, due to the hastily manufactured reduction gears. Continued engine troubles meant that production was severely delayed. Although No. 56 Squadron, Royal Flying Corps, received its first aircraft in June 1917, by the end of that year there were still only five squadrons operating the aircraft (Nos. 40, 41, 56 and 60). This was despite the fact that more than 800 SE5 and SE5a aircraft had been completed by then.

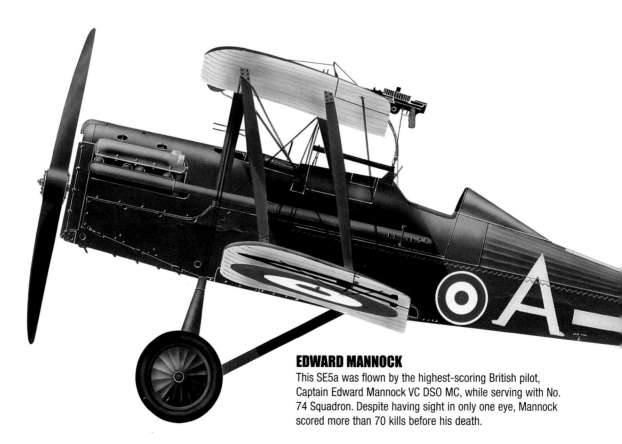

EDWARD MANNOCK
This SE5a was flown by the highest-scoring British pilot, Captain Edward Mannock VC DSO MC, while serving with No. 74 Squadron. Despite having sight in only one eye, Mannock scored more than 70 kills before his death.

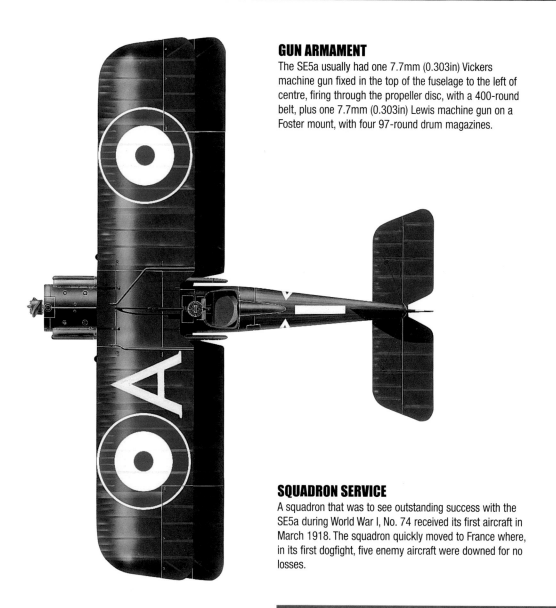

GUN ARMAMENT

The SE5a usually had one 7.7mm (0.303in) Vickers machine gun fixed in the top of the fuselage to the left of centre, firing through the propeller disc, with a 400-round belt, plus one 7.7mm (0.303in) Lewis machine gun on a Foster mount, with four 97-round drum magazines.

SQUADRON SERVICE

A squadron that was to see outstanding success with the SE5a during World War I, No. 74 received its first aircraft in March 1918. The squadron quickly moved to France where, in its first dogfight, five enemy aircraft were downed for no losses.

SPECIFICATIONS

Crew: 1

Length: 6.38m (20ft 11in)

Wingspan: 8.12m (26ft 7.5in)

Empty weight: 696kg (1535lb)

Powerplant: 1 × Hispano-Suiza 8 inline piston engine

Maximum speed: 212km/h (132mph) at 1980m (6500ft)

Armament: 1 x fixed 7.7mm (0.303in) machine gun firing through propeller, 1 x trainable 7.7mm (0.303in) machine gun

Compared to other fighting scouts of the period, the SE5a appeared slightly under-armed, with only a single synchronized Vickers gun and a Lewis gun of the same calibre on a Foster mounting on the upper wing. However, the SE5a made up for its slight deficiency in armament on account of its high top speed of between 203 and 212km/h (126–132mph). Other advantages of the SE5a included the fact that its designers had made efforts to ensure that it was easy to fly – a response to the fact that wartime pilots would have only minimal flying training before being posted to operational units.

MANUFACTURING EFFORT

Production was undertaken under a variety of sub-contracts issued to Austin, Air Navigation Company, Martinsyde, Grahame-White, Vickers, Whitehead and Wolseley, in addition to manufacture by the Royal Aircraft Factory at Farnborough. After the war, a further batch was assembled in the United States by Eberhart Steel Products.

In total, around 5000 aircraft were manufactured, most of these in the course of 1918. SE5a fighters served with Nos. 1, 24, 29, 32, 40, 41, 56, 60, 64, 74, 84, 85, 92 and 94 Squadrons of the Royal Flying Corps and subsequently Royal Air Force in France, Nos. 111 and 145 Squadrons in Palestine, Nos. 17, 47 and 150 Squadrons in Macedonia, and No. 72 Squadron in Mesopotamia. The SE5a also equipped the 25th and 148th Aero Squadrons of the US Air Service.

The most celebrated of British scout pilots flew the SE5 and SE5a, of whom the greatest exponent was Major James McCudden, whose total score of 57 aerial victories included 50 while serving with No. 56 Squadron. Other Allied aces to have flown the SE5 and/or SE5a included Mannock, Bishop, Beauchamp-Proctor and Ball. The last of these, Albert Ball, preferred the French Nieuport, but eventually settled on the SE5a, in which he was to lose his life.

Compared to its British contemporary, the Camel, the SE5a enjoyed the benefits offered by a static engine, the whirling mass of the Camel's rotary creating serious torque problems that could be of benefit only to a highly skilled pilot. While lacking the manoeuvrability of the Camel, the SE5a offered inherent stability. This also lent the SE5a to the ground support role. In the closing stages of the war these aircraft were also used extensively for close support, armed with lightweight bombs.

P.D. LEAROYD
This SE5a was flown by Second Lieutenant P.D. Learoyd of No. 40 Squadron, RFC, based at Bray Dunes aerodrome in the spring of 1918. No. 40 Squadron was formed in 1916 at Gosport; its ranks included two dozen World War I aces, including Mannock.

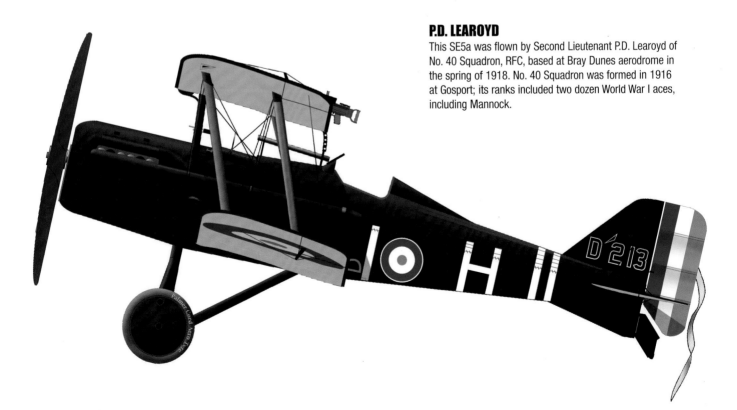

GRADUAL IMPROVEMENTS

The SE5a was subject to continuous refinement. Towards the end of 1917, a stronger landing gear became standard with substantially tapered forward legs, while other modifications included additional braces to the leading edge of the fin, and strengthened trailing edges.

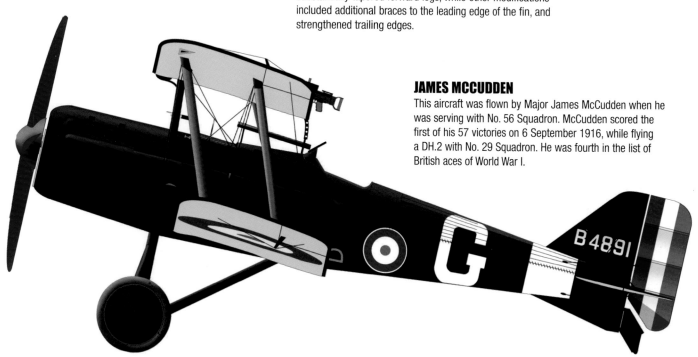

JAMES MCCUDDEN

This aircraft was flown by Major James McCudden when he was serving with No. 56 Squadron. McCudden scored the first of his 57 victories on 6 September 1916, while flying a DH.2 with No. 29 Squadron. He was fourth in the list of British aces of World War I.

Wearing the colours of No. 24 Squadron, RFC, this is one of a number of replica SE5a aircraft that operate as warbirds, some having been produced for film work. At least one original airframe is also still airworthy, and can be seen flying with the Shuttleworth Collection at Old Warden in the United Kingdom.

Focke-Wulf Fw 190

Most pilots considered the Fw 190 to be superior to the Luftwaffe's other major single-engine fighter of World War II, the Bf 109. The Fw 190 entered development as early as 1937, but the realities of the war meant that it would never completely displace its Messerschmitt rival. Despite that, the 'Butcher Bird' excelled in a variety of combat roles.

Development of the Fw 190 was launched in autumn 1937, when the German air ministry placed a contract with Focke-Wulf. Chief designer Kurt Tank submitted two proposals, one powered by a Daimler-Benz DB 601 liquid-cooled inverted-Vee engine and the other by the new BMW 139 air-cooled radial. The radial unit was chosen, and detail design work began in summer 1938.

The resulting Fw 190 was a low-wing cantilever monoplane of light alloy stressed-skin construction. The first prototype, the Fw 190 V1, was rolled out in May 1939 and made its initial flight on 1 June of the same year.

Refinement of the basic design continued with the Fw 190 V2 second prototype, flown in October 1939 with an armament of two 13mm (0.51in) and two 7.92mm (0.312in) machine guns. Even before the first prototype's initial flight,

SPECIFICATIONS (FW 190D-9)

Crew: 1

Length: 10.2m (33ft 5.5in)

Wingspan: 10.5m (34ft 5.5in)

Empty weight: 3490kg (7694lb)

Powerplant: 1 × Junkers Jumo 213A-1 inverted-Vee piston engine

Maximum speed: 685km/h (426mph) at 6600m (21,655ft)

Armament: 2 x 13mm (0.51in) machine guns, 2 x 20mm (0.78in) cannon, plus up to 500kg (1102lb) of disposable stores

BELOW: WALTER NOWOTNY

An Fw 190A-4 of Leutnant Walter Nowotny. Probably the most famous Fw 190 pilot, Nowotny was the first past the 250-kill mark, achieving 258 by the time of his death. Most of these were scored flying the 'Butcher Bird' with JG 54.

A pair of Fw 190s from II Gruppe, Schlachtgeschwader 1 cruise somewhere on the Eastern Front. Both have bomb racks fitted for ground attack operations.

ABOVE: JOSEF JENNEWEIN

This Fw 190A-4 displays one of several colour schemes worn by Fw 190s on the Russian Front, consisting of a brown and tan disruptive pattern. The aircraft belonged to 3/JG 51 and is depicted as it appeared while at Orel in June 1943.

ABOVE: HANNES TRAUTLOFT

An Fw 190A-4 flown by Oberstleutnant Hannes Trautloft, who was Geschwaderkommodore of JG 54 'Grunherz' when the unit was at Krasnogvardeisk in December 1942. It was Trautloft who introduced the famous green heart symbol.

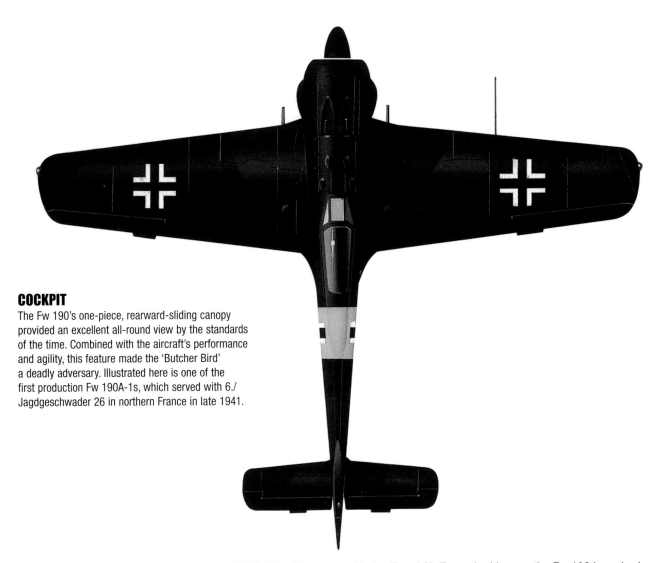

COCKPIT

The Fw 190's one-piece, rearward-sliding canopy provided an excellent all-round view by the standards of the time. Combined with the aircraft's performance and agility, this feature made the 'Butcher Bird' a deadly adversary. Illustrated here is one of the first production Fw 190A-1s, which served with 6./Jagdgeschwader 26 in northern France in late 1941.

a decision had been taken to replace the BMW 139 with the more powerful but longer and heavier BMW 801 radial engine, which in turn demanded a redesign of the fuselage.

The third and fourth prototypes were abandoned, and the Fw 190 V5 with the new engine was completed early in 1940. A pre-production batch of Fw 190A-0 aircraft was followed by deliveries in February 1941 to Erprobungskommando 190 for service evaluation. In August, the first aircraft began to be received by a front-line Luftwaffe unit, Jagdgeschwader 26 in northern France.

Once in service, the Fw 190 soon demonstrated its superiority over the Supermarine Spitfires then in service

with the Royal Air Force. In this way, the Fw 190 launched its service career, which would include production of almost 20,000 aircraft. The many versions of the Fw 190 were completed not only by Focke-Wulf, but also by Ago, Arado, Fieseler and Dornier.

Such was the Fw 190's success in the ground-attack role that a dedicated version was produced for this task. The Fw 190F-1 ground-attack variant was introduced early in 1943 as a development of the Fw 190A-4 with the engine and cockpit given additional armour protection, the outboard 20mm (0.78in) cannon removed and a bomb rack added beneath the fuselage. The final production series in Germany was

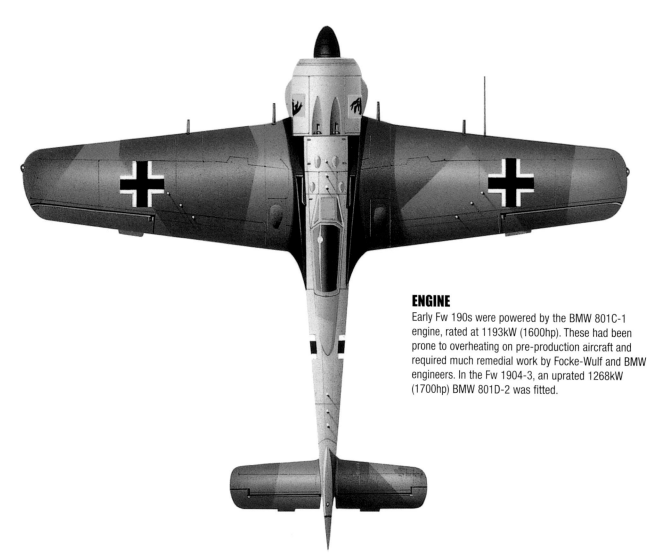

ENGINE

Early Fw 190s were powered by the BMW 801C-1 engine, rated at 1193kW (1600hp). These had been prone to overheating on pre-production aircraft and required much remedial work by Focke-Wulf and BMW engineers. In the Fw 1904-3, an uprated 1268kW (1700hp) BMW 801D-2 was fitted.

the Fw 190G. This included the Fw 190G-1 fighter-bomber, which could carry an 1800kg (3968lb) bomb that required strengthened landing gear; the wing-mounted armament was reduced to two 20mm (0.78in) cannon.

'LONG-NOSE DORA'

In late 1943, several Fw 190A-7s were completed with the Jumo 213A inverted-Vee engine as the Fw 190D-9. Known popularly as the 'long-nose 190' or 'Dora 9', the Fw 190D-9 was armed with two wing-mounted 20mm (0.78in) cannon and two machine guns above the engine, and had water/ methanol fuel injection.

Key 'Dora' derivatives included the Fw 190D-10 with the Jumo 213C engine and a 30mm (1.1in) cannon firing through the spinner instead of the two machine guns, and the Fw 190D-12 ground-attack version with engine-mounted 30mm (1.1in) cannon and two 20mm (0.78in) cannon in the wings, plus armour protection for the engine.

The Fw 190D airframe underwent further improvement to provide even better performance at high altitude. This led to the introduction of the Ta 152, which saw service in the final months of the war, most notably as an escort for Luftwaffe Me 262 jet fighters.

F-22 Raptor

Although its production run was cut short, the F-22A Raptor is generally considered to be the finest air superiority fighter in the world today. Combat proven, the Raptor offers an unrivalled combination of low observability, breathtaking performance and agility, with an array of advanced sensors and weapons for air-to-air and air-to-ground missions.

In 1981, the US Air Force launched its Advanced Tactical Fighter (ATF) programme with the aim of fielding a new-generation air superiority fighter to succeed the F-15. The requirement called for a fighter that would combine low observability (or 'stealth') with 'supercruise' (the ability to cruise at supersonic speed without afterburning), a very high level of agility to defeat the Soviet MiG-29 and Su-27, a triplex fly-by-wire flight control system, and an advanced navigation/attack system based around a powerful radar.

Concept definition contracts were issued in September 1983 to Boeing, General Dynamics, Grumman, McDonnell Douglas, Northrop and Rockwell. Requests for proposals

followed in September 1985, and in October the following year it was announced that Lockheed and Northrop had been selected to proceed to the demonstration and validation phases of the programme.

The two companies' prototype aircraft (YF-22 and YF-23) completed their first flights in late 1990. Ultimately, the YF-22 was selected as the better of the two. Engineering and manufacturing development (EMD) efforts began in 1991 with development contracts to Lockheed/Boeing (airframe) and Pratt & Whitney (engines). EMD included extensive subsystem and system testing as well as flight testing with nine aircraft at Edwards Air Force Base, California.

RADAR
The F-22's AN/APG-77 radar has an active electronically scanned array that has long range and high resolution for the early detection of opposing fighters. It can provide detailed information about multiple threats, allowing the pilot to rapidly assimilate targets.

A 27th Fighter Squadron pilot prepares for his F-22 flight at Langley Air Force Base, Virginia. The Raptor's combination of sensor capability, integrated avionics, situational awareness and weapons provides first-kill opportunity against threats and ensures its position as the most capable in-service fighter.

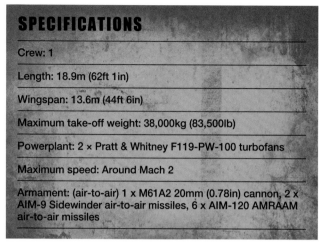

SPECIFICATIONS

Crew: 1

Length: 18.9m (62ft 1in)

Wingspan: 13.6m (44ft 6in)

Maximum take-off weight: 38,000kg (83,500lb)

Powerplant: 2 × Pratt & Whitney F119-PW-100 turbofans

Maximum speed: Around Mach 2

Armament: (air-to-air) 1 x M61A2 20mm (0.78in) cannon, 2 x AIM-9 Sidewinder air-to-air missiles, 6 x AIM-120 AMRAAM air-to-air missiles

The first EMD flight was in 1997, and at the completion of its flight test life this aircraft was used for live-fire testing.

The programme received approval to enter low-rate initial production in 2001. Initial operational and test evaluation by the Air Force Operational Test and Evaluation Center was completed successfully in 2004. Based on maturity of design and other factors, the programme received approval for full-rate production in 2005.

SHORT-RANGE WEAPONS

For dealing with close-quarters targets, the F-22A is armed with the proven M61A2 Vulcan 20mm (0.78in) cannon provided with 480 rounds, while internal side weapon bays are provided for the carriage of two AIM-9 infrared-guided air-to-air missiles, including the most recent AIM-9X version with high off-boresight capability.

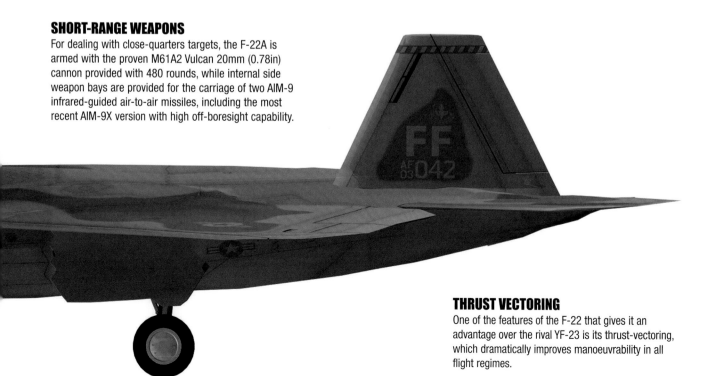

THRUST VECTORING

One of the features of the F-22 that gives it an advantage over the rival YF-23 is its thrust-vectoring, which dramatically improves manoeuvrability in all flight regimes.

On 15 December 2005 — the same day the aircraft achieved initial operational capability with the 27th Fighter Squadron — it was declared that the previous F/A-22A designation had been dropped and the F-22A designation reinstated. The primary operators of the F-22A are found within the USAF's Air Education and Training Command, Air Combat Command and Pacific Air Forces and the type never received an export licence.

PRODUCTION CURTAILED

At one time, the USAF planned to order 750 ATFs at a total cost of $26.2 billion. In 1990, the number of F-22s was reduced to 648. Subsequent reductions were made to the planned total, primarily as a result of cost overruns in the development phase. The total was therefore reduced to 438 in 1994, and to 339 in 1997. By 2003, a Congressional Cost Cap was understood to limit the total to just 277 aircraft, and in 2006 then Secretary of Defense Donald Rumsfeld reduced the number to 183 aircraft.

A key part of the Raptor's lethality is its avionics suite, built around the Northrop Grumman AN/APG-77 active electronically scanned array (AESA) radar and the BAE Systems AN/ALR-94 passive receiver system. The ALR-94 incorporates more than 30 antennas blended into the wings and fuselage that provide 360-degree all-round coverage and detection for radar signals.

The powerplant is a pair of 156kN (35,000lb st) Pratt & Whitney F119 engines, enabling the Raptor to accelerate to and cruise at speeds of about Mach 1.8 without using afterburners. With afterburning engaged, the Raptor is able to attain speeds of Mach 2.0 and altitudes in excess of 18,288m (60,000ft), and climbs faster than the F-15.

Despite its status as the USAF's pre-eminent air superiority fighter, the Raptor's combat debut came in an air-to-ground role. On the night of 23 September 2014, as the US and Arab coalition air power struck targets of the so-called Islamic State in Syria, F-22As from the 27th FS employed GPS-guided munitions to target a facility located in northern Syria, about 121km (75 miles) from the Turkish border. Since then, F-22s have maintained an almost-constant deployed presence with US Central Command (CENTCOM) as well as providing a powerful deterrent in other theatres around the world.

RADAR-DEFEATING DESIGN

The F-22A's angular but clean external shape features jagged edges on any portion of the airframe that could reflect electro-magnetic energy back towards a hostile radar. While stores can be carried on four external hardpoints, the primary weapons are concealed in three internal weapons bays (one large centreline bay and two smaller lateral bays).

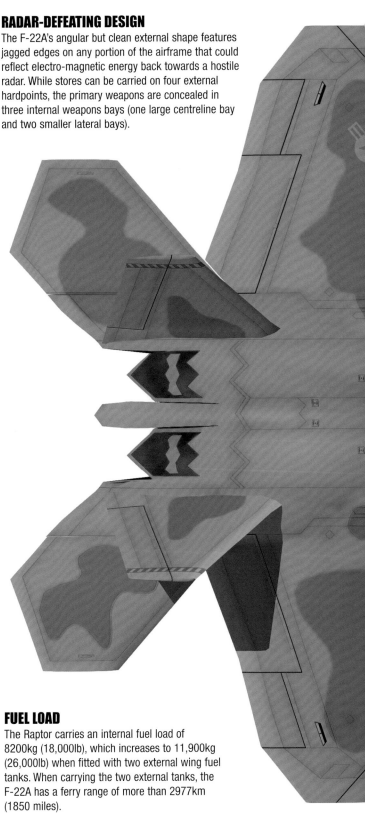

FUEL LOAD

The Raptor carries an internal fuel load of 8200kg (18,000lb), which increases to 11,900kg (26,000lb) when fitted with two external wing fuel tanks. When carrying the two external tanks, the F-22A has a ferry range of more than 2977km (1850 miles).

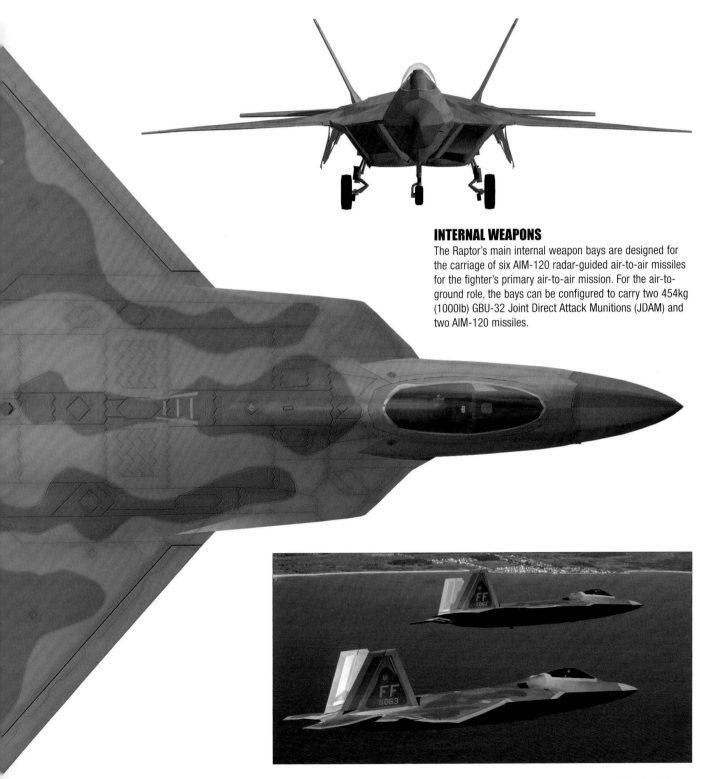

INTERNAL WEAPONS

The Raptor's main internal weapon bays are designed for the carriage of six AIM-120 radar-guided air-to-air missiles for the fighter's primary air-to-air mission. For the air-to-ground role, the bays can be configured to carry two 454kg (1000lb) GBU-32 Joint Direct Attack Munitions (JDAM) and two AIM-120 missiles.

In March 2006, the first two F-22A Raptors were delivered to the famous 94th Fighter Squadron. The 94th was the second squadron at Langley Air Force Base to receive the new stealth fighter.

F-16 Fighting Falcon

The F-16 started life as a simple, lightweight counter-air fighter with limited capabilities in the long-range air-to-air and attack roles. Today, it is the most successful Western warplane in its class, and advanced variants continue to equip the US and many other air forces.

The F-16 was originally developed by General Dynamics as a lightweight air-combat fighter, but today production is undertaken by Lockheed Martin. First flown on 20 January 1974, the service-test YF-16 was selected in favour of Northrop's YF-17 in a fly-off competition for the US Air Force. The first of eight full-scale development F-16A airframes flew in 1975, followed in 1977 by the first example of the combat-capable F-16B two-seat trainer.

The design of the Fighting Falcon (almost universally known as the 'Viper' in service) stressed high agility. Features include a shock-inlet air intake located under the forward fuselage below the cockpit. A blended wing/body shape is combined with prominent leading-edge root extensions to generate lift at high angles of attack. The

SPECIFICATIONS (F-16A)

Crew: 1

Length: 14.8m (49ft 5in)

Wingspan: 9.8m (32ft 8in)

Empty weight: 7070kg (15,586lb)

Powerplant: 1 × General Electric F110-GE-100 or Pratt & Whitney F100-PW-220 turbofan

Maximum speed: More than 2125km/h (1321mph) at altitude

Armament: 1 x M61A1 20mm (0.78in) cannon with 500 rounds; external stations can carry up to 9276kg (20,450lb) of stores

CANOPY
The one-piece canopy provides superb visibility for the pilot. Parameters are 360 degrees all-round view, 195 degrees fore and aft, 40 degrees down over each side and 15 degrees over the nose. Pilots have widely praised the exceptional view from the cockpit.

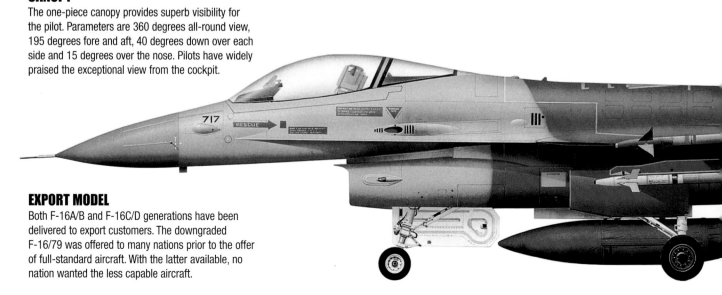

EXPORT MODEL
Both F-16A/B and F-16C/D generations have been delivered to export customers. The downgraded F-16/79 was offered to many nations prior to the offer of full-standard aircraft. With the latter available, no nation wanted the less capable aircraft.

PAKISTANI 'VIPER'

This F-16A Block 15R was one of those delivered to the Pakistan Air Force under the Peace Gate II programme. The aircraft wears the markings of No. 14 Squadron 'Shaheens' and carries an air-to-air load-out of AIM-9 Sidewinder air-to-air missiles plus a centreline fuel tank.

aircraft is statically unstable and relies upon a fly-by-wire system for controllability, and the pilot's ejection seat is angled back by 30 degrees to improve G tolerance.

Delivery of production-standard F-16A/Bs to the USAF began in January 1979.

'SALE OF THE CENTURY'

When NATO came to look for a replacement for the F-104 Starfighter, the F-16A/B was selected in June 1975 under an agreement between Belgium, Denmark, the Netherlands and Norway. This saw licence production of the Fighting Falcon in Belgium and the Netherlands and launched the aircraft's export success.

Despite teething troubles with engine malfunctions and structural cracks, the F-16 developed into an excellent multi-role fighter. With production Block 15 for the USAF, a portion of F-16A/Bs were converted to the F-16A/B

An F-16C Fighting Falcon assigned to the US Air Force's 522nd Fighter Squadron, from Cannon Air Force Base, New Mexico, fires an AGM-65H Maverick air-to-ground missile at a target located over the Utah Test and Training Range. The mission was part of an air-to-ground weapons system evaluation programme mission commonly referred to as Combat Hammer.

ADF standard that featured an upgraded AN/APG-66 radar and the medium-range AIM-7 Sparrow air-to-air missile. These aircraft were supplied to Air National Guard squadrons.

First flown on 19 June 1984, the F-16C single-seater and its F-16D two-seat counterpart brought new equipment including the APG-68 multi-mode radar, a wide-angle head-up display (HUD) and an improved data display for the pilot, plus compatibility to interface with the AGM-65D Maverick and AIM-120 AMRAAM missiles.

The Block 30/32 and Block 40/42 versions of the F-16C/D featured a 'configured' engine bay that allowed customers to opt for the General Electric F110-GE-100

rated at 128.93kN (28,984lb st) or the Pratt & Whitney F100-PW-220 rated at 106.05kN (23,840lb st). Block 30/32 aircraft also added the ability to carry AGM-45 Shrike and AGM-88 HARM anti-radiation missiles for the defence suppression role.

By the early 1990s, the production standard was the F-16C/D Block 50/52 aircraft with the APG-68(V)5 radar with improved memory and more modes, a HUD compatible with night vision googles, ALE-47 chaff/flare dispenser, and full HARM integration. These F-16s were also powered by the IPE (Improved Performance Engine) versions of two standard. Around 100 USAF F-16C/D Block 50/52 aircraft were also brought up to Block 50/52D

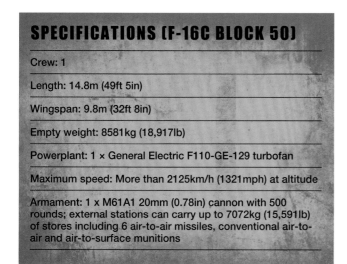

SPECIFICATIONS (F-16C BLOCK 50)

Crew: 1

Length: 14.8m (49ft 5in)

Wingspan: 9.8m (32ft 8in)

Empty weight: 8581kg (18,917lb)

Powerplant: 1 × General Electric F110-GE-129 turbofan

Maximum speed: More than 2125km/h (1321mph) at altitude

Armament: 1 x M61A1 20mm (0.78in) cannon with 500 rounds; external stations can carry up to 7072kg (15,591lb) of stores including 6 air-to-air missiles, conventional air-to-air and air-to-surface munitions

SAM-KILLER

A distinguishing feature of some F-16Ds operated by Israel is the extended dorsal spine. Fitted inside are avionics that allow the F-16 to operate as a Wild Weasel defence suppression aircraft. The indigenous equipment was developed following significant losses sustained by the Israeli Air Force at the hands of enemy surface-to-air missiles.

ISRAELI F-16D

The tail of this Israeli Air Force two-seater displays the markings of No. 105 Squadron – a large scorpion painted on either side. Positioned above this is a smaller badge comprising a red scorpion on a red, white and blue disc. Since the mid-1990s, the markings on Israeli fighters have become much more elaborate.

standard with provision for the ASQ-213 HARM Targeting System.The latest production version of the 'Viper' is the F-16E/F Block 60 that was produced for the United Arab Emirates. Changes include an active electronically scanned array (AESA) radar, internal forward-looking infrared (FLIR) sensor, an advanced cockpit and internal electronic self-protection suite.

As of early 2017, F-16s had been delivered to 28 customers around the world and Lockheed Martin was promoting its F-16V for both domestic and export use. This advanced variant, available as a new-build aircraft or via upgrade, includes AESA radar, more modern avionics, and a large-format, high-resolution cockpit display.

Messerschmitt Me 262

The Me 262 is assigned its place in history as the first jet aircraft to enter service anywhere in the world. As well as the quantum leap in performance guaranteed by its powerplant, it was also remarkable for its use of advanced aerodynamics, including a swept wing.

The Messerschmitt Me 262 that entered Luftwaffe service in late 1944 originated in pre-war German research into gas turbine propulsion. Design of the aircraft began in 1938 and prototype airframes were ready as early as 1941. At this stage, however, the required jet engines were not yet available.

A maiden flight was achieved by the Me 262 V1 prototype on 18 April 1941, but utilized a single Jumo 210G piston engine as powerplant. This proved that the general handling characteristics were good, and allowed the Me 262 to be flown for development of the aircraft systems. On 25 March 1942, the Me 262 V1 took to the air under the power of a pair of BMW 003 turbojets, each of which produced 840kg (1852lb) of thrust. After taking off on the power of all three engines (the nose-mounted Jumo 210G being retained for emergency use), both the turbojets failed, and test pilot Flugkapitan Fritz Wendel was forced to land on piston power alone.

The earlier engine failure was attributed to compressor blade failures, which caused the engines to seize, and

Germany experienced extreme difficulties in maintaining engine production for the Me 262, the factories producing the jet engines being primary targets for Allied bombers. This led to poor reliability of the powerplants, while shortages of chrome and nickel prevented the turbine blades from being manufactured with sufficient strength to withstand the extreme temperatures encountered, thus making the life of the engines very short.

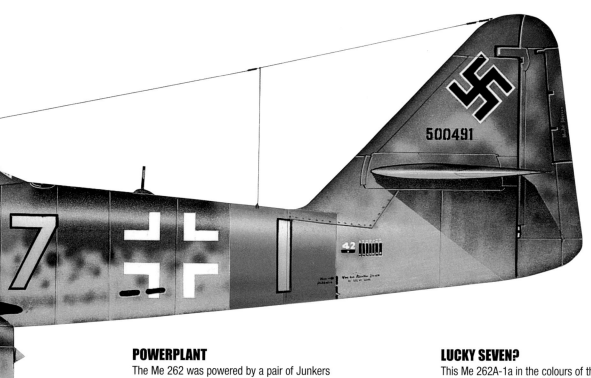

POWERPLANT

The Me 262 was powered by a pair of Junkers Jumo 004B-1 axial flow turbojets, each rated at about 8.82kN (1984lb) static thrust. This gave a maximum speed of approximately 869km/h (540mph) at 6096m (20,000ft). The aircraft could exceed this speed in a dive, soon reaching its limiting Mach number.

LUCKY SEVEN?

This Me 262A-1a in the colours of the 9. Staffel Jagdgeschwader 7 was based at Parchim in early 1945 under I. Jagddivision of I Jagdkorps in the defence of the Reich. After capture at the end of the war, this aircraft was given the code FE-111 by the technical branch of the USAAF for evaluation. In the course of 1979, the aircraft was stripped down, refurbished and and put on display at the Air and Space Museum, Washington DC.

SPECIFICATIONS (ME 262A-1A)

Crew: 1

Length: 10.61m (34ft 9.5in)

Wingspan: 12.5m (41ft)

Empty weight: 4000kg (8818lb)

Powerplant: 2 × Junkers Jumo 109-004B-4 turbojets

Maximum speed: 870km/h (541mph) at 7000m (26,965ft)

Armament: 4 x 30mm (1.1in) cannon in nose

required a complete redesign of the engine. However, development of the Me 262 had continued under the power of two Junkers turbojets.

The Junkers engines were larger and heavier than the BMW engines, and the Me 262 airframe had to be modified to accept them. The third (V3) prototype flew with two 8.24kN (1852lb) thrust Jumo 004A turbojets on 18 July 1942.

The Me 262 was a cantilever low-wing monoplane, with the engines nacelle-mounted below the wing at approximately one-third span. Early prototypes featured retractable tailwheel landing gear, but this gave way to a tricycle arrangement by the time production began in 1944.

SCHNELLBOMBER

The Me 262's fortunes are frequently described as having been thwarted by Hitler's misguided efforts to put the Me 262 into service as a bomber for reprisal raids on the United Kingdom. Although Hitler did indeed envision the Me 262

NIGHT-FIGHTER

Me 262B-1a/U1 Werk/nr 111980 was assigned to 10./NGJ 11, better known as Kommando Welter. 'Red 12' was operated from Burg bei Magdeburg until May 1945. After the end of the war, it was evaluated by a team from Farnborough led by test pilot Captain Eric 'Winkle' Brown.

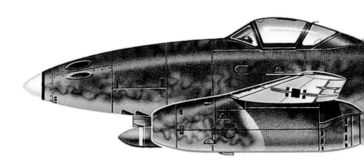

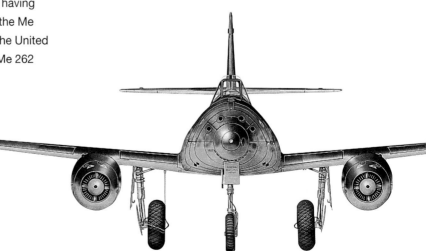

FIGHTER-BOMBER

Bomb-armed Me 262A-2a of 1./KG 51, 9K+FH (Werk/nr 111625). Command of Kampfgeschwader 51 came under Major Wolfgang Schenk in November 1944: during the summer of that year, Schenk took his Kommando into action with Me 262s on the Normandy war front.

ELEVATORS AND AILERONS

Pre-production Me 262s were fitted with fabric-covered elevators, but these proved highly susceptible to ballooning in high-speed dives, and on several occasions the fabric actually tore. Thereafter, all production aircraft were fitted with metal-skinned elevators.

as a Schnellbomber ('fast bomber') rather than a defensive interceptor, it is arguable whether his intervention in the programme had a significant impact on the delay in bringing the aircraft into service. Of greater concern was the difficulty in refining the engines to provide the required thrust and, above all, reliability.

In late 1944 the Me 262 entered service, initially in Me 2624-1a fighter form, armed with four 30mm (1.1in) cannon in the nose. The first of these aircraft joined Kommando Nowotny in October 1944. They were followed by the Me 262A-1a/U1 with two additional 20mm (0.78in) cannon, the Me 262A-1a/U2 bad-weather fighter and the Me 262A-1a/U3 unarmed reconnaissance aircraft.

The Me 262A-2a bomber variant could carry up to 500kg (1102lb) of bombs in addition to the four 30mm (1.1in) guns. A two-seat version (with prone bomb-aimer), the Me 2624-2a/U2, was also produced.

Before the end of the war, Me 262s were being flown with some success against Allied bombers both as day- and night-fighters (the latter were radar-equipped Me 262B-1a/U1, developed from the Me 262B-1a two-seat conversion trainer), and air-to-air rockets were being developed. Using this latter weapon, a salvo of 24 R4M rockets would be launched against a bomber formation and followed up with 30mm (1.1in) cannon fire. Enemy fighters were altogether trickier foes for the Me 262, which although considerably faster than any Allied fighter opposition, was inferior in terms of manoeuvrability, especially during the approach to land. In this way, a number of Me 262s were destroyed in combat, and the Luftwaffe was forced to provide additional (piston-engined) escort to the jets in the vicinity of their operating airfields.

At this late stage in the war, the Me 262 was always going to have the odds stacked against it; as well as the overwhelming dominance of Allied air power in the skies over Europe, Allied bombing raids on factories and airfields ensured that production and deployment of the new fighter was haphazard.

Total production of the Me 262 amounted to around 1430; there is little doubt that if the type had entered service at a much earlier date, it could well have turned the war in the air in Germany's favour by making the Allied daylight bombing offensive too hazardous.

SR-71 'Blackbird'

Best known by its unofficial 'Blackbird' nickname, the Lockheed SR-71 is assured its place in history as the fastest air-breathing manned aircraft, and its Mach-3 performance meant that the spyplane was effectively immune to interception during the Cold War.

Revealed to the public in February 1964 by US President Johnson, the 'Blackbird' was, at that time, a Central Intelligence Agency project identified as the A-11. Johnson disclosed that the aircraft had already achieved speeds in excess of 3219km/h (2000mph) and flown at altitudes greater than 21,335m (70,000ft).

In reality, the 'A-11' was the Lockheed A-12, a single-seat strategic reconnaissance aircraft that was first flown on 30 April 1962. A total of 15 A-12s were completed and flown by both CIA and US Air Force pilots. As well as the standard A-12, two aircraft were modified to the M-21 standard, as drone carriers for the ramjet-powered D-21 remotely piloted vehicle. Another development path produced the YF-12A, a prototype interceptor, only three examples of which were completed.

SERIES PRODUCTION

Lockheed's Clarence 'Kelly' Johnson further developed his original A-12 design to produce a two-seat strategic reconnaissance aircraft for the USAF. Originally schemed

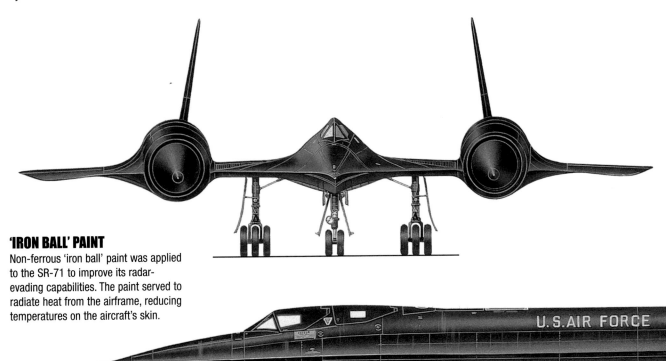

'IRON BALL' PAINT
Non-ferrous 'iron ball' paint was applied to the SR-71 to improve its radar-evading capabilities. The paint served to radiate heat from the airframe, reducing temperatures on the aircraft's skin.

U.S.AIR FORCE

An air-to-air right overhead view of an SR-71A strategic reconnaissance aircraft. Unofficially known as the 'Blackbird', the SR-71's highly classified reconnaissance missions saw the aircraft's sensor systems collect material that helped to formulate US foreign policy for more than 20 years. Throughout that time, the exclusive US Air Force operator of the aircraft was the 9th Strategic Reconnaissance Wing at Beale Air Force Base, California.

REFUELLING
Most 'Blackbird' missions involved at least one refuelling, from a specially equipped tanker. Standard procedure was to launch the tanker(s) ahead of the SR-71, which would follow and top up its tanks after take-off, at 7925m (26,000ft).

MISSION RECORDER
An on-board mission recorder system kept a record of all aircraft and system performance, in addition to recording all communications, sensor actions and navigational data. The recorder was in a crashworthy box.

ELINT
The SR-71A was equipped for gathering electronic intelligence (ELINT) as part of its 'synergistic' approach to intelligence, in which radar imagery was combined with signals intelligence and photographic images. The aircraft could carry various different signals intelligence payloads, mainly for recording radar signals.

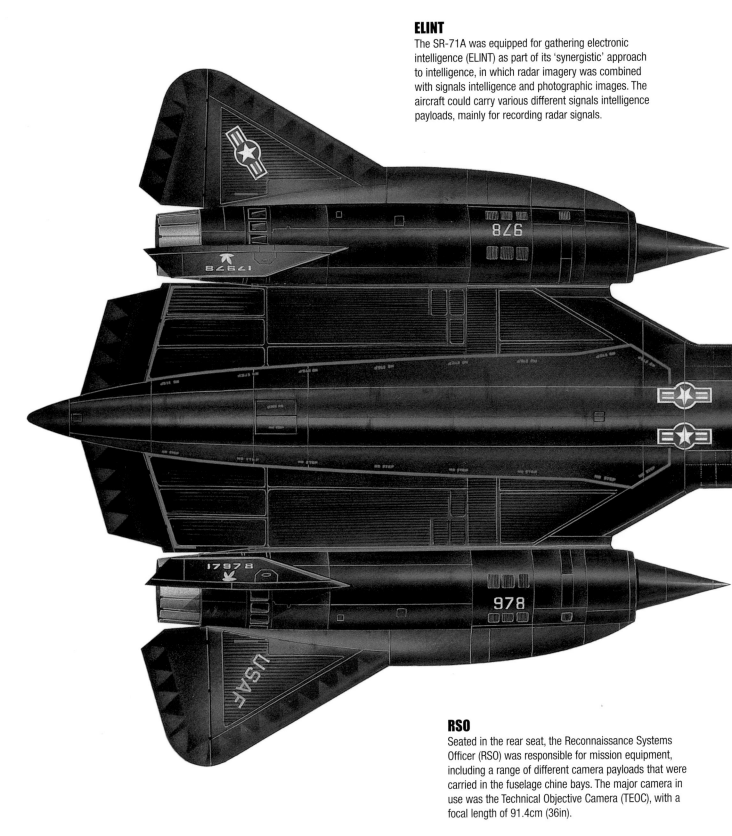

RSO
Seated in the rear seat, the Reconnaissance Systems Officer (RSO) was responsible for mission equipment, including a range of different camera payloads that were carried in the fuselage chine bays. The major camera in use was the Technical Objective Camera (TEOC), with a focal length of 91.4cm (36in).

as a strike/reconnaissance aircraft, this was planned to have resulted in R-12 and RS-12 versions. In the event, only the single-role R-12 spyplane was pursued, and this led to production as the SR-71. Sharing much in common with the A-12 and the YF-12A, the SR-71A was manufactured mainly using titanium in order to maintain structural integrity when subjected to kinetic heating at operating speeds in the region of Mach 3.

In terms of design, the SR-71A employed a very slim fuselage and a thin delta wing to combat aerodynamic drag encountered at high speed. Integral lifting 'chines' were incorporated in order to prevent the forward fuselage pitching down as speed increased. The twin Pratt & Whitney J58 turbojet engines produced all the required low-speed thrust, but at Mach 3 their thrust was reduced to 18 per cent of the total, with the remainder provided by ingenious

inlet and nozzle design, the inlets themselves incorporating movable cones known as 'spikes'. In this way, air entering the inlets bypassed the engines, going directly to the afterburners and ejector nozzles, thus acting as ramjets.

Throughout its career of almost 24 years, the SR-71 was the world's fastest and highest-flying operational aircraft. Operating at an altitude of 24,384m (80,000ft), it was able to conduct surveillance of an area measuring 258,999 square km (100,000 square miles) each hour. On 28 July 1976, an SR-71 set two world records for its class – an absolute speed record of 3529.56km/h (2193.167mph), and an absolute altitude record of 25,929m (85,068.997ft).

The SR-71 entered USAF service in 1966 and was soon employed operationally over Vietnam. Within two years, the original A-12s had been retired. Two examples of the two-seat SR-71B trainer were completed, the loss of one

SPECIFICATIONS (SR-71A)

Crew: 2

Length: 32.74m (107ft 5in)

Wingspan: 16.94m (55ft 7in)

Empty weight: 30,617kg (67,500lb)

Powerplant: 2 × Pratt & Whitney J58 afterburning turbojets

Maximum speed: Mach 3.2 (3380km/h/2100mph) sustained cruising speed at 24,385m (80,000ft)

Armament: None

of these leading to contruction of a single SR-71C as replacement. This latter combined the rear fuselage of one of the YF-12As with a forward fuselage taken from a static test airframe. The 29 SR-71As flew missions in some of the most well-defended airspace of the Cold War period, detachments being maintained at Okinawa, Japan and at RAF Mildenhall in the UK. Although retired in 1989, the aircraft were briefly returned to service after Desert Storm, the first example being reactivated in June 1995. However, the USAF finally abandoned the SR-71 in 1998, after which its use was continued by NASA for test work.

The last four SR-71s flown by NASA during the 1990s flew for the last time on 9 October 1999.

Tupolev Tu-95

The remarkable turboprop-powered Tupolev 'Bear' appeared anachronistic when it was first revealed to Western observers in the 1950s, but the quality of the basic design has ensured that it remains in front-line service today as the most numerous long-range strategic bomber within the Russian Air Force inventory.

'BEAR-D'

Known to NATO as the 'Bear-D', the Tu-95RTs was a maritime reconnaissance version that was among the most likely to be encountered by Western air defences during the Cold War. The combination of turboprop engines, capacious internal fuel tanks and in-flight refuelling capability ensured a very long range for overwater patrol.

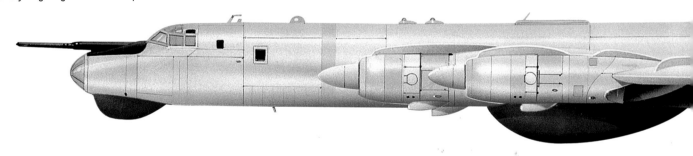

The Tu-95 was originally designed purely as a long-range strategic bomber — with nuclear capability — competing against the four-jet Myasishchev M-4. Initially, the M-4 was the preferred choice of Soviet Long-Range Aviation, but flight-testing showed that it could not meet the specified radius of action and it was never a major combat weapon. In contrast, while nobody was very surprised that the Tupolev aircraft could meet the range requirement, its speed and altitude capability proved better than expected. All-round performance was far higher than that of any previous propeller aircraft in history, and it still is today, more than half a century later.

No other aircraft so fully exploits the potential of the turboprop, to the extent that jet speed is combined with the economy of slow-turning propellers. Along with the C-130 Hercules, it is part of a select number of military aircraft to have achieved a production in excess of 35 years. In that time, the basic free-fall bomber has spawned missile-carrier,

maritime reconnaissance, missile targeting, and other derivatives. In the early 1980s, the 'Bear' received a new lease of life when it was adapted as a launch platform for a new generation of low-flying cruise missiles, the updated airframe also being adapted for anti-submarine warfare as the Tu-142.

The Tu-95 'Bear-A' made its first flight in prototype form on 12 November 1952, but was lost in a crash in May 1953. After a definitive prototype flew in February 1955, the initial production version of the bomber began to roll off the line in October that year.

While the initial 'Bear-A' had been limited to carrying free-fall ordnance, the first of the missile-carrying 'Bears' was the Tu-95K, armed with a single example of Mikoyan's powerful Kh-20 (AS-3 'Kangaroo'). The Tu-95K 'Bear-B' entered service in 1959. With the carriage of a large cruise missile compromising radius of action, Tupolev set about creating a long-range version of its missile-carrier. The

SPECIFICATIONS (TU-95MS)

Crew: 7

Length: 49.13m (161ft 2.25in)

Wingspan: 50.04m (164ft 2in)

Empty weight: 91,800kg (202,380lb)

Powerplant: 4 × Kuznetsov/Samara NK-12MP turboprops

Maximum speed: 830km/h (516mph)

Armament: 6–12 x Kh-55 (AS-15 'Kent') cruise missiles in internal bay and on underwing pylons, or 8 x Kh-101/Kh-102 cruise missiles, and 2 x twin-barrelled 23mm (0.9in) GSh-23 cannon

NK-12 TURBOPROPS
The Tu-95/142 series is powered by four Kuznetsov/Samara NK-12MP turboprops, each developing a maximum of 11,185kW (15,000hp). Each eight-blade propeller unit consists of two four-blade co-axial contra-rotating reversible-pitch propellers.

The final production version of the Tu-142 'Bear-F' maritime patrol aircraft was the Tu-142MZ that introduced a new radio sonobuoy system and a revised electronic countermeasures system. It was flight-tested in prototype form in 1985, and manufactured between 1993 and 1994.

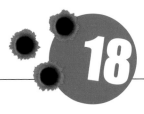

Blessed with very long range and economic operation, the 'Bear' was an obvious candidate for the maritime mission. Successful experience with the Tu-95RTs 'Bear-D' in the oceanic surveillance and targeting role would lead to the subsequent development of the Tu-142 'Bear-F', dedicated to hunting submarines.

LANDING GEAR

The 'Bear' family features typical Tupolev landing gear, with the four-wheel bogies on each main unit retracting into large fairings on the wing trailing edges, in line with the inner engines. The steerable nose gear comprises twin nosewheels.

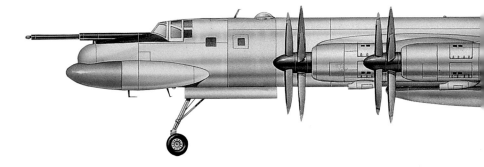

result was the Tu-95KD, with in-flight refuelling probe, which entered production as the Tu-95KM 'Bear-C' in 1965.

In 1964, the Soviet Navy introduced to service the Tu-95RTs 'Bear-D', a dedicated maritime reconnaissance and missile-targeting version. Equipped with passive and active sensors to provide over-the-horizon targeting for submarine-launched anti-shipping missiles, this version was derived from the original 'Bear-A' free-fall bomber and was identified by Western intelligence in 1967. In addition to a suite of passive ELINT and SIGINT receivers, the Tu-95RTs relied upon a powerful active sensor in the form of the Uspekh ('Big Bulge') maritime search and targeting radar.

Using surplus Tu-95M 'Bear-A' bomber airframes, a number of aircraft were adapted for the maritime reconnaissance role as the Tu-95MR 'Bear-E'. In contrast

to the 'Bear-D', this model combined electronic intelligence (ELINT) equipment with a package of optical cameras in a bulged bomb-bay installation. The Tu-95M was superseded by the much-improved Tu-142 in the early 1980s.

MISSILE CARRIERS

The final incarnation of the first-generation 'Bear' was the Tu-95K-22 missile-carrier, armed with up to three Kh-22M (AS-4 'Kitchen') stand-off missiles. The first aircraft, a converted Tu-95KM, made its maiden flight on 30 October 1975. A primary target was US Navy carriers. The first Kh-22M was launched from an operational Tu-95K-22 in 1981.

After production of the Tu-95 ceased in Samara, production of Tu-142 maritime patrol aircraft – based on a thoroughly upgraded Tu-95 airframe – was continued in

DEFENSIVE ARMAMENT

Unlike later models, the original Tu-95 free-fall bomber was provided with three gun installations, positioned dorsally, ventrally and at the tail. Each of these installations was equipped with a pair of 23mm (0.9in) AM-23 cannon, normally provided with 700 (dorsal), 800 (ventral) and 1000 (tail) rounds, respectively.

STANDOFF MISSILE CARRIER

The Kh-20 (AS-3 'Kangaroo') missile was intended to strike both critical land installations and naval targets. During an attack on a warship, the Tu-95K's YaD radar would first determine the position of the target. For missile launch, the Kh-20 would be lowered from its semi-recessed installation into the slipstream below the bomber and its turbojet engine spooled up.

Beginning in 2007, Russian heavy bombers resumed their long-distance 'patrol' flights, and Tu-95MS and Tu-160 aircraft began to be increasingly intercepted by Western fighters. The 'Bear-H' is equipped for air-to-air refuelling. The location of the fixed refuelling probe directly in front of the cockpit makes this process straightforward.

Taganrog. By the end of the 1970s, a new generation of long-range cruise missiles had appeared. As well as the supersonic Tu-160, the Soviets selected the Tu-142 airframe to carry the Kh-55 (AS-15 'Kent') missiles. In series production, the aircraft was designated Tu-95MS. The first aircraft were delivered in December 1982. During the first production period, the Samara plant built 173 aircraft. Then, 88 Tu-95MS bombers were produced during 1982–92 – the first 12 in Taganrog and the rest in Samara. As well as the Soviet Union and Russia, the 'Bear' has been operated by Ukraine (before being sold back to Russia) and by the Indian Navy, which flew the Tu-142.

Currently, Russia retains around 60 Tu-95MS bombers, which are being upgraded, plus two squadrons of Tu-142 maritime patrol aircraft and a handful of Tu-142MR strategic radio-relay aircraft.

Junkers Ju 88

Often compared against the British de Havilland Mosquito, the Junkers Ju 88 was, if anything, even more versatile than its Allied counterpart. As well as fulfilling a wide variety of operational and second-line roles, the Ju 88 was subject to continued improvement right up until the end of the war.

The Ju 88 was first schemed as a three-seat high-speed bomber. The first prototype, powered by two Daimler Benz Db 600Aa engines, each developing 746kW (1000hp), took to the air on 21 December 1936. Additional prototypes were engaged in testing alternative powerplants, including the Junkers Jumo of similar rating. Once equipped with the new engines, a prototype displayed an impressive speed of 520km/h (323mph), leading to several record-breaking attempts made in the pre-war years.

After a total of 10 prototypes had been completed, the pre-production Ju 88A-0 bomber flew in early 1939, then

SPECIFICATIONS (JU 88A-4)

Crew: 4

Length: 14.4m (47ft 2.75in)

Wingspan: 20m (65ft 7.5in)

Empty equipped weight: 9860kg (21,737lb)

Powerplant: 2 × Junkers Jumo 211J-1 piston engines

Maximum speed: 470km/h (292mph) at 5300m (17,390ft)

Armament: 1 x 13mm (0.51in) or 2 x 7.92mm (0.312in) forward-firing machine guns, 2 x similar guns in rear cockpit, 2 x below the fuselage, plus 2000kg (4409lb) of bombs

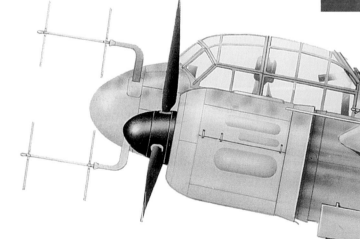

NIGHT-FIGHTER FATE
This Ju 88G-1 was operated by 7./NJG 2. After its crew became lost on the night of 12–13 July 1944, it landed by accident at RAF Woodbridge in the United Kingdom. It provided the British with valuable intelligence.

WING AERIALS
The dipole aerials carried on the wing allowed the crew to receive emissions from the Monica tail-warning radars carried by RAF bombers. This information was then fed into the night-fighter's Flensburg direction finder.

Of all the theatres in which the Ju 88 fought, the one most closely associated with the type is the Mediterranean. This aircraft is armed with four SC 250 bombs on the external racks inboard of the engine nacelles. A further 10 of these 250kg (551lb) weapons could be carried internally.

UPWARD-FIRING GUNS

Although this aircraft was not fitted with the installation, many Ju 88Gs were equipped with upward-firing guns in the rear fuselage, to tackle British night-bombers flying above them. Instead, this Ju 88G-1 was armed with four MG 151 cannon in a ventral box.

entered service in September that year as the Ju 88A-1 initial production version. While initial combat experience emphasized the aircraft's good performance and useful bombload, the defensive armament was found wanting. This led to the development of the improved Ju 88A-4 bomber, with wings of increased span, strengthened structure to enable greater loads to be carried and beefed

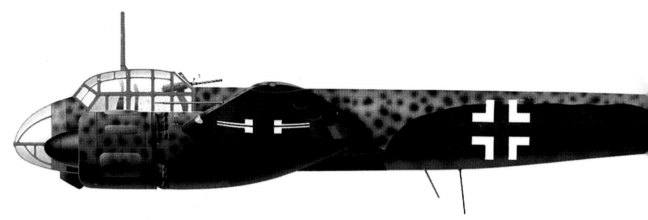

NIGHT BOMBER

This Ju 88S-1 three-seat fast bomber was finished in standard 1944 night camouflage. It operated from Dedelsdorf in the final months of the war, on lone missions against the United Kingdom and the Channel ports with I./KG 66. The Ju 88S-1 was equipped to fly radio-beam pathfinder missions.

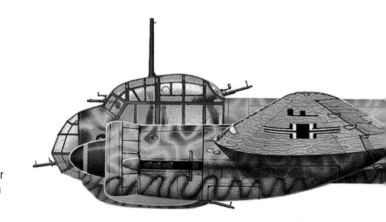

'TOTENKOPF' GESCHWADER

Operated by the 'Totenkopf' (Death's head) Geschwader, I./KG 54, this Ju 88A-4 was based at Bergamo in Italy in September 1943. The 'Wellenmuster' camouflage pattern was applied over the standard Mediterranean two-tone scheme for anti-invasion missions over Sicily and Salerno.

up defensive armament. Such was the success of the basic Ju 88A that it spawned a variety of sub-variants up to and including the Ju 88A-17.

While production of the Ju 88A series continued, work began on an improved Ju 88B, with a more extensively glazed nose and two 1193kW (1600hp) BMW 801MA radials. Limited improvements in performance meant only 10 pre-production machines were completed.

FIGHTER VERSIONS

Such was the speed offered by the airframe that it was soon adapted for fighter missions, initially in the form of

the Ju 88C series. While the Ju 88C-1 with BMW 801MA engines was abandoned, the first production model in this series was the Ju 88C-2, essentially a Ju 88A-1 with a solid nose containing three 7.92mm (0.312in) machine guns and a 20mm (0.78in) cannon. Sub-variants included the Ju 88C-4 heavy fighter/reconnaissance aircraft, Ju 88C-5 improved heavy fighter, Ju 88C-6a (an improved Ju 88C-5), Ju 88C-6b and Ju 88C-6c night-fighters, Ju 88C-7a and Ju 88C-7b intruders and the Ju 88C-7c heavy fighter. Other night-fighters included the Ju 88R-1 and Ju 88R-2, which were powered by BMW 801MA engines once these became available.

A captured Ju 88A-4 is prepared for a flight up at Collyweston, Northamptonshire. Originally operated by 3./KG 30, the aircraft landed by mistake at Broadfield Down, near Bristol, after a night raid on Birkenhead on 23–24 July 1941. It was taken on charge by the Royal Aircraft Establishment for tactical trials.

DEFINITIVE DAY BOMBER

The Ju 88A-4 entered development in early 1940 and was intended to exploit the advantage offered by the more powerful Jumo 211F and 211J engines. At the same time, Junkers engineers added a further 1.63m (5ft 4.25in) in wingspan to improve load-carrying ability.

For the long-range reconnaissance role, Junkers developed the Ju 88D series, based on the Ju 88A-4 bomber. The Ju 88D-1 to Ju 88D-5 variants differed in their use of engines and equipment.

The ultimate night-fighter version was the Ju 88G, which appeared in the summer of 1944 and replaced the earlier Ju 88C and Ju 88R. The Ju 88G was among the finest night-fighters of the war, with airborne intercept radar and a range of different weapons options.

Towards the end of the war, the Luftwaffe introduced the long-range Ju 88H, which featured a lengthened fuselage carrying additional fuel. Specific variants included the Ju

88H-1 reconnaissance aircraft and the Ju 88H-2 fighter. A dedicated anti-tank aircraft, the Ju 88P, was a development of the Ju 88A-4, the Ju 88P-1 version carrying a hard-hitting 75mm (2.9in) PaK 40 anti-tank gun. The successive Ju 88P-2 to Ju 88P-4 versions offered different combinations of offensive weapons for the same role.

The final production versions represented efforts to wring additional performance out of the basic design as the tide of the war turned increasingly in favour of the Allies. The Ju 88S was a high-performance bomber version, while the Ju 88T was a photo-reconnaissance aircraft. Total production amounted to almost 15,000 aircraft.

SPAD XIII

The pace of development during World War I was such that few fighters remained dominant for long. Of all the fighting scouts on the Western Front, the best all-rounder was probably the French-designed SPAD XIII, famously flown by the American 'Hat in the Ring' Squadron.

The Société Pour l'Aviation et ses Dérivés – better known as SPAD – first made its mark with the SPAD VII fighting scout, which was first flown in April 1916 and soon demonstrated its superiority over the German Albatros and Fokker scouts.

Such was the success of the SPAD XIII that a further development of the basic design was a logical next step. Compared to the SPAD VII, the SPAD XIII, which was first flown in 4 April 1917, differed primarily in its use of a geared 164kW (220hp) Hispano-Suiza 8Ba engine that not only provided more power but drove a propeller in the opposite direction to that on the direct-drive Hispano 8Aa as found on the SPAD VII. Much of the success of both the SPAD VII and XIII can be attributed to the exceptional

EDDIE RICKENBACKER
This aircraft, serial S4523, was intended for the squadron commander, but was claimed by Rickenbacker for himself. He flew it from Rembercourt airfield near St Mihiel, France, in autumn 1918.

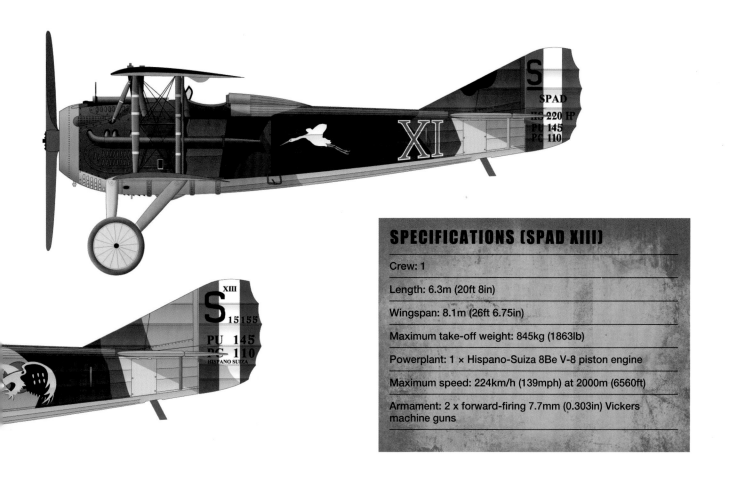

SPECIFICATIONS (SPAD XIII)

Crew: 1

Length: 6.3m (20ft 8in)

Wingspan: 8.1m (26ft 6.75in)

Maximum take-off weight: 845kg (1863lb)

Powerplant: 1 × Hispano-Suiza 8Be V-8 piston engine

Maximum speed: 224km/h (139mph) at 2000m (6560ft)

Armament: 2 x forward-firing 7.7mm (0.303in) Vickers machine guns

FRANK LUKE (ABOVE)

SPAD XIII serial S15155 was flown by the fast-scoring Frank Luke Jr, who was the second most successful American Expeditionary Force pilot during World War I. He served with the 27th Aero Squadron and, at the time of his death in combat in September 1918, he had scored 18 officially credited victories.

RENÉ FONCK (TOP)

René Fonck flew this SPAD XIII in 1917. The aircraft carries the 'Cigognes' (stork) markings of Escadrille SPA 103, a tradition that continues in the French Air Force today. When he received the Légion d'Honneur, Fonck was described as 'A fighting pilot of great value, combining outstanding bravery and exceptional qualities of skill and sang-froid.'

Hispano engine, a pioneering V-8 unit that was designed by the Swiss Marc Birkigt. Other changes were made to the SPAD XIII, too, including inverse tapered-chord ailerons on a wing of slightly increased span, rounded tailplane tips and vertical tail surfaces of increased area. Armament comprised twin 7.7mm (0.303in) Vickers machine guns.

ALLIED ACE OF ACES

The first examples of the aircraft were delivered to units on the Western Front in May 1917, replacing Nieuports and the SPAD VII within the French fighter squadrons. The SPAD XIII gained a certain notoriety as it was the mount of the French ace Georges Guynemer, the national hero with 54 victories, who disappeared in mysterious circumstances while flying one of the first examples of the aircraft over Poelkapelle in September 1917. Despite this setback, the SPAD XIII would soon show its prowess in the hands of other aviators, including René Fonck, who ended World War I as the top

Allied fighter ace, with 75 victories. Fonck, an expert marksman, found an ideal mount in the SPAD XIII, and on one occasion was credited with destroying three enemy aircraft with just 27 rounds of ammunition.

EXTENSIVE SERVICE

During the final 14 months of the war, SPAD XIIIs equipped no fewer than 81 French escadrilles (squadrons) as well as numerous units of the Belgian and Italian air services, and Nos. 19 and 23 Squadrons of the Royal Flying Corps. Among other nationalities that flew the SPAD XIII, the most celebrated was Francesco Baracca, who was Italy's top fighter ace of World War I, credited with 34 aerial victories. After a handful of victories in the SPAD XIII in October 1917, Baracca's aircraft was 'shot up and its longeron broken into pieces by enemy machine gun fire in an aerial dogfight.' As a result, Baracca returned to the SPAD VII for a period, and then switched between the two machines.

In July 1918, the Americans decided to procure the SPAD XIII to equip their fighting formations after expressing disappointment in the Nieuport 28. The SPAD XIII was thus flown by Captain Eddie Rickenbacker, the leading ace of the Expeditionary Force. Flying with the famed 94th Aero Squadron 'Hat in the Ring', Rickenbacker racked up a considerable number of kills in the final weeks of the war. Joining him in the Expeditionary Force was Frank Luke Jr, the fastest-scoring American pilot of the war, whose final tally of 18 included a number of observation balloons that were shot down at the controls of a SPAD XIII.

Production of the SPAD XIII was somewhat sluggish and by the end of the war the SPAD VII was still in large-scale service despite it being outclassed by the German Fokker D.VII. At the time of the major German offensives of March 1918, the SPAD VII continued to outnumber its superior successor.

A total of 8472 SPAD XIIIs were built. Production could have been much greater had it not been terminated by the end of the war: prior to the cessation of hostilities, the Allies had outstanding orders for some 10,000 aircraft, which were all cancelled. Nevertheless, the aircraft's post-war career saw it exported to Belgium, Czechoslovakia, Japan and Poland.

Leading American ace of World War I, Captain Eddie Rickenbacker is seen alongside his SPAD XIII, which he flew with the 94th Aero Squadron in 1918. Note the famous 'Hat in the Ring' insignia on the rear fuselage and the rough and muddy airstrip that was typical of conditions on the Western Front.

SPAD 13

An airworthy SPAD XIII operated as part of the Cole Palen Old Rhinebeck Aerodrome collection. Powered by a Wright-Hispano engine, it was once displayed at Roosevelt Field and is seen in the markings of Captain Robert Soubiran of the 103rd Pursuit Squadron, formerly the famous Lafayette Escadrille. Palen is seen flying the preserved SPAD during 1960. The aircraft is now on display at the Air Force Museum in Dayton, Ohio.

GEORGE GUYNEMER

SPAD XIII serial S504 was flown by Georges Guynemer in September 1917. It is an early series aircraft with rounded wings and armed with twin machine guns. France's most popular ace, Guynemer was killed in combat near Poelkapelle, Belgium on 11 September 1917.

'CIGOGNES'

SPA 3's history dates back to when Escadrille 3 formed in July 1912. In April 1916, the unit was amalgamated with Escadrilles 26, 73, and 103. In November 1916, the four became Groupe de Combat 12, better known as the 'Cigognes'. Once re-equipped with SPADs, the original escadrille became SPA 3.

P-38 Lightning

The mighty P-38 was something of an anomaly among the US Army Air Force in World War II: a genuinely successful heavy fighter that was equally capable in the long-range escort role or as a hard-hitting ground-attack aircraft in both European and Pacific theatres. After a successful combat debut, it was soon dubbed the 'fork-tailed devil'.

The success of the P-38 is more remarkable considering it was the first fighter design from the Lockheed stable. The twin-engine, twin-boom aircraft was originally designed to meet a 1937 specification calling for a high-altitude interceptor, a role in which it would see little use. First flown on 27 January 1939, the XP-38 prototype was followed

by the first production P-38s. Powered by a pair of Allison V-1710-27/29 engines, these possessed a top speed that was in excess of any other twin-engine fighter at that time: 628km/h (390mph). The production aircraft was equipped with armament of one 37mm (1.4in) cannon and four 12.7mm (0.5in) machine guns in the nose, providing

FIGHTER ESCORT

The P-38J resulted in a new lease of life for the Lightning, particularly during the 1943 daylight raids by USAAF B-17 and B-24 bombers over Europe. However, in 1944, as deliveries of the P-51 stepped up, the P-38J and the more powerful P-38M came to be used increasingly in the ground-attack role.

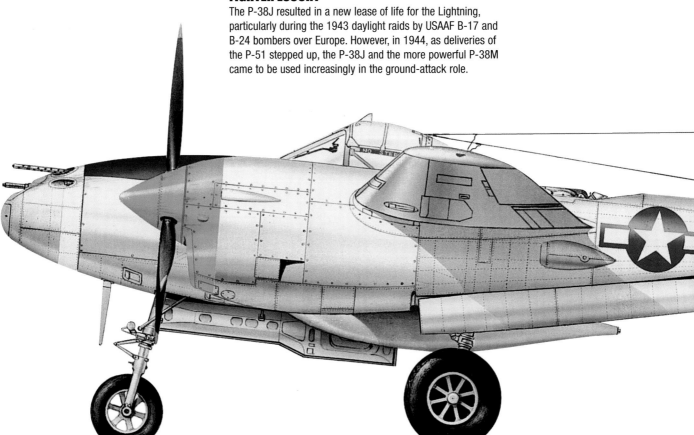

SPECIFICATIONS (P-38L)

Crew: 1

Length: 11.53m (37ft 10in)

Wingspan: 15.85m (52ft)

Empty weight: 5806kg (12,800lb)

Powerplant: 2 × Allison V-1710-111/113 inline piston engines

Maximum speed: 667km/h (414mph) at 7620m (25,000ft)

Armament: 1 x 20mm (0.78in) cannon, 4 x 12.7mm (0.5in) machine guns in the nose, plus a bombload of 2 x 726kg (1600lb) bombs or 10 x 70mm (2.75in) rockets

A Royal Australian Air Force photo-reconnaissance Lightning, assigned to No. 1 Photographic Reconnaissance Unit. The RAAF initially received only two F-4s, while a third example was subsequently delivered as an attrition replacement.

'LOCO GROUP'

This P-38J-15 was assigned to the 55th Fighter Squadron, 20th Fighter Group based at Kingscliffe. The unit was known as the 'Loco Group' on account of its train-busting prowess. The 55th used a triangle on the tailfins as its squadron marking. RAF-style letter codes on the tailbooms also indicated the squadron.

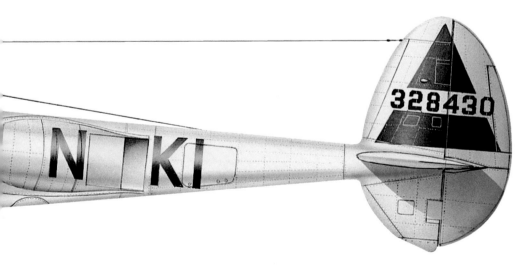

P-38J

The P-38J was generally similar to the P-38H that preceded it, but with many detail changes introduced throughout the 2970-aircraft production run. The P-38J first saw combat service in August 1943 and was used for long-range penetration fights into the heart of Europe.

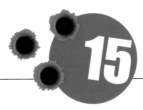

a concentrated battery of fire. The first fully operational version of the Lightning was the P-38D, which began to see squadron service with the US Army Air Force around the time of the Japanese attack on Pearl Harbor. In the same month, the first of 138 aircraft ordered for the Royal Air Force began to arrive in the United Kingdom. After evaluation, the UK cancelled its order, prompted by the continued ban on the export of turbochargers and the adverse effect this had on the aircraft's performance.

The next version to see quantity production was the P-38E for the USAAF. This differed primarily in substituting the original 37mm (1.4in) cannon for a 20mm (0.78in) weapon. The P-38F, meanwhile, was a fighter-bomber development, with provision for a bombload of up to 907kg (2000lb) on racks under the wings. The P-38F began to enter service in mid-1942 with fighter groups in Europe and North Africa. Although its initial combat with Luftwaffe fighters was disappointing, it

excelled in the ground-attack role during the final stages of the Tunisian campaign. Next in line was the P-38G, with minor equipment changes.

INCREASED BOMBLOAD

The Lightning's utility as a fighter-bomber was given a boost with the appearance of the P-38H, which could carry up to 1452kg (3200lb) of bombs, including a pair of 726kg (1600lb) weapons. The P-38J model, of which 2970 examples were produced, featured deep 'chin' fairings for the radiators immediately aft of the propellers. Other changes included increased fuel capacity via external tanks; with a full fuel load, the aircraft's endurance was increased to around 12 hours. The P-38J was the mount of Major Richard I. Bong, the leading American ace of World War II. Bong scored most of his 40 victories at the controls of the P-38J. The P-38J possessed the range required for the escort mission and could accom-

BARE METAL
By mid-1944, most USAAF fighters operating in Europe had shed their olive drab/neutral grey finish in favour of natural metal. This provided fractionally more speed in combat. Unit markings remained. The 20th Fighter Group received natural metal P-38s from February 1944.

LIGHT BOMBER
While this P-38J is equipped with the standard 'fighter' nose, a number of J-models were adapted for use in the light bomber role, for which they were fitted with an alternative glazed nose to the centre nacelle for use by a bomb aimer. A bombing radar was another option for this role.

EXTRA FUEL
On the P-38J-5 model and after, the space previously occupied by the intercoolers in the wing leading edges now accommodated two additional 208-litre (255-gallon) fuel tanks, increasing total internal fuel capacity to 1552 litres (410 gallons).

The P-38H introduced uprated 1063kW (1425hp) V-1710-89/91 engines. This variant also introduced automatic oil radiator flaps to solve a major engine overheating problem. In other respects, the P-38H was essentially identical to the P-38G, though it had B-33 instead of B-13 turbochargers.

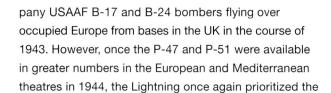

pany USAAF B-17 and B-24 bombers flying over occupied Europe from bases in the UK in the course of 1943. However, once the P-47 and P-51 were available in greater numbers in the European and Mediterranean theatres in 1944, the Lightning once again prioritized the ground-attack role.

The ultimate wartime development of the Lightning was the P-38L, which was also the most prolific. Compared to the P-38J, the only difference in the P-38L was the adoption of -111/113 engines in place of the -89/91s previously used. Both versions were widely used in the ground support role, the more powerful P-38L being modified to carry 10 70mm

(2.75in) rockets under the wings. The same version was also the first Allied aircraft to drop napalm bombs on German forces in the second half of 1944.

In addition to the fighter and fighter-bomber versions, the Lightning also excelled in the photo-reconnaissance role. The F-4 and F-5 conversions were employed widely in both Europe and the Far East. Another niche role involved two-seat P-38s used as 'lead ships', carrying a bombardier and a Norden bombsight and flying ahead of a formation of single-seat fighter-bombers. A further refinement added a radar for all-weather bombing raids. Production of all Lightnings amounted to 9394 aircraft.

Hawker Hurricane

The Hurricane was the most successful British fighter during the Battle of Britain in 1940. Although soon superseded by the Supermarine Spitfire, it remained in service until the end of the war and served in a variety of roles, including night-fighter and tank-buster.

The Hurricane was the Royal Air Force's first monoplane fighter and the first with a top speed of over 483km/h (300mph). Designed by Sydney Camm, the prototype Hurricane first flew on 6 November 1935 and entered RAF service in December 1937. The initial Hurricane Mk I was powered by a Rolls-Royce Merlin II developing 768kW (1030hp) and was armed with eight 7.7mm (0.303in) machine guns. At the time of the Battle of Britain in summer 1940, the Hurricane Mk I was the RAF's primary fighter

and destroyed more enemy aircraft than all other defences combined. Although it was not the fastest fighter of its day, the Hurricane made up for this in combat with its excellent agility and ability to withstand considerable battle damage.

The Hurricane Mk IIA, which was the next version to enter service, was powered by a 955kW (1280hp) Merlin XX and arrived with squadrons before the end of 1940. The similar Hurricane Mk IIB differed in its armament of 12 7.7mm (0.303in) machine guns, while the Hurricane Mk IIC

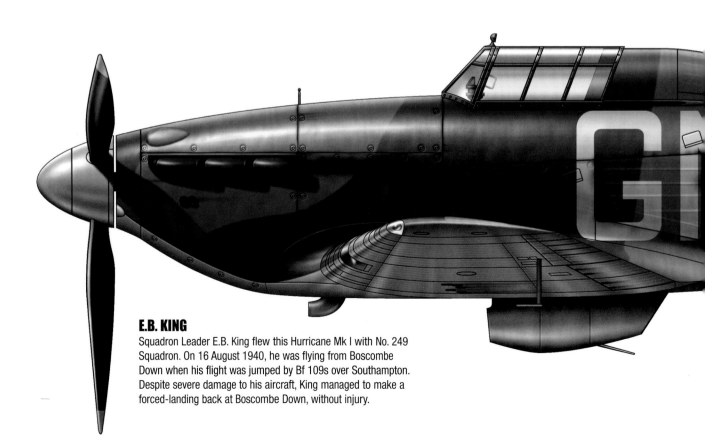

E.B. KING
Squadron Leader E.B. King flew this Hurricane Mk I with No. 249 Squadron. On 16 August 1940, he was flying from Boscombe Down when his flight was jumped by Bf 109s over Southampton. Despite severe damage to his aircraft, King managed to make a forced-landing back at Boscombe Down, without injury.

SPECIFICATIONS (MK IIC)

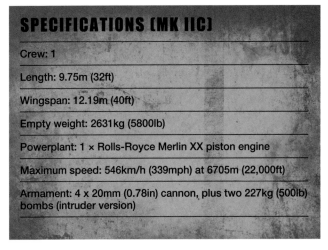

Crew: 1

Length: 9.75m (32ft)

Wingspan: 12.19m (40ft)

Empty weight: 2631kg (5800lb)

Powerplant: 1 × Rolls-Royce Merlin XX piston engine

Maximum speed: 546km/h (339mph) at 6705m (22,000ft)

Armament: 4 x 20mm (0.78in) cannon, plus two 227kg (500lb) bombs (intruder version)

One of an increasing number of airworthy Hurricanes, this Mk I, R4118, was delivered new to No. 605 (County of Warwick) Squadron at Drem in August 1940. During the Battle of Britain it flew 49 sorties from Croydon and shot down five enemy aircraft. It now flies with Hurricane Heritage in the UK.

MACHINE GUN ARMAMENT
The rifle-calibre machine guns that armed Hurricanes in the Battle of Britain were found to be ineffective against the Luftwaffe bombers' self-sealing tanks. As a result, cannon soon found their way into British fighters, and were included in the Hurricane Mk IIC.

BATTLE OF BRITAIN
The Battle of Britain began in July 1940, at which time the Hurricane equipped no fewer than 26 squadrons of the Royal Air Force, compared to 17 with Spitfires, eight with Blenheims and two with Defiants.

entered service in 1941 and was armed with four 20mm (0.78in) cannon. The Mk IIs could also carry up to two 227kg (500lb) bombs to service in the fighter-bomber role. In the West, the Hurricane Mk II remained a front-line type until 1943. However, in the Far East the aircraft remained in front-line use until the end of the war. A specialist anti-tank variant, the Hurricane Mk IID introduced a pair of 40mm (1.5in) anti-tank weapons in 1942. The tank-busting Hurricane saw notable success in the North African theatre.

The Hurricane Mk II was also the principal night-fighter version, supplementing the twin-engine Bristol Blenheim in this role early in the war. As well as homeland defence, the night-firing Hurricanes flew intruder missions over occupied Europe. Apart from its matt black paint scheme, the night-fighter/ intruder Hurricane was no different from its day-fighter counterparts.

The introduction of a 'universal' wing resulted in the Hurricane Mk IV, which could carry up to eight 27.2kg (60lb) rocket projectiles or any of the external stores carried by the Hurricane Mk II, including bombs and drop tanks.

A total of 14,321 Hurricanes were produced in factories in the UK and in Canada (the Hurricane Mks X, XI and XII).

HURRICANE AT SEA

The production total includes the Sea Hurricane for the Royal Navy, which first went to sea in catapult-launched form on board converted merchant ships. It was later provided with catapult and arrestor gear for service on board conventional aircraft carriers.

The first version, the Sea Hurricane Mk IA, was fitted with catapult spools for launch from merchant ships in the event of enemy aircraft appearing, after which the pilot would likely have to ditch into the sea. The Sea Hurricane Mk IB added deck arrestor gear for carrier operations. A few examples of the Sea Hurricane Mk IC were completed, with four 20mm (0.78in) wing cannon. After the introduction of the Merlin XX, the Sea Hurricane Mk IIB was the standard machine-gun-armed fighter, while the Sea Hurricane Mk IIC was the cannon-armed version.

The first Sea Hurricanes entered service in February 1941; the type remained in service, primarily in the Arctic and Mediterranean theatres, until 1943.

OPERATING UNIT

P3059, a Hurricane Mk I typical of the Battle of Britain, served with No. 501 (County of Gloucester) Squadron during August 1940. The squadron operated from Croydon, Middle Wallop, Gravesend and Kenley between June and September 1940.

GLOSTER PRODUCTION

This aircraft was built by Gloster under sub-contract and was part of a batch equipped from the outset with Rotol constant-speed propellers. They began to be delivered to the RAF's fighter squadrons in May 1940; deliveries continued throughout the Battle of Britain.

Messerschmitt Bf 109

Despite it increasingly being supplemented by the Focke-Wulf Fw 190 from the end of 1941, the Bf 109 provided the backbone of the Luftwaffe's single-seat fighter force throughout World War II. It also served as the equipment for the Luftwaffe's leading aces, including the highest-scoring fighter ace of all time, Erich Hartmann.

The development of the Messerschmitt Bf 109 parallelled the establishment of a modern and powerful Luftwaffe in Germany in the mid-1930s. Designed by Willy Messerschmitt, who had already completed the Bf 108 cantilever low-wing cabin monoplane with retractable landing gear, the Bf 109 single-seat fighter prototype saw off competition from the Arado Ar 80, Focke-Wulf Fw 159 and Heinkel He 112 to be selected for the Luftwaffe. As originally flown on 28 May 1935, the prototype Bf 109 was powered by a Rolls-Royce Kestrel engine developing 518kW (695hp). The second prototype introduced a 455kW (610hp) Junkers Jumo 210A for which it had originally been designed.

The pre-production prototypes were used to trial a range of different armament options. The initial three of these aircraft were designated Bf 109A, while the remainder served as prototypes for the forthcoming Bf 109B. The early iterations of the Bf 109B included the Bf 109B-1, with a 474kW (635hp) Jumo 210D engine, and the Bf 109B-2, with a 477kW (640hp) Jumo 210E, later superseded by a 500kW (670hp) Jumo 210G.

In early 1937, the first production Bf 109B-1s began to be delivered to the Luftwaffe's Jagdgeschwader 132 'Richthofen'. The Bf 109 first saw combat in the Spanish Civil War, where it served with the German Condor Legion beginning in summer 1937. In the meantime, the aircraft

SPECIFICATIONS (BF 109G-6)

Crew: 1

Length: 9.02m (29ft 7.1in)

Wingspan: 9.92m (32ft 6.6in)

Empty weight: 2700kg (5952lb)

Powerplant: 1 × Daimler-Benz DB605A piston engine

Maximum speed: 623km/h (387mph) at 7000m (22,966ft)

Armament: 2 x 13mm (0.59in) machine guns, 1 x 30mm (1.1in) cannon in the nose, 2 x 20mm (0.78in) cannon under the wings

The early Bf 109F could be distinguished by its rounded wingtips and angular undercarriage bays. In a dive, the speed of the Bf 109F was superior to that of the Royal Air Force's Spitfire Mk V. This version spearheaded the Luftwaffe single-seat fighter arm during the invasion of the Soviet Union.

POWERPLANT
The Bf 109E-4 was powered by a DB 601a 12-cylinder inverted-Vee engine with direct fuel injection. This feature allowed the Bf 109 to perform negative-G manoeuvres without the engine cutting out.

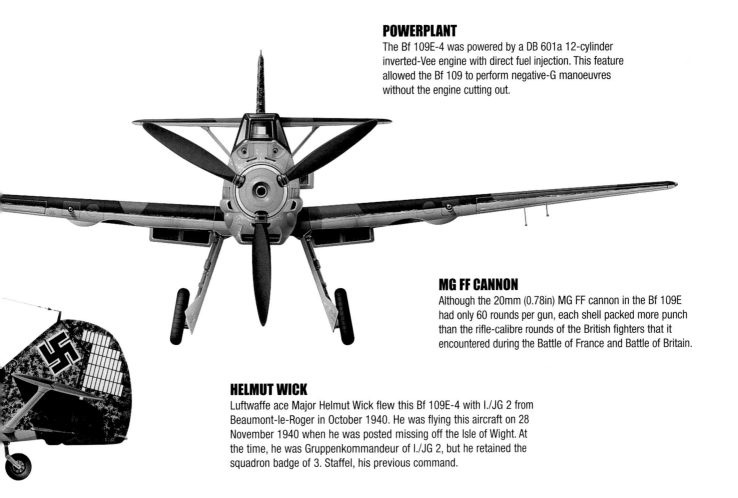

MG FF CANNON
Although the 20mm (0.78in) MG FF cannon in the Bf 109E had only 60 rounds per gun, each shell packed more punch than the rifle-calibre rounds of the British fighters that it encountered during the Battle of France and Battle of Britain.

HELMUT WICK
Luftwaffe ace Major Helmut Wick flew this Bf 109E-4 with I./JG 2 from Beaumont-le-Roger in October 1940. He was flying this aircraft on 28 November 1940 when he was posted missing off the Isle of Wight. At the time, he was Gruppenkommandeur of I./JG 2, but he retained the squadron badge of 3. Staffel, his previous command.

was also used to gain the world landplane speed record, being timed at 610.55km/h (379.38mph) after being re-engined with a boosted Daimler-Benz DB 601.

The Bf 109B was supplemented by the Bf 109C-1 with a 522kW (700hp) Jumo 210Ga engine and with armament increased from three to four machine guns. The Bf 109D was the first production model to introduce the DB 601D engine and direct fuel-injection, and armament variations included between two and four machine guns and one hub-cannon. Fighter-bomber and reconnaissance versions were produced in 1940 and the Bf 109E saw large-scale service during the Battle of Britain.

The next production series was the Bf 109F, initially powered by a DB 601N engine and later by a DB 601E. Other new additions included nitrous-oxide power boosting, faster-firing 15mm (0.59in) machine guns and optional underwing gun pods. Both the Bf 109E and Bf 109F were also completed in tropicalized form for service in North Africa in 1941–42.

PROLIFIC 'GUSTAV'

Powered by the DB 605 engine, the Bf 109G served with the Luftwaffe on all fronts between 1942 and the end of the war. The most numerous series, the Bf 109G, introduced various different armament options, including 30mm (1.1in) cannon, and had the option of cabin pressurization. Perhaps the ultimate iteration of the G-series was the Bf 109G-10, which was also the fastest at 690km/h (429mph).

The last of the Bf 109s to see quantity production was the Bf 109K, which was powered by a boosted DB 605. Other versions included the Bf 109H high-altitude fighter with an increased-span wing and the shipboard Bf 109T that was designed for service on Germany's abortive aircraft carrier *Graf Zeppelin*.

More than 33,000 Bf 109s were built by the time production came to an end. Such was the utility of the Bf 109 that it remained in front-line service for some years after World War II. As well as German production, the Bf 109 was licence-built in Spain as the Hispano Aviación HA-1112, which served with the Spanish air force as late as 1965. Additional post-war production was undertaken in Czechoslovakia. The Czech Avia S-199 was the first fighter acquired by the Israeli Air Force, and saw combat during the 1948 Arab–Israeli War.

'STAR OF AFRICA'

This Bf 109F-4 was flown by Hauptmann Hans-Joachim Marseille, who managed to claim 158 official victories before his death west of El Alamein on 30 September 1942. On one occasion, Marseille scored 14 victories in a single day. No other pilot claimed as many Western Allied aircraft as Marseille.

E-7 MODIFICATIONS

The Bf 109E-7 version was introduced to Luftwaffe service in the middle of the Battle of Britain in August 1940. The aircraft featured a modified fuel system and attachments for a drop tank below the belly. Additional fuel meant the aircraft was well suited to the role of providing escort for daylight bomber raids over the UK.

Ilyushin Il-2

The most numerous warplane ever built, the Il-2 Shturmovik is remembered as the aircraft that helped turn the tide of the war in the East, and, as the Red Army went on the offensive, it accompanied it all the way to the gates of Berlin. The Il-2 introduced the Shturmovik concept, and its emphasis on ground attack and tank-busting proved influential.

The Il-2 relied on structural strength and durability, armour protection and heavy armament – combined with tactics that saw it thrown into battle in exclusive support of the troops on the ground – to ensure that it became a decisive weapon in the war on the Eastern Front. Although other nations had previously attempted to field close support aircraft, the Ilyushin design was perhaps the first to offer the required balance of attributes to succeed in the role.

Development of the Shturmovik (attacker) began in the late 1930s, under a team headed by Sergei Ilyushin. From the start, the aircraft, initially known as the TsKB-55 or BSh-2, was to be based around an armoured shell

that would form an integral part of the fuselage structure, offering protection to its two crew, engine, radiators and fuel tank. At this early stage, however, the Soviet military was unconvinced of the utility of a two-seat attack aircraft, and the two-seat design was rejected in favour of continued development of a single-seat version. This emerged as the TsKB-57, with the pilot seated below a raised, faired canopy. Powerplant was a Mikulin AM-38 developing 1268kW (1700hp). Other changes in the TsKB-57 included two 20mm (0.78in) cannon in place of two of the previous four machine guns in the wing. The first prototype flew on 12 October 1940.

FLYING SURFACES
Most early Il-2s combined all-metal wings, tailplanes and control surfaces with a wooden tailfin. Some, however, incorporated a wooden outer wing and tailplane structure. The sweep angle of the wing was increased to 15 degrees in time for combat over Stalingrad in early 1943. The aim of this modification was to decrease drag.

INTERNAL BOMBS
The Il-2 had provision for carriage of external and internal disposable stores. This included two bomb cells in each wing, each covered by a pair of doors with manual opening by the pilot. Each cell typically carried a 100kg (220lb) high-explosive general-purpose bomb.

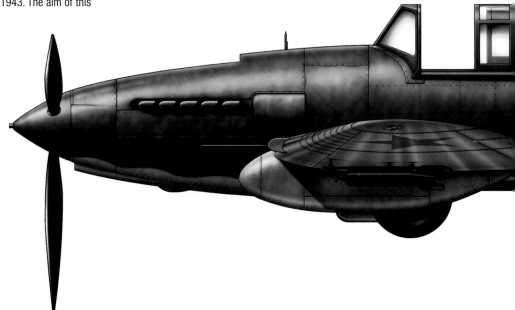

SPECIFICATIONS (IL-2M3)

Crew: 2

Length: 11.65m (38ft 2.5in)

Wingspan: 14.6m (47ft 10.75in)

Empty weight: 4525kg (9976lb) equipped

Powerplant: 1 × Mikulin AM-38F inline piston engine

Maximum speed: 410km/h (255mph) at 1500m (4920ft)

Armament: 2 x 23mm (0.9in) cannon and 2 x 7.62mm (0.3in) machine guns in the wing, 1–2 x 12.7mm (0.5in) machine gun for the gunner, plus 4 x 100kg (220lb) bombs or rockets

The Il-2 was initially fielded in single-seat form, and as such proved very vulnerable to attack from behind. The first efforts to provide the Il-2 with a defensive armament for the rear sector involved a field modification of the rear fuselage, with a cut-out for a gunner on a canvas seat with a 12.7mm (0.5in) UBT machine gun on an improvised mounting.

Evaluation of the prototype was completed just three months before the German invasion of June 1941, by which time the aircraft was in full-scale production as the Il-2. Initial deliveries were made in May 1941. Compared to the TsKB-57, the early production aircraft featured additional protection for the pilot.

Although only 249 aircraft had been taken on charge by the time the invasion began, the Il-2 would go on to serve

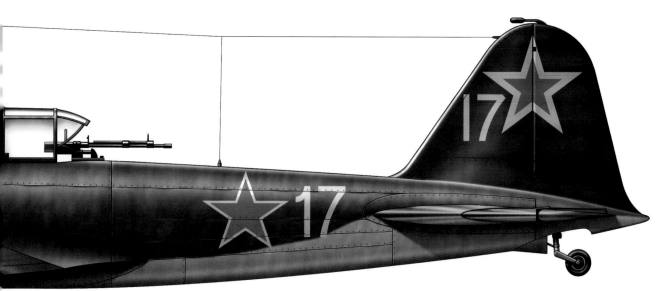

STRENGTHENING
From 1944, the Il-2M3 was provided with an all-Dural fuselage structure that was much tougher than the previous wooden monocoque rear fuselage of earlier models. The Dural version featured four steel strengthening elements that were first introduced as a field expedient before becoming standard on production aircraft.

in huge numbers: a total of 36,163 of all variants would eventually be completed. However, early losses and a lack of fighter cover encouraged the authorities to revisit the original two-seat concept in February 1942.

IMPROVED SHTURMOVIK

The Il-2M added provision for a rear gunner under an extended canopy. After two conversions were tested in March 1942, the aircraft appeared in service from September of that year. Other changes included replacing the 20mm (0.78in) cannon with harder-hitting 23mm (0.9in) weapons, aerodynamic refinements and a new powerplant in the form of the more powerful AM-38F.

By the time of the Battle of Stalingrad in early 1943, a new version of the Shturmovik had entered service. This was the Il-2 Type 3 (or Il-2M3). This featured redesigned wings with 15 degrees of weep on the outer panels, leading

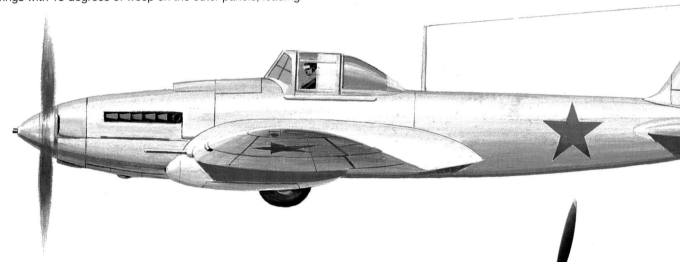

to much improved flying qualities and handling. This aircraft would become the most numerous of the Il-2 line.

Other changes introduced in the course of the war included revised armament, such as cassettes for the carriage of 200 hollow-charge anti-tank bomblets. A relatively small number of aircraft were adapted as dedicated tank-busters, the Il-2 Type 3M being armed with a pair of 37mm (1.4in) cannon in fairings outboard of the main undercarriage.

The Shturmovik also saw service with the Soviet naval air arm, the Il-2T being developed as a torpedo-bomber specifically for this service.

REAR GUNNER

In the Il-10, the armoured cockpits were closer together and the gunner had a 20mm (0.78in) canon rather than a machine gun in an improved mounting that was provided with a glazed cupola fairing. On the earlier Il-2, the glazed hood for the rear gunner had often been removed for combat operations.

IMPROVED IL-10

Compared to the Il-2, the Il-10 was greatly cleaned up, and also differed significantly in airframe shape, structure and systems. The fuselage was deeper and better streamlined. Although it was heavier, the Il-10 had simpler main landing gear, with single legs and wheels that rotated to lie flat inside the wing.

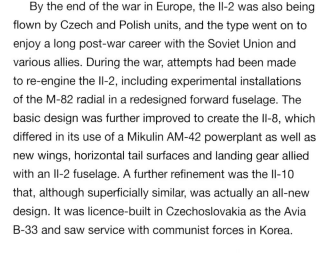

By the end of the war in Europe, the Il-2 was also being flown by Czech and Polish units, and the type went on to enjoy a long post-war career with the Soviet Union and various allies. During the war, attempts had been made to re-engine the Il-2, including experimental installations of the M-82 radial in a redesigned forward fuselage. The basic design was further improved to create the Il-8, which differed in its use of a Mikulin AM-42 powerplant as well as new wings, horizontal tail surfaces and landing gear allied with an Il-2 fuselage. A further refinement was the Il-10 that, although superficially similar, was actually an all-new design. It was licence-built in Czechoslovakia as the Avia B-33 and saw service with communist forces in Korea.

Il-2s depart from a forward base on the Eastern Front for a combat mission, probably in 1942. While most of these aircraft are early ShVAK-armed single-seaters, the aircraft in the foreground is equipped with VYa cannon, which were fitted with longer barrels than the ShVAK weapons.

WINTER SCHEME

This early Il-2, still lacking the rear gunner's position, has been finished in a temporary winter distemper to provide improved camouflage when operating on snowy airfields. Such schemes rapidly became weathered and dirty when operating on the more primitive airstrips encountered on the Eastern Front.

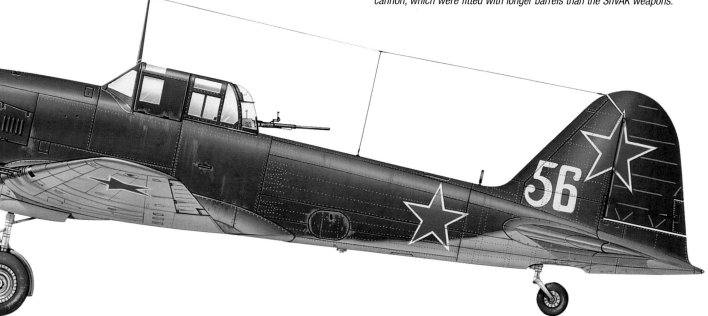

P-47 Thunderbolt

Rivalled only by the superb P-51 Mustang as the finest single-seat US Army Air Force fighter of World War II, the P-47 was one of the heaviest fighters of the war and could carry a potent load of offensive weapons for the ground-attack role as well as serving as an escort.

The P-47 represented a further evolution of the Alexander Seversky-designed Republic P-43 radial-powered fighter and was developed under a team led by Alexander Kartveli. The prototype XP-47B was first flown on 6 May 1941, and was built around the Pratt & Whitney R-2800 developing 1492kW (2000hp) provided with an exhaust-driven turbocharger in the rear fuselage. Armament comprised eight 12.7mm (0.5in) machine guns in the wings.

The initial production aircraft was the P-47B, 171 of which were completed. These incorporated minor refinements compared to the prototype and were capable of a top speed of 691km/h (429mph). In January 1943,

the P-47B arrived with the USAAF in the United Kingdom, and the 56th and 78th Fighter Groups began to fly escort missions for B-17 bombers in early April. The early-model Thunderbolt proved very resistant to battle damage, but was lacking in terms of agility and rate of climb. The next production version, the P-47C, differed in its adoption of a lengthened fuselage and provision for a 568-litre (125-gallon) drop tank under the fuselage.

POST-WAR 'JUG'

This dorsal-fin-equipped P-47D-30 served in occupied Germany immediately after the end of World War II. The operator was the 512th Fighter Squadron of the 406th Fighter Group, based at Nordholz in the north of the country.

SPECIFICATIONS (P-47D)

Crew: 1

Length: 11m (36ft 1in)

Wingspan: 12.42m (40ft 9in)

Empty weight: 4536kg (10,000lb)

Powerplant: 1 × Pratt & Whitney R-2800-59 radial engine

Maximum speed: 689km/h (428mph) at 9145m (30,000ft)

Armament: 8 x 12.7mm (0.5in) machine guns, plus 2 x 454kg (1000lb) bombs or 6 x 70mm (2.75in) rocket projectiles under the wings

A prototype P-47N, the fastest and heaviest of all the wartime Thunderbolts. Equipped with eight machine guns in the wing and capable of carrying impressive loads of bombs and rocket projectiles, the P-47N was well suited to the ground attack role and saw extensive service in the Pacific.

IMPROVEMENTS

The P-47 incorporated a range of improvements including a refined engine, a better turbocharger, improved cockpit armour, and multi-ply tyres that did not burst on rough strips when the aircraft was heavily loaded with bombs.

D-MODEL

The P-47D was the major production version, the first example being flown in December 1942. It was powered by either a 1716kW (2300hp) R-2800-21W or a 1891kW (2535hp) water-injected radial.

'BUBBLE' HOOD

The P-47D was the first of the Thunderbolts to incorporate a cut-down rear fuselage combined with a 'bubble' hood on later sub-variants. The P-47D was the major production model, with 12,606 examples being built. Other changes included a water-injection power boost. As well as flying from the UK, initially on bomber escort duties, the P-47D also saw combat in the Mediterranean and the Far East. After flying for a year or so on fighter escort duties, the Thunderbolt began to be adapted for the ground-attack role. The P-47D was the first model with provision for offensive missions, in the form of underwing racks capable of carrying a pair of 474kg (1000lb) bombs, as well as the centreline drop tank. Later-production P-47Ds had their offensive armament increased to 1134kg (2500lb) including up to 10 127mm (5in) rocket projectiles. The P-47D initially saw use in the ground-attack role with the 348th Fighter Group. Based in Australia, the unit flew its Thunderbolts against Japanese targets in New Guinea. Subsequent

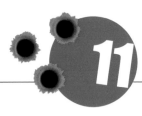

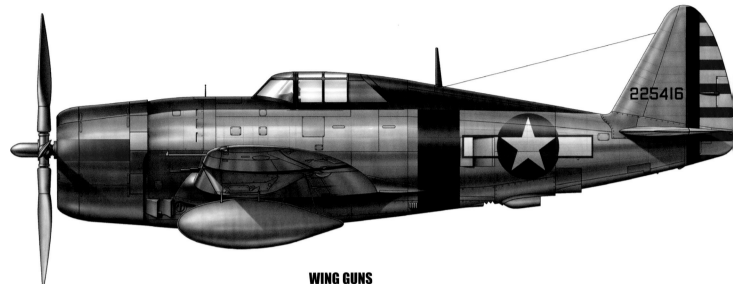

'RAZORBACK' (ABOVE)

The P-47C and early P-47Ds had 'razorback' fuselages, the early 'D' being externally almost identical to the P-47C-5. However, it featured various internal refinements as well as a redesigned exhaust gas duct for the turbocharger, changes in the engine accessory compartment, and a paddle-bladed propeller.

WING GUNS

The eight machine guns in the wing were mounted in a staggered formation. These reliable 12.7mm (0.5in) weapons provided a good weight of fire, even if they lacked the destructive force of cannon. In some instances, they could even be used for destroying enemy tanks.

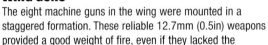

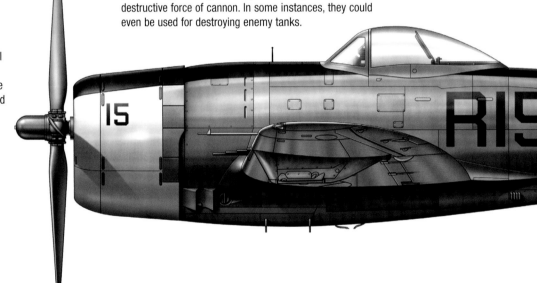

deliveries were made to the US 9th and 15th Air Forces in the UK and the Mediterranean.

The Thunderbolt saw service with the Royal Air Force, with no fewer than 16 squadrons equipped with the fighter in Burma. The RAF adopted the P-47B as the Thunderbolt Mk I, and the P-47D as the Thunderbolt Mk II, a total of 826 being delivered. Close support tactics developed in this theatre included the use of Thunderbolts in 'cab rank' patrols, which provided support to the 14th Army as it

advanced on Rangoon. From mid-1944, as the pace of P-51 deliveries increased, the P-47 was switched from escort duties to the ground-attack role and came to the fore once the Allies had landed in northwest Europe. After D-Day, the P-47 became a familiar sight to Allied ground troops to which it provided close air support. Similar missions were also flown after the Allied invasion of Italy. The aircraft had an impressive loss rate of just 0.7 per cent per mission.

A P-47D of the 376th Fighter Squadron, 361st Fighter Group. The 361st was the last P-47 group to join the Eighth Air Force operating in the United Kingdom. Between January 1944 and April 1945, the group flew 441 missions, most of which saw it escort daylight bombing raids flying over occupied Europe.

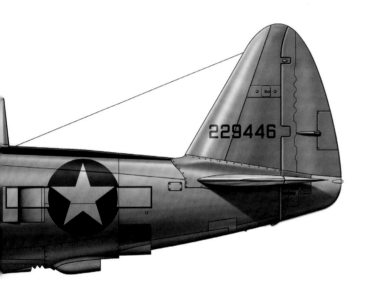

'BUBBLE HOOD' (LEFT)

From the P-47D-25 onwards, the 'razorback' fuselage gave way to a new teardrop canopy that defined the shape of future models and greatly increased visibility from the cockpit. At the same time, the development of an external fuel tank also provided greater endurance.

In an effort to address the P-47's relative lack of straight-line performance, Republic developed the P-47M, which was a 'sprint' model that utilized an improved turbocharger to boost top speed to 762km/h (473mph) at an altitude of 9755m (32,000ft). Deliveries of the P-47M to Europe began in late 1944.

While the P-47M was optimized for the European theatre, the P-47N was dedicated to service in the Pacific. This version featured an enlarged wing with blunt tips and increased fuel capacity. A total of 1186 P-47Ns were completed, and these were used as escorts for B-29s during raids against mainland Japan in 1945.

By the time production came to an end, a total of 15,675 P-47s of all versions had been completed.

Although the Thunderbolt did not enjoy the long post-war service career of the Mustang, the type remained in US Air Force service (as the F-47 from 1948), serving latterly with the Air National Guard before finally being retired in 1955. Thereafter, it remained in use with a variety of mainly Latin American operators.

F-4 Phantom II

The F-4 Phantom II was probably the best all-round Cold War fighter: a true multi-role warplane that could take on roles as diverse as fleet air defence, nuclear strike and low-level reconnaissance. It served with distinction in Vietnam and in Middle East conflicts.

The Phantom II began life as a twin-engine all-weather carrier fighter to replace the F3H Demon in US Navy service. Design studies were launched in September 1953, but with the Navy satisfied with the F8U Crusader, the McDonnell design reworked their new design for the carrier-based attack role. By July 1955, plans had changed again, and the team was instructed to redesign the aircraft as an all-weather attack fighter. A July 1955 contract called for two YF4H-1 prototypes, the first of which made a maiden flight on 27 May 1958.

The Phantom II immediately demonstrated great potential and was ordered by the US Navy as the F4H-1, which was redesignated as the F-4A in September 1962.

The initial carrier-based model was the F-4B, 649 of which were built, including 12 F-4G aircraft (the first use of this designation) with revised radio equipment. First deployed in August 1962, the F-4B became the standard all-weather fighter with the US Navy and Marine Corps, the heart of its firepower being the APQ-72 radar and radar-guided AIM-7 Sparrow air-to-air missiles.

US AIR FORCE 'RHINOS'

The aircraft also attracted interest from the US Air Force, which initially placed orders for the F-110A. A change in designation systems meant that this aircraft entered service as the F-4C, a minimum-change version of the US Navy's

MIG-KILLER
This F-4J was flown by VF-96 pilots Lieutenants Randall Cunningham and William P. Driscoll on 10 May 1972, when they shot down three North Vietnamese MiGs using three Sidewinder missiles. The Phantom was then shot down by a surface-to-air missile.

POWERPLANT

The F-4J owed its performance to the two J79-GE-19 turbojets, rated at 8119kg (17,000lb) thrust with afterburning. As with previous Phantoms, a movable splitter plate controlled airflow into the air intakes, separating undisturbed airflow from the sluggish boundary layer close to the skin of the aircraft.

WEAPONS LOAD

For its MiG-killing mission, this F-4J carried a full complement of AIM-9 Sidewinder heat-seeking missiles, but only two radar-guided AIM-7 Sparrows. The Sparrow proved somewhat disappointing in aerial combat over Southeast Asia.

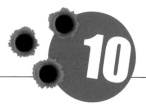

F-4B, with APG-72 radar. The subsequent F-4D was more closely tailored to Air Force requirements, and received the APG-109A radar that featured additional attack modes.

The US military's primary tactical reconnaissance aircraft for much of the Cold War, the RF-4 family was launched by the RF-4B for the US Marine Corps, followed by the RF-4C for the USAF and the RF-4E for export customers.

The USAF's Phantom II was further improved with the introduction of the F-4E. This had improved radar (APG-120 with solid-state technology in a smaller radome), additional internal fuel, a slatted wing for improved agility at high weights, and – importantly for combat in Southeast Asia and the Middle East – an internal 20mm (0.78in) cannon.

SPEY PHANTOMS

The Phantom II was a remarkable export success. Among the customers was the United Kingdom, for which the manufacturer developed the F-4K for the Fleet Air Arm, designated Phantom FG.Mk 1 in Royal Navy service, and the F-4M (Phantom FGR.Mk 2) for the Royal Air Force. Both these versions were powered by Rolls-Royce Spey engines. Other specific export versions included the F-4F for the West German Luftwaffe, which was later adapted to carry AIM-120 Advanced Medium-Range Air-to-Air Missiles (AMRAAM). The F-4EJ version was built by Mitsubishi for the Japan Air Self-Defense Force.

The last new-build Phantom II model for the US Navy and the Marine Corps was the F-4J. This version featured more powerful engines, a slotted tailplane, dropping ailerons and improved avionics, including AWG-10 fire-control radar and a new bombing system. An upgrade of the F-4J produced the F-4S, with avionics improvements and leading-edge slats. The F-4N was a similar upgrade applied to the F-4B.

The final sub-type for the USAF was the F-4G Wild Weasel, a dedicated electronic warfare aircraft that combined sensors, emissions analyzers and jamming equipment with anti-radiation missiles to home in on hostile air defence systems.

A total of 5177 Phantom IIs were produced and the type saw extensive combat service in Southeast Asia and the Middle East. The F-4 remained in front-line service in early 2017 with Greece, Iran, Japan, South Korea and Turkey.

SPECIFICATIONS (F-4B)

Crew: 2

Length: 17.75m (58ft 3in)

Wingspan: 11.71m (38ft 5in)

Empty weight: 12,700kg (28,000lb)

Powerplant: 2 × General Electric J79-8B afterburning turbojets

Maximum speed: 2390km/h (1485mph) clean at 14.63m (48,000ft)

Armament: 4–6 x AIM-7 Sparrow III AAMs, up to 4 x AIM-9B/D Sidewinder AAMs, up to 7257kg (16,000lb) of offensive weapons

LUFTWAFFE RECONNAISSANCE

At peak strength, the RF-4E served with two Luftwaffe tactical reconnaissance wings, including Aufklärungsgeschwader 52 based at Leck, and assigned to the 2nd Allied Tactical Air Force.

US MARINE CORPS RECONNAISSANCE

The USMC tactical reconnaissance version was the RF-4B. This example served with VMFP-3. The squadron was based at El Toro, California. Later in their career, the aircraft wore this low-visibility scheme with muted national insignia.

A US Air Force Reserve F-4D lands during Exercise Gunsmoke, a fighter gunnery competition, in 1985. The store carried under the fuselage centreline is a 20mm (0.78in) Vulcan gun pod, making up for the fact that the F-4D lacked an internal cannon.

RF-4B

The RF-4B was generally similar in appearance to the USAF's RF-4C. First flown on 12 March 1965, the RF-4B was based on the F-4B airframe but added a recce nose housing cameras, an infrared linescan and a side-looking radar. The last 12 examples of the 46 built in total featured the thick wing of the F-4J. The final examples were retired by VMFP-3 in 1990.

F-86 Sabre

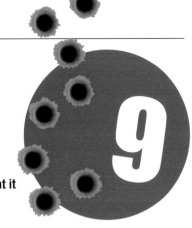

Best remembered for its starring role during the Korean War in the early 1950s, the North American F-86 was the first of the American swept-wing fighters. Such was its quality that it remained in front-line service into the early 1980s with some operators.

The Sabre originated in a US Army Air Force requirement for a day fighter that could also serve in roles including escort fighter and dive-bomber.

The North American response was the NA-140 design, which originally featured straight wings and was first contracted in late 1944. However, once German research into swept wings became available at the end of the war, the XP-86 prototypes were reconfigured accordingly. The revised design first flew on 1 October 1947, with swept wings and tail surfaces.

The new fighter soon displayed its potential, and after being re-engined with a General Electric J47 turbojet, the pre-production YP-86A broke the sound barrier in April

SPECIFICATIONS (F-86D)

Crew: 1

Length: 12.29m (40ft 4in)

Wingspan: 11.3m (37ft 1in)

Empty weight: 5656kg (12,470lb)

Powerplant: 1 × General Electric J47-GE-17B or -33 turbojet

Maximum speed: 1138km/h (707mph)

Armament: 24 x 70mm (2.75in) air-to-air rocket projectiles

'ALL-FLYING' TAIL
The F-86E was the first of the Sabres to feature an 'all-flying' tail, in which the horizontal stabilizer became the primary control surface for the tailplane. The result was a dramatic improvement in aircraft control throughout the transonic flight regime.

ARMAMENT
The F-86A, E and most Fs were armed with six Colt-Browning 12.7mm (0.5in) machine guns in the sides of the nose. The exceptions were a number of specially modified F-86Fs that carried four 20mm (0.78in) cannon for service in Korea.

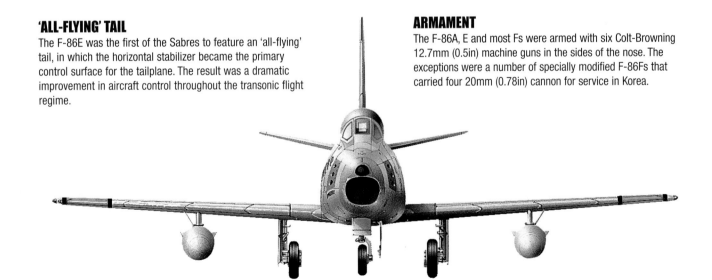

F-86E-10

Although originally planned to come off the
production line as F-86Fs, the F-86E-10
batch was completed to the earlier standard
due to supply problems. First manufactured
in September 1951, the F-86E-10 retained
the older GE-13 engine, but some examples
received the new GE-27 during overhauls.

*As well as front-line duties, the versatile F-86 turned its hand to
a variety of support roles. This F-86F served with the NACA High-
Speed Flight Station (HSFS) at Edwards Air Force Base, California,
in the mid-1950s, where it was used as a chase plane.*

ACE PILOT

This F-86E, 51-2735, was flown in Korea by
Major William T. Whisner, who served with the
25th Fighter Interceptor Squadron, 51st Fighter
Interceptor Wing. A World War II ace with 15.5 kills,
Whisner added another 5.5 in Korea.

ENGINE

The General Electric J47-GE-27 was planned to
have powered the 132 F-86E-10, but instead
joined the production effort with the subsequent
F-86F model. The new engine developed 27.05kN
(6090lb) of thrust.

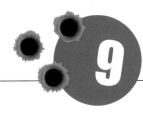

An F-86 of the 4th Fighter Interceptor Wing forms the backdrop to a US Fifth Air Force Easter service in Korea during a break in combat operations by the wing. Early on in the conflict, Sabres quickly replaced the USAF's straight-wing F-80 Shooting Star and F-84 Thunderjet fighters, which stood little chance in aerial clashes with the communist-flown MiG-15s.

1948, flying in a shallow dive. The YP-86A was adopted for production as the P-86A, first flown in May 1948. Just a month later, the US Air Force modified its designation system, and the P-86 became the F-86, later named Sabre.

INITIAL OPERATOR

Service entry of the F-86A was with the USAF's 1st Fighter Group in February 1949. It was the F-86A model that first went to war in Korea, where its primary opponent was the Soviet-built MiG-15. By the end of hostilities, F-86 pilots had shot down 792 MiGs, according to USAF records, achieving a kill ratio of about 8:1.

After 554 examples of the F-86A had been completed, production switched to the F-86E, with an all-moving

SABRE VERSUS MIG

In terms of armament, the F-86E was at a disadvantage compared to the cannon-armed MiG-15. Although the four machine guns provided a three-second burst of more than 300 rounds, each projectile was so light that it failed to cause much damage to the MiG.

tailplane, and the F-86F, which featured a modified wing. Both these models again saw Korean duty.

Although commonly known as a day-fighter, it was the all-weather/night-fighter version of the Sabre that proved most prolific. A total of 2054 examples of the F-86D, or 'Sabre Dog', were completed, followed by a nuclear-capable fighter-bomber, the F-86H (477 built). The F-86K was a simplified version of the F-86D intended primarily for export customers.

Much of the Sabre's success came from its widespread adoption by export customers, and production lines were set up in Canada and Australia. Canadair produced the local Sabre Mk 2 for the Royal Canadian Air Force and for US allies. This was followed by the Sabre Mk 4, built to meet an urgent Royal Air Force fighter requirement and featuring a General Electric engine. An indigenous Orenda 10 turbojet was included in the Sabre Mk 5, while the ultimate Canadian Sabre was the Mk 6, with an Orenda 14.

Australian production was undertaken by the Commonwealth Aircraft Corporation and yielded the Sabre Mk 30 and Mk 31 for the Royal Australian Air Force, these being powered by Rolls-Royce Avon engines and armed

with 30mm (1.1in) Aden cannon. The Sabre Mk 32 differed in its use of a locally built engine.

In addition to these foreign production lines, American-made kits were supplied to Italy and Japan for local assembly. The Italian Fiat company assembled 221 examples of the F-86K for domestic and export customers. In Japan, Mitsubishi led a group of companies that first assembled, and then increasingly built, 300 examples of the F-86F and the reconnaissance-configured RF-86F.

By the end of production, more than 5500 examples of the F-86 day-fighter alone had been completed.

The basic design of the Sabre also found success in the naval realm. When the US Navy and US Marine Corps issued a requirement for a successor to the straight-wing North American FJ Fury, the result was the FJ-2, essentially an F-86E with modifications for naval service, including launch and recovery from aircraft carrier decks. The Fury was further refined in the FJ-3, which featured a characteristically deeper fuselage and a more powerful Wright J65 engine; the FJ-4 (later designated F-1E), which was entirely redesigned; and the FJ-4B (AF-1E), which was adapted to better suit the ground-attack role.

FUEL TANKS

In order to provide a welcome increase in range, the Korean Sabres often carried underwing drop tanks. The additional fuel allowed the fighters to extend their duration in the 'MiG Alley' combat zone, but they were always in short supply. A production line was set up Japan in an effort to increase provision of the tanks.

WINDSCREEN

A feature of the F-86E-10 model was a new windscreen. This was a flat transparency of armoured glass, which provided much-improved protection for the pilot. It was also easier to see through than the previous V-shaped windscreen.

B-29 Superfortress

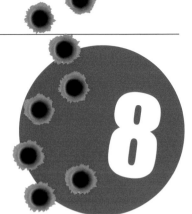

Forever associated with its role in delivering the two atomic bombs that were dropped on the Japanese cities of Hiroshima and Nagasaki, the Boeing B-29 was the ultimate bomber of World War II. It combined a number of highly advanced features with a huge bombload.

Remarkably, design work on what became the B-29 began as early as 1938, long before the United States was involved in the conflict that many would credit the Superfortress as having ended. For the late 1930s, Boeing's Model 345 was a radical proposition: the design envisaged an operational range, structural loads, skin thickness, defensive armament and crew accommodation that were state of the art. It was not until early 1940, however, that the US Army Air Corps issued requests for proposals for a new, very long range bomber, to which Boeing submitted its XB-29.

On 21 September 1942, a first prototype took to the air, and with the aid of an unprecedented manufacturing effort, more than 2000 B-29s had been completed by the end of World War II. The primary target of the Superfortress was the Japanese home islands, which were attacked first from air bases in China and India, and subsequently from islands that took the Allies ever closer to Tokyo. A first B-29 mission was flown from India against Bangkok on 5 June 1944. The first of the large-scale raids against Japan were launched once the aircraft had arrived in the

'BOCKSCAR'
Operated by the 509th Composite Group's 393rd Very Heavy Bomber Squadron at Tinian, Marianas, the B-29 named 'Bockscar' was captained by Major Charles W. Sweeney for the Nagasaki mission on 9 August 1945.

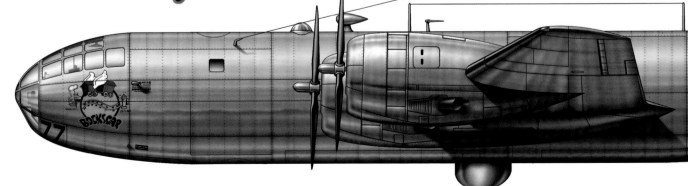

Marianas in October 1944; these soon increased in size until as many as 300 aircraft were being launched in the course of a single mission.

Beginning in March 1945, the B-29s used a new and more devastating tactic, in which a loose stream of aircraft flew under the cover of darkness and dropped incendiary weapons from low level. Some of these raids caused more casualties than the two atomic raids that targeted Hiroshima and Nagasaki, on 6 and 9 August 1945 respectively. In these two missions, specially prepared B-29s dropped 20-kiloton weapons, ushering in the age of nuclear warfare and ensuring that Japan surrendered.

EXTENSIVE PRODUCTION

Boeing eventually completed 3960 examples of the B-29, and the type was followed by the improved B-50, which featured more powerful engines and other changes. While the nuclear-armed B-50 provided Strategic Air Command with its initial post-war equipment, the B-29 remained in use during the Korean War, where aircraft from the 22nd and 92nd Bomb Groups began flying missions on 13 July 1950. By the end of the conflict on the Korean peninsula, a force

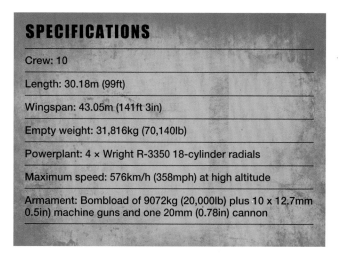

SPECIFICATIONS

Crew: 10

Length: 30.18m (99ft)

Wingspan: 43.05m (141ft 3in)

Empty weight: 31,816kg (70,140lb)

Powerplant: 4 × Wright R-3350 18-cylinder radials

Maximum speed: 576km/h (358mph) at high altitude

Armament: Bombload of 9072kg (20,000lb) plus 10 x 12.7mm 0.5in) machine guns and one 20mm (0.78in) cannon

DEFENSIVE ARMAMENT

The B-29 was provided with pairs of 12.7mm (0.5in) machine guns in four remotely controlled turrets and a manned turret in the tail. The tail position was also armed with a 20mm (0.78in) cannon.

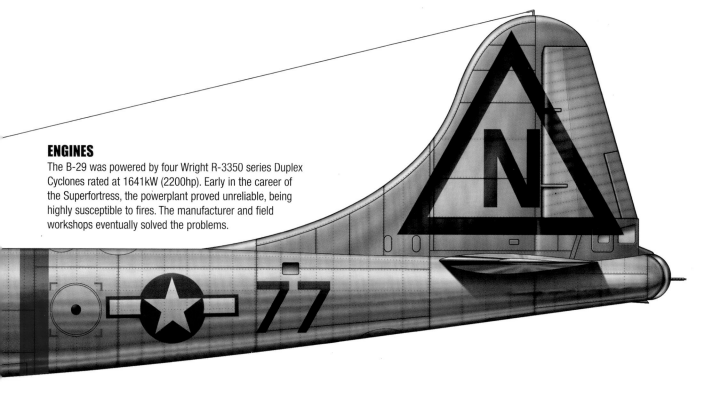

ENGINES

The B-29 was powered by four Wright R-3350 series Duplex Cyclones rated at 1641kW (2200hp). Early in the career of the Superfortress, the powerplant proved unreliable, being highly susceptible to fires. The manufacturer and field workshops eventually solved the problems.

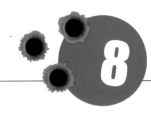

In addition to the two nuclear weapons dropped in combat, the B-29 played an important role in the development of such weapons after World War II. This aircraft was photographed heading for Bikini Atoll to drop the first atomic bomb of the post-war era, on 1 July 1946.

of no more than a hundred B-29s at any one time delivered 151,590 tonnes (167,100 tons) of bombs in the course of 21,000 sorties. This was more ordnance than had been delivered by Superfortress units during World War II. The B-50's combat service included the Vietnam War, but when it had been relegated to use as an aerial refuelling tanker.

Three B-29s that landed in Soviet territory during World War II served as pattern aircraft for the reverse-engineered Tupolev Tu-4 that were operated as the Soviet Union's first true strategic bomber.

SECOND LINE AND EXPORT

While the B-29A and B-29B versions incorporated only minor differences compared to the initial B-29 bomber, the Superfortress was also developed to undertake other roles, including strategic reconnaissance. The RB-29 and RB-29A were both equipped for photo-reconnaissance work. Another variant that saw active service during the Korean War was the SB-29, which comprised a B-29 bomber converted for the air/sea rescue role with a lifeboat that

could be dropped by parachute. The B-29D designation applied to an improved version with Pratt & Whitney R-4360 engines, later redesignated as the B-50.

Apart from the unofficial adoption of the type by the Soviet Union, the only true export operator of the B-29 was the Royal Air Force, which took delivery of 88 examples under the name Washington B.Mk 1, operating these on loan for a period of five years until it was able to field bombers of indigenous production.

FLIGHT DECK

The bombardier was accommodated in the extensively glazed nose, with the pilot and co-pilot seated side by side behind him. The flight engineer faced aft, immediately behind the co-pilot, with the radio operator facing starboard behind him. The navigator's station was located on the port side, behind the pilot's seat.

BOMBLOAD

The B-29 could carry a total of 20 227kg (500lb) bombs in each of its two bomb bays, for a total load of 9072kg (20,000lb). With such a load, the aircraft had a range of around 1609km (1000 miles). As well as high-explosive bombs, the B-29 carried incendiary and, eventually, nuclear bombs.

PRESSURIZED FUSELAGE

Boeing pioneered the use of pressurized cabins with its Model 307 Stratoliner. In the B-29, the pressurized front and rear cabins were connected by a pressurized tunnel that ran above the unpressurized bomb bay. The tailgunner sat in a separate pressurized compartment.

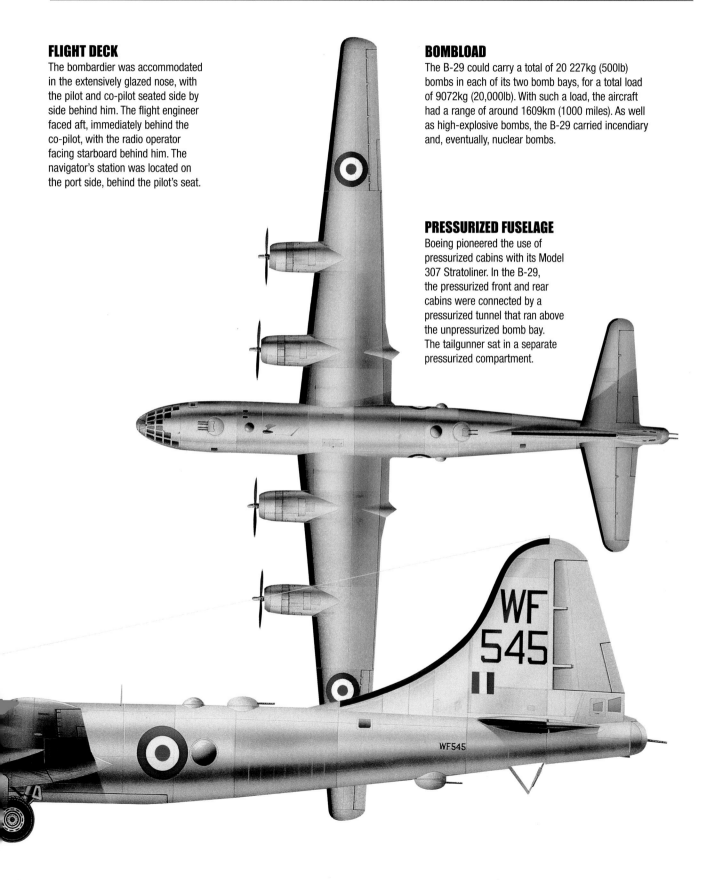

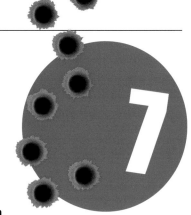

C-47 Skytrain

The remarkable C-47 – the military version of the famous Douglas DC-3 airliner – became the standard Allied transport aircraft of its class during World War II and remains in front-line service to this day. In the process, it has served in countless roles and in theatres as diverse as the jungles of Southeast Asia and the frozen wastes of the Arctic and Antarctica.

The C-47 Skytrain – which received the familiar Dakota name in British service – was a military evolution of the Douglas DC-3, which had set the standard for airliners in the mid-1930s, thanks to its levels of speed and comfort. In commercial form, the DC-3 was first flown on 17 December 1935, but it was not until 1940 that an order was placed by the US Army Air Corps. Such was the utility of the basic design that only straightforward changes were required for the military version, including more powerful engines, a strengthened rear fuselage and cabin floor, and provision of large loading doors.

Once in military service, the airliner interior of the DC-3 gave way to utilitarian bucket seats along the sides of the cabin, and the powerplant was revised from the original Wright Cyclones to Pratt & Whitney R-1830-92 radials. After a total of 94 of the initial C-47 version had been built, production switched to the C-47A, which added a 24-volt electrical system in place of the previous 12-volt system.

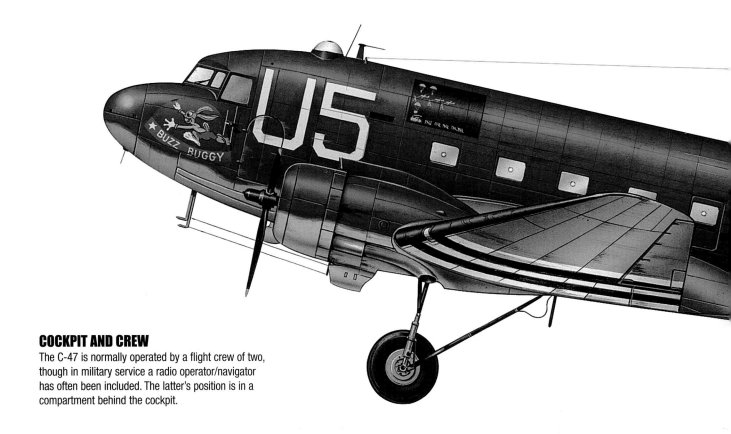

COCKPIT AND CREW
The C-47 is normally operated by a flight crew of two, though in military service a radio operator/navigator has often been included. The latter's position is in a compartment behind the cockpit.

SPECIFICATIONS

Crew: 3

Length: 19.43m (63ft 9in)

Wingspan: 29.11m (95ft 6in)

Empty weight: 8255kg (18,200lb)

Powerplant: 2 × Pratt & Whitney R-1830-92 radials

Maximum speed: 370km/h (230mph) at 2591m (8500ft)

Armament: None

British paratroops from the Allied 1st Airborne Army board a USAAF C-47A on 17 September 1944 as part of Operation Market Garden, the airborne assault on Eindhoven, Nijmegen and Arnhem. More than 1500 Allied aircraft participated in the assault.

CARGO DOORS

Most military C-47s have a large two-part cargo door in the port side of the rear fuselage. A smaller door within one side of the main door allows deployment of airborne troops. The cabin floor of the Skytrain was strengthened for military work.

RUDDER

Shared with the DC-3, the unpowered rudder has extremely broad chord, providing excellent control authority at low speed. This is essential when delivering troops or supplied by parachute. The rudder itself has a simple trailing-edge trim tab for fine control.

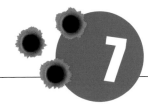

HELLENIC DAKOTA

Among the last C-47s in Hellenic Air Force service was this former RAF Dakota, delivered to Greece immediately after World War II. The final examples served with 355 Mira and other miscellaneous units and survived into the late 1980s.

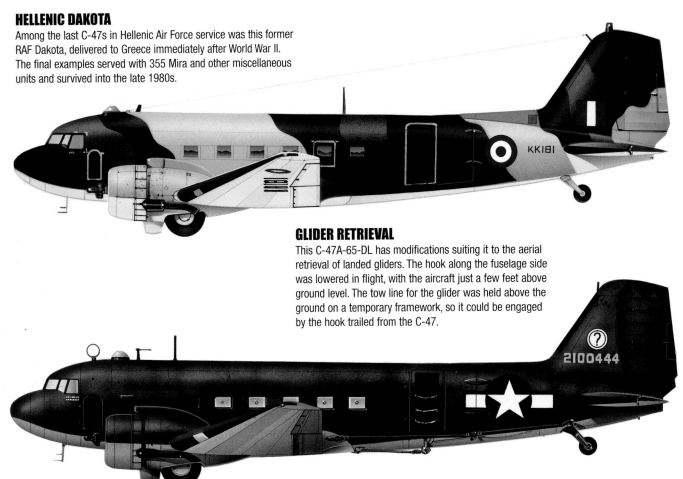

GLIDER RETRIEVAL

This C-47A-65-DL has modifications suiting it to the aerial retrieval of landed gliders. The hook along the fuselage side was lowered in flight, with the aircraft just a few feet above ground level. The tow line for the glider was held above the ground on a temporary framework, so it could be engaged by the hook trailed from the C-47.

After a production run that took in 4931 C-47As, this model was superseded by the C-47B, which was equipped with high-altitude superchargers for its R-1830-90 engines. The 3241 examples of the C-47B included some that were completed as TC-47B crew trainers. Among the other major wartime versions, the most important was probably the 28-seat C-53 Skytrooper – a rapid reconfiguration of the commercial-standard aircraft for issue to military units. By the end of the war, total C-47 production reached 10,048. Licence production took place in both Japan and the Soviet Union, resulting in the L2D and the Lisunov Li-2.

WARTIME MISSIONS

During World War II, the C-47 became best associated with airborne operations, during which it delivered paratroopers and worked as a glider tug. In the latter role, C-47s saw

distinguished service in airborne operations over Sicily, Burma, Normandy, Arnhem and the crossing of the Rhine. As well as service with the US Army Air Force, the C-47 was a familiar sight in Royal Air Force service. The RAF's Dakota Mk I was equivalent to the original C-47, while the Dakota Mk II corresponded to the C-53. The Dakota Mk III was the RAF's designation for the C-47A, while the C-47B was known as the Dakota Mk IV. Dakotas – as well as their USAF C-47 counterparts – played an important role in the Berlin Airlift that began in 1948.

The C-47 and Dakota saw extensive post-war service, during which its global footprint increased dramatically. In the process it became perhaps the most widely used military aircraft of all time. With the US Air Force, the C-47 was involved in the Korean War and soldiered on in various roles into the 1960s. At the start of that decade, there were

Very early production C-47-DL Skytrains from the Long Beach factory towing Waco Hadrian gliders during a training flight in the United States. 41-18365, the C-47 nearest the camera, was part of the first batch of 956 aircraft manufactured at Long Beach.

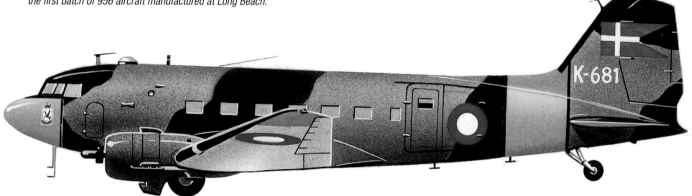

SCANDINAVIAN C-47

A Royal Danish Air Force C-47 in the colours of Eskadrille 721, as it appeared in the mid-1960s. The squadron was formed in October 1950, through a merger of Danish Naval Air Service and Danish Army Air Corps units, and has always been tasked with transport.

more than 1000 examples still on the USAF's books. In US Navy service the aircraft was known as the R4D.

GUNSHIPS

American involvement in Vietnam beginning in the mid-1960s saw the Skytrain adopt a new role, as a heavily armed gunship that was used to conduct interdiction of communist supply lines at night. In 1965, the USAF intro-duced the AC-47D gunship conversion that was armed with three 7.62mm (0.3in) Miniguns firing through doors and windows on the port side of the fuselage. Known by the nickname 'Puff the Magic Dragon', the AC-47D proved the gunship concept and subsequently found favour with operators in Latin America. Today, many surviving C-47s have been re-engined with turboprop engines, as pioneered by Basler Turbo Conversions Inc.

F6F Hellcat

Holding the honours for the most successful carrier fighter of World War II, the US Navy's Hellcat was another excellent product of the Grumman 'Iron Works' and built upon the reputation established by its F4F Wildcat forerunner.

Although the F4U Corsair enjoyed a longer service career, and was in many ways more advanced, the fact that it initially proved unsuitable for carrier operations confirms the Hellcat's status as finest shipborne fighter of World War II.

A logical development of the F4F Wildcat, the Hellcat was first flown in prototype XF6F-3 form on 26 June 1942. Most importantly, combat experience with the Wildcat in the Pacific theatre was incorporated in the design of the new fighter, which carried the Grumman in-house designation G-50. The most obvious change compared to its successor was the shift from a mid-wing configuration

to a new low-wing layout. Successive prototypes tested different engine installations before the Pratt & Whitney R-2800 Double Wasp was selected. In early 1943, the first production F6F-3 aircraft began to be delivered to VF-9, which was on board the carrier USS *Essex*. Sub-variants of the initial production model were the F6F-3E night-fighter and the F6F-3N, which carrier a radar in a wing pod.

FIGHTER-BOMBER VERSION

The next major production version appeared in 1944. The F6F-5, added provision for offensive stores, in the form of up to 907kg (2000lb) of bombs and two 20mm (0.78in) can-

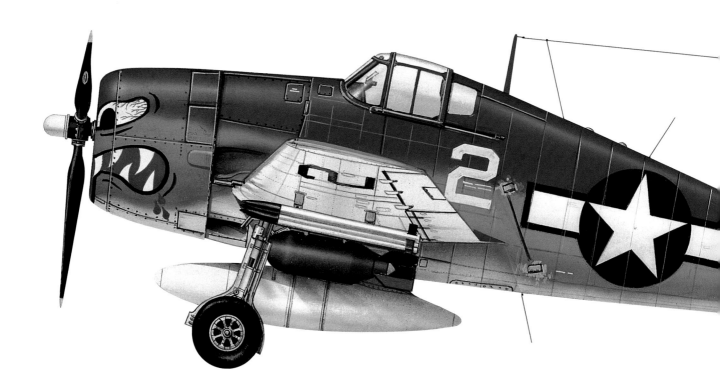

Proving to be the outstanding fighter of the US Navy during World War II, the F6F Hellcat was mass-produced at a rate unequalled by any other aircraft manufacturing programme and went on to help turn the tide against the Japanese.

UNDERWING WEAPONS

This Hellcat carries a mixed load of six 127mm (5in) rocket projectiles, mounted on zero-length launch rails under the wing. The inner hardpoints each carry a single bomb. Rockets in particular were a favoured ground-attack weapon during the latter stages of the Pacific war, especially during the assault on Okinawa.

GUN ARMAMENT

The standard fixed armament comprised six 12.7mm (0.5in) Browning machine guns. Mounted in a staggered formation, each weapon was provided with 400 rounds of ammunition. Later-production F6F-5s often replaced two of the machine guns with two harder-hitting 20mm (0.78in) cannon.

COLOUR SCHEME

The standard Pacific scheme of sea blue and pale undersides ultimately gave way to all-over midnight blue during the later stages of the war. White markings on the fin denoted individual units. The markings on the cowling were associated with VF-27.

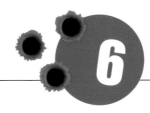

non that replaced the inboard 12.7mm (0.5mm) wing guns. The radar-equipped night-fighter version was the F6F-5N. Production of the F6F-5N amounted to 6435 aircraft; 252 F6F-3s and 930 F6F-5s served with the British Fleet Air Arm as the Hellcat Mk I and Hellcat Mk II respectively. In all, production of the Hellcat ran to 12,275 of all versions, completed between June 1942 and November 1945.

COMBAT DEBUT

The first Hellcat unit to take the aircraft into combat was VF-5 on board the USS *Yorktown*, in August 1943. Official figures credit US Navy and US Marine Corps Hellcats with the destruction of 5156 enemy aircraft in air combat – equivalent to around 75 per cent of all US Navy air combat victories in the war. One of the Hellcat's greatest successes came in the huge carrier operation at the Battle of the Philippine Sea, during which 15 US carriers embarked 480 F6F fighters (plus 222 dive-bombers and 199 torpedo-bombers). In the space of a week of fighting, Task Force 58 had destroyed more than 400 Japanese aircraft and sunk three aircraft carriers. Compared to its major Japanese foe, the A6M Zero, the Hellcat was more

survivable and possessed greater endurance, allowing it to stay in the fight.

Dozens of Hellcat pilots made ace status; the leading US Navy ace, Captain David McCampbell, scored 34 aerial kills and received the Medal of Honor. During one mission on 24 October 1944, McCampbell shot down no fewer than nine enemy aircraft. With no lack of understatement, the Navy's 'ace of aces' described the Hellcat as 'a satisfying performer and a stable gun platform'.

The only other wartime operator of the Hellcat was the Fleet Air Arm, which flew the aircraft over Norway (including top cover flown during the strikes against the German battleship *Tirpitz*), the Mediterranean and the Far East. From a total of 455 kills logged by the FAA during World War II, the Hellcat was responsible for 52.

The Hellcat remained in US Navy service for several years after the war and was also converted as a drone. At least 120 ex-US Navy F6F-5 and F6F-5N aircraft were supplied to the French Navy for use in Indochina, and survivors later served in North Africa. Other post-war operators were Argentina, Paraguay and Uruguay; the last of these continued to fly the aircraft as late as 1961.

US Navy Hellcats in service with a post-war Reserve unit serving at a base near New York. The aircraft nearest the camera, BuNo 79603, was part of a batch of 3000 F6F-5 models, which represented the last major Hellcat variant. More than 7000 Dash 5s were built in total.

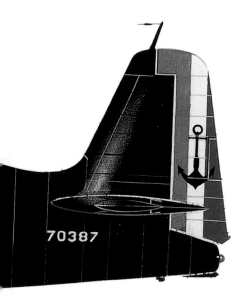

FRENCH SERVICE

French Hellcats were flown by both land-based (French Air Force) and Naval Aviation units. The first naval Hellcats went aboard a French carrier in spring 1950, replacing Seafires with Flottilles 1F and 12F. They served in Indochina until the fall of Dien Bien Phu.

COCKPIT

The Hellcat pilot was seated high in the fuselage under a sliding canopy. Well protected by armour plating, particularly at his rear, the pilot did, however, suffer from poor rear-quadrant visibility. A reflector gunsight ahead of him was provided for weapons aiming.

Supermarine Spitfire

The best-remembered British fighter of World War II, the Supermarine Spitfire is immediately associated with the Battle of Britain in 1940. However, such was the quality of the basic design that the aircraft was continually refined throughout the war, and the type remained in service in a front-line capacity well into the 1950s.

Designed by R.J. Mitchell, the Spitfire drew upon the successful heritage of Supermarine's racing seaplanes, which were developed to compete in the Schneider Trophy.

The Spitfire was first flown in prototype form on 5 March 1936 and entered Royal Air Force service as the Spitfire Mk I powered by a Rolls-Royce Merlin II engine. Armament comprised eight machine guns. The Spitfire Mk I saw service during the Battle of Britain in 1940 together with the Spitfire Mk II, which introduced a Merlin XII engine. These were joined in September 1940 by the

Spitfire Mk IIB that was armed with two 20mm (0.78in) cannon and four machine guns. Early on in development, the Spitfire was adapted for the photo-reconnaissance mission, and the Spitfire Mk IV was the first major production version for this mission.

The 'second generation' of Spitfire development was marked by the appearance of the Spitfire Mk V, which entered service in March 1941 and led to an impressive production run of 6479 aircraft. The Mk Vs were powered by a Merlin 45 engine that developed 1074kW (1440hp).

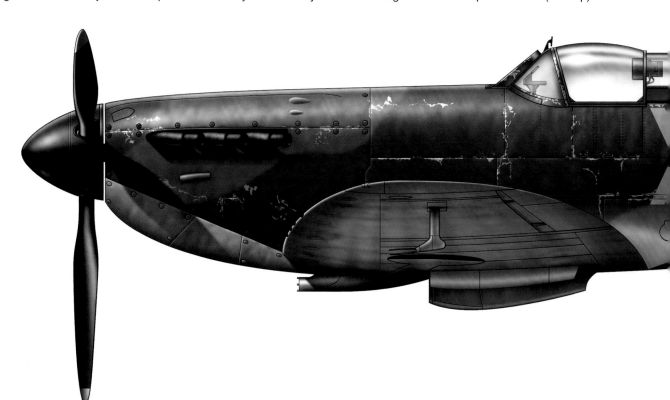

Powered by a 1294kW (1735hp) Griffon II engine, the Spitfire Mk XII had a speed of 599km/h (372mph) at 1737m (5700ft) and excellent performance at low altitude. Like the Spitfire Mk IX before it, the Mx XII was intended to counter the Fw 190.

Sub-variants included the Spitfire Mk VC, which was a fighter-bomber development with provision for the carriage of a single 227kg (500lb) bomb or two 113kg (250lb) bombs. From mid-1941 until mid-1942, RAF Fighter Command was spearheaded by the Spitfire Mk VB. This model was superseded by the Spitfire Mk IX, a quick-change adaptation of the Mk V designed to accommodate a 1238kW (1660hp) Merlin 61/66 engine featuring a two-stage, two-speed supercharger. 5665 Mk IXs were built, making it the second most prolific model after the Mk V.

HIGH FLYERS

While most of the Spitfire Mk VCs featured clipped wings for improved performance at low altitude, two high-altitude

BATTLE OF BRITAIN MK I
Spitfire Mk Ia X4250 was first flown in August 1940 and served with No. 603 Squadron during the Battle of Britain. On 27 September 1940, it was force-landed on the beach at Folkestone, when flown by Pilot Officer Peter Dexter.

GUN ARMAMENT
With its armament of eight Browning Mk II 7.7mm (0.303in) machine guns, the Spitfire Mk I had a lighter weight of fire than the Luftwaffe's Bf 109E with its two cannon and two machine guns. Cannon were trialled in combat on the Spitfire Mk Ib version, but were found to be prone to jamming.

UNDERCARRIAGE
The Spitfire's main undercarriage featured a notably narrow track, which made for tricky ground handling and led to many accidents. This was a trait that was shared with its rival, the Bf 109.

fighter versions took the opposite approach. In order to
intercept high-flying Luftwaffe aircraft, the Spitfire Mk VI and
Spitfire Mk VII were developed, these featuring extended
wingtips. Clipped-wing Spitfire Mk IXs were also completed
for low-altitude operations as the LF.Mk IX, which served
with no fewer than 27 RAF squadrons in the UK, Middle
East and Far East. In a further attempt to improve the basic
design, the Spitfire Mk VIII was introduced, and this model
saw extensive service in the Mediterranean and Far East.
While the Mk IX represented a hasty adaptation of the Mk V
to accommodate the Merlin 61/66, the Spitfire Mk VIII was
intended to be powered by this engine from the outset. In
addition to a retractable tailwheel, the Spitfire Mk VIII also
introduced as standard the various tropicalized features that
had been added to earlier variants when required.

Further, unarmed photo-reconnaissance derivatives were
the Spitfire Mk X and the Spitfire Mk XI. They were followed
by a dual-role fighter and fighter-bomber, the Spitfire Mk XVI,
which boasted a maximum speed of 652km/h (405mph). The
Spitfire Mk XVI was the last of the mass-produced variants
to retain the Merlin powerplant, which was superseded by
the Rolls-Royce Griffon. Total production of Merlin Spitfires
amounted to 18,298 examples.

GRIFFON SPITFIRES

The first of the Griffon-powered Spitfires, the Mk XII was
introduced in 1943 as a counter to the Focke-Wulf Fw 190.
It was followed by the Spitfire Mk XIV fighter and fighter-
bomber powered by a Griffon 65 that developed 1529kW
(2050hp). Appearing in service in mid-1944, the Spitfire Mk
XIV was involved in the heaviest single RAF fighter-bomber
attack of the war when, on 24 December 1944, 33 examples
attacked a V-2 rocket-launching site in the Netherlands.
Last of the wartime fighter-bombers, the Spitfire Mk XVI was
powered by a Packard Merlin 266, and was produced in
similar sub-variants as the Spitfire Mk IX.

By the end of the war, the RAF was receiving the Spitfire
Mk XVIII, which was equipped for fighter-reconnaissance
work and had a top speed of 712km/h (442mph). Although
less successful than its land-based counterparts, the Seafire
was produced in large numbers for the Fleet Air Arm and
was similarly developed in both Merlin- and then Griffon-
powered versions. A total of 2334 Seafires were completed,
adding to the total of 20,351 Spitfires of all variants.

FEAF SERVICE

MV349 was a Spitfire F.Mk XIVE built
by Supermarine and delivered in late
1944. It wears the markings of the
Far East Air Force. After being shipped
to Bombay, it was flown to Burma,
and served in the hands of No. 28
Squadron, fighting on the Malayan
front until the end of the war.

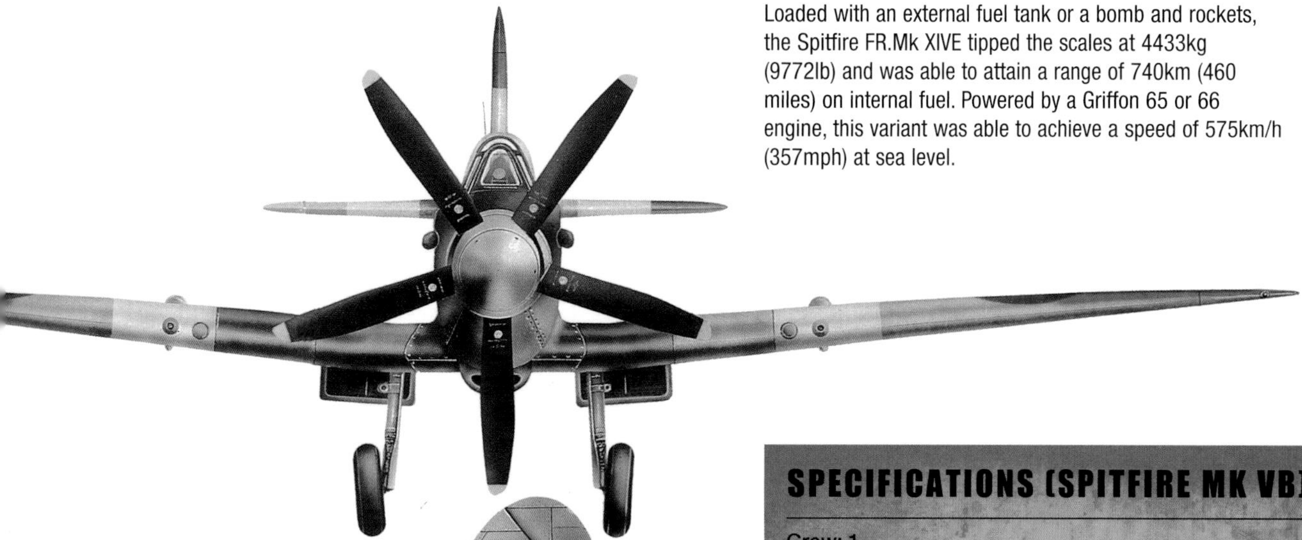

PERFORMANCE

Loaded with an external fuel tank or a bomb and rockets, the Spitfire FR.Mk XIVE tipped the scales at 4433kg (9772lb) and was able to attain a range of 740km (460 miles) on internal fuel. Powered by a Griffon 65 or 66 engine, this variant was able to achieve a speed of 575km/h (357mph) at sea level.

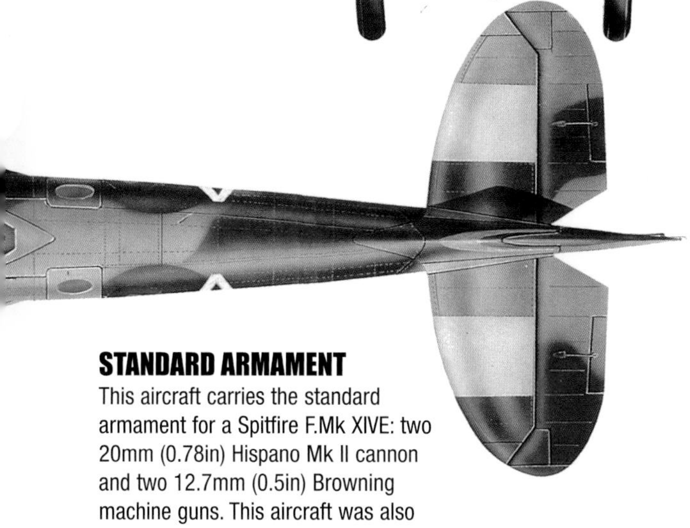

SPECIFICATIONS (SPITFIRE MK VB)

Crew: 1

Length: 9.11m (29ft 11in)

Wingspan: 11.23m (36ft 10in)

Empty weight: 3313kg (5100lb)

Powerplant: 1 × Rolls-Royce Merlin 45/46/50 V-12 piston engine

Maximum speed: 602km/h (374mph) at 3960m (13,000ft)

Armament: 2 x 20mm (0.78in) cannon and 4 x 7.7mm (0.303in) machine guns

STANDARD ARMAMENT

This aircraft carries the standard armament for a Spitfire F.Mk XIVE: two 20mm (0.78in) Hispano Mk II cannon and two 12.7mm (0.5in) Browning machine guns. This aircraft was also fitted with a low-level oblique camera aft of the cockpit, as in the Spitfire FR.Mk XIVE, but lacked this model's clipped wings.

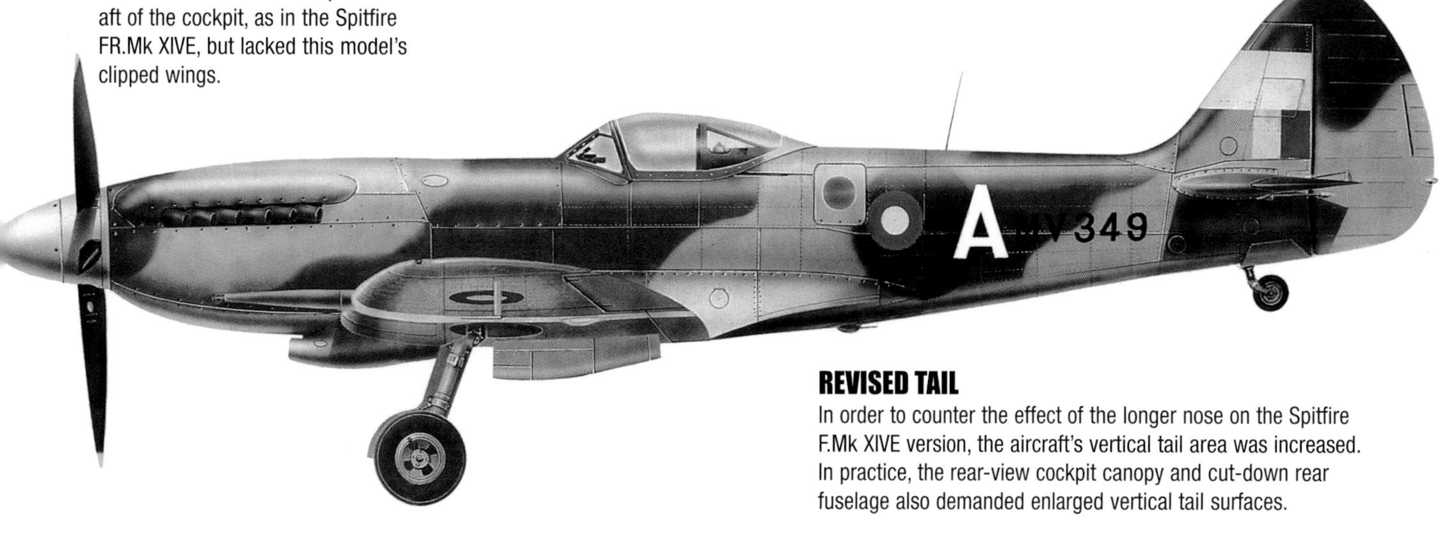

REVISED TAIL

In order to counter the effect of the longer nose on the Spitfire F.Mk XIVE version, the aircraft's vertical tail area was increased. In practice, the rear-view cockpit canopy and cut-down rear fuselage also demanded enlarged vertical tail surfaces.

B-52 Stratofortress

An enduring symbol of US military power, the role the remarkable B-52 plays today is just as important as it was when it led the ranks of Strategic Air Command in the 1960s. By the time it is finally withdrawn from service, the 'BUFF' will likely have served for more than 80 years.

The Stratofortress was first planned soon after World War II, as the Boeing Model 464. As originally envisaged, it would have been powered by turboprop engines. By 1948, the design had been revised to include a powerplant of eight Pratt & Whitney J57 turbojets. First flown in XB-52 prototype form on 15 April 1952, the second prototype YB-52 was followed by three B-52As used for test duties and then the first true production model, the B-52B, which entered service in 1955.

Of the 50 B-52Bs built, 27 were converted as RB-52 reconnaissance aircraft. The B-52C was considerably improved in terms of performance and equipment and was followed by 170 B-52Ds, with an improved fire control system for the defensive armament. The B-52E (100 built) featured a more advanced navigation and weapons delivery system. After 89 B-52Fs, with uprated J57s, production switched to the B-52G in 1959. This offered a much increased fuel capacity and provision to carry two Hound Dog standoff cruise missiles. Another change was the accommodation of the entire crew in the nose, and a new structure that featured a shortened tailfin.

DEFINITIVE H-MODEL

A total of 744 B-52s were built, with the last, a B-52H, delivered in October 1962. The first of 102 B-52Hs was delivered to Strategic Air Command in May 1961 and production of

B-52F

B-52F Stratofortress 57-0169 was one of 89 F-models, which were produced in Seattle and Wichita (44 and 45 aircraft respectively). The B-52F flew for the first time on 6 May 1958. This example, named 'Thunder Express', operated from Anderson AB, Guam. It recorded 68 combat missions over Vietnam.

HOUND DOG

The GAM-77 (later AGM-28) Hound Dog standoff missile was a main weapon of the SAC B-52G/H force between 1961 and 1976. The Hound Dog employed an inertial guidance system and electronic countermeasures and carried a 1-megaton thermonuclear warhead.

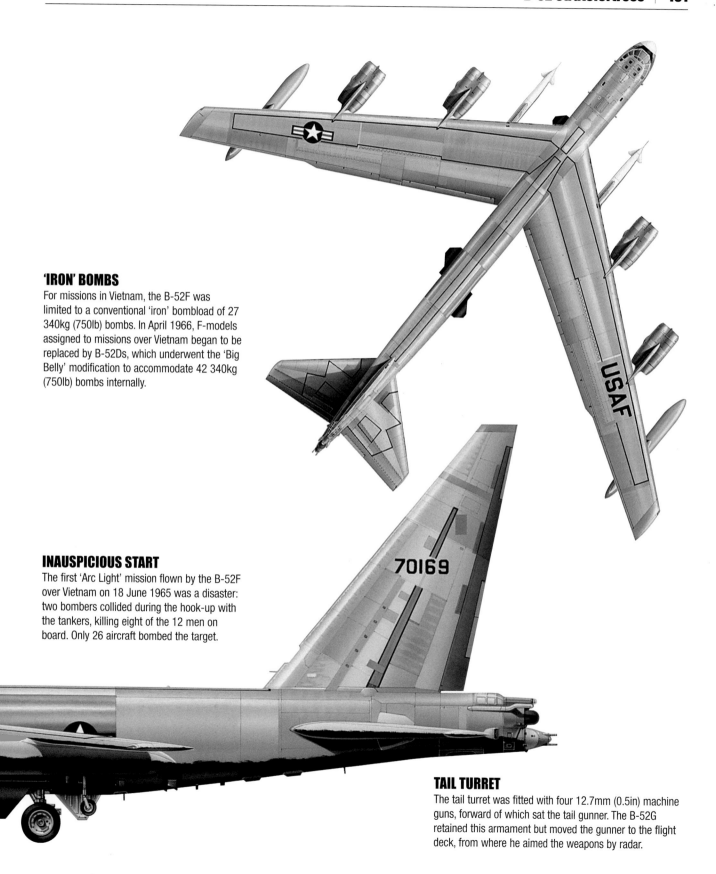

'IRON' BOMBS

For missions in Vietnam, the B-52F was limited to a conventional 'iron' bombload of 27 340kg (750lb) bombs. In April 1966, F-models assigned to missions over Vietnam began to be replaced by B-52Ds, which underwent the 'Big Belly' modification to accommodate 42 340kg (750lb) bombs internally.

INAUSPICIOUS START

The first 'Arc Light' mission flown by the B-52F over Vietnam on 18 June 1965 was a disaster: two bombers collided during the hook-up with the tankers, killing eight of the 12 men on board. Only 26 aircraft bombed the target.

TAIL TURRET

The tail turret was fitted with four 12.7mm (0.5in) machine guns, forward of which sat the tail gunner. The B-52G retained this armament but moved the gunner to the flight deck, from where he aimed the weapons by radar.

A B-52H from the 5th Bomb Wing at Minot AFB, North Dakota, refuels from a Utah Air National Guard KC-135 Stratotanker over the western United States. The B-52 continues to be the primary manned strategic bomber for the USAF.

this version was terminated in 1963. The B-52H introduced a new powerplant in the form of the much more powerful TF33 engine, eliminating the need for water injection, and instead of four 12.7mm (0.5in) tail guns it had a six-barrel cannon (since removed and replaced with electronic countermeasures gear).

During the Vietnam War, B-52D and B-52F aircraft were modified to carry enormous loads of conventional bombs.

Today's B-52H has a dual nuclear and conventional role and can carry up to 20 Air-Launched Cruise Missiles (ALCMs). As well as nuclear ALCMs, it can carry the Conventional Air-Launched Cruise Missile (CALCM) that was first employed in combat during Operation Desert Storm in 1991.

DESERT STORM AND ALLIED FORCE

The aircraft's flexibility was evident in Operation Desert Storm and again during Operation Allied Force. B-52s struck wide-area troop concentrations, fixed installations and bunkers, and decimated the morale of Iraq's Repub-

lican Guard. On 2–3 September 1996, two B-52Hs struck Baghdad power stations and communications facilities with 13 AGM-86C CALCMs as part of Operation Desert Strike. At that time, this was the longest distance flown for a combat mission, involving a 34-hour, 25,750-km (16,000-mile) round trip from Barksdale Air Force Base, Louisiana.

In 2001, the B-52 contributed to the success in Operation Enduring Freedom, providing the ability to loiter high above the battlefield and provide close air support through the use of precision-guided munitions. The B-52 also played a role in Operation Iraqi Freedom. On 21 March 2003, B-52Hs launched approximately 100 CALCMs during a night mission.

SPECIFICATIONS (B-52H)

Crew: 5

Length: 49.05m (160ft 11in)

Wingspan: 56.39m (185ft)

Empty weight: 88,450kg (195,000lb)

Powerplant: 8 × Pratt & Whitney TF33-P-1 turbojets

Maximum speed: 1011km/h (628mph)

Armament: Approximately 31,751kg (70,000lb) of ordnance, comprising bombs, mines and missiles

A B-52G of the 1708th Bomb Wing (Provisional) takes off on a mission during Operation Desert Storm. On 16 February 1991, seven B-52s from Barksdale Air Force Base, Louisiana, carried a total of 39 AGM-86C Conventional Air-Launched Cruise Missiles on this mission. The strikes were launched against eight high-priority Iraqi targets. The B-52Gs then returned to Barksdale after 35 hours in the air.

Today, only the H-model is still in the USAF inventory. It is assigned to the 5th Bomb Wing at Minot AFB, North Dakota, and the 2nd Bomb Wing at Barksdale AFB, which fall under Air Force Global Strike Command. The aircraft is also assigned to the Air Force Reserve Command's 307th Bomb Wing at Barksdale AFB.

VIETNAM CAMOUFLAGE

This 2nd Air Force B-52D has Vietnam-era two-tone green and tan over gloss black camouflage. It also illustrates the tailfin associated with all models prior to the B-52G. The D-model served over Southeast Asia from bases in Guam and at U-Tapao, Thailand.

EARLY FEATURES

As well as the tall vertical tail surfaces, all early variants of the B-52 featured a manned gun turret in the tail; J57 engines were standard throughout these versions. The D-model was the most common of the early variants. Once rebuilt as a conventional bomber, 105 340kg (750lb) bombs could be carried.

MiG-21

It is unlikely that any jet fighter in history will see as much combat in so many different corners of the world as the Soviet-designed MiG-21. The aircraft was still in production into the 21st century and remains a capable front-line asset with a number of air forces.

First flown in Ye-2 prototype form in February 1955, Mikoyan-Gurevich's new fighter incorporated swept wings and tailplanes and an interim RD-9 engine. Later the same year, the basic configuration was revised to produce the Ye-4, now allying the swept tail surfaces with a delta wing. In 1956, the Ye-5 appeared with the definitive R-11 engine, while the Ye-50 proved to be an evolutionary dead end, combining the old RD-9 engine with a supplementary rocket booster. The original swept-wing configuration was then tested with the R-11 (Ye-2A) before a decision was made to put the delta-winged version into production.

The first pre-series aircraft were completed in Tbilisi in 1957.

The first of the 'Fishbed' to attain quantity production was the MiG-21F, a basic day-fighter that was trialled in prototype form as the Ye-6, with the definitive delta wing and R-11 combination. One Ye-6 was specially adapted to take a number of closed-circuit speed records in 1959. The same year saw the appearance of the Ye-7, a prototype for the MiG-21PF production version, which was characterized by its increased-size engine intake. Series production commenced in Tbilisi in 1959, with initial deliveries to the

INDIAN VERSION

The MiG-21FL is an export version of the MiG-21PF that was built in India by Hindustan Aeronautics Limited. This example served with No. 1 Squadron 'Tigers' until 1973. Despite its age, the MiG-21FL remained in Indian Air Force service in early 2017.

SPECIFICATIONS (MIG-21BIS)

Crew: 1

Length: 14.7m (48ft 2.75in)

Wingspan: 7.15m (23ft 5in)

Empty weight: 5895kg (12,996lb)

Powerplant: 1 × Tumanskii R-35-300 afterburning turbojet

Maximum speed: Mach 2.1 (2230km/h/1386mph)

Armament: 1 x 23mm (0.9in) GSh-23L twin-barrel cannon plus up to 1500kg (3307lb) of disposable stores on four underwing hardpoints

The Indian Air Force has operated a range of MiG-21 variants over a period of 50 years, including this MiG-21FL. Following completion of the latest upgrade programme, the type remains in service as the MiG-21UPG, known in IAF service as the Bison.

ARMAMENT

As well as a GP-9 cannon pack carried on the centreline, this MiG-21FL is armed with a pair of K-13A (AA-2 'Atoll') heat-seeking air-to-air missiles. Although proving unreliable in combat, these weapons comprised the main missile armament of the early MiG-21s.

Soviet Union in 1960. In order to meet the new demands of crew training, a two-seat version was flown in prototype Ye-6U form in 1960, before this entered production as the MiG-21U. Subsequent two-seat versions for training were the MiG-21US and UM.

The first generation of single-seat production machines comprised the MiG-21, of which only a handful were built as the pre-series; the MiG-21F, of which 93 were built as the first true production aircraft; and the MiG-21F-13, the first to be built in quantity and the first with missile armament.

The second generation of 'Fishbeds' were all-weather fighters heralded by the MiG-21PF with RP-21 radar and optional missile armament. The MiG-21FL was a downgraded export version of the PF, with less capable radar and a less powerful engine. The MiG-21PFS added a blown-flap system to the PF with boundary layer control. The ultimate expression of this development line was the MiG-21PFM, with upgraded radar and avionics and reintroduction of cannon armament.

Next in line was a third generation of jets, with the first suggestion of a multi-role capability and a dedicated reconnaissance model, the MiG-21R. The MiG-21S was a tactical fighter, with RP-22 radar and additional fuel capacity. The 'S' was exported as the MiG-21M, with a return to RP-21 radar and built-in cannon. Built-in cannon was also a feature of the MiG-21SM, which featured the R-13-300 engine. The same was exported as the MiG-21MF. Introducing additional fuel capacity to the SM produced the MiG-21SMT with an enlarged spine.

The ultimate, fourth-generation 'Fishbed' was the MiG-21bis. This was completed in two sub-variants, the bis LASUR and the bis SAU, and was also licence-built in India. The main feature was the all-new R-25 turbojet.

CHINESE PRODUCTION

For many years, the 'Fishbed' provided the backbone of China's fighter fleet in the form of the Chengdu J-7. The type remains in widespread service in China and with export operators (as the F-7). Production of the 'true' J-7 series finally ended in May 2013 when a batch of F-7s was delivered to Bangladesh, but the latest JL-9 trainer is a much-modified derivative of the J-7, and is still being manufactured.

GOODWILL VISIT

This MiG-21bis provided Western observers with a valuable intelligence coup during a friendly visit by the type to the Finnish air base of Kuopio-Rissala in August 1974. The operating unit was the 34th 'Proskurovskiy' Guards Fighter Aviation Regiment.

ENGINE

The definitive MiG-21bis was powered by the R-25, the ultimate development of the R-11 series, which could provide a maximum output of 97.1kN (21,828lb) thrust when operating at low level.

AVIONICS ADVANCES
While the LASUR version was equipped with ground-control intercept (GCI) equipment for compatibility with the Soviet Air Defence Force, this was substituted in the SAU for an instrument landing system.

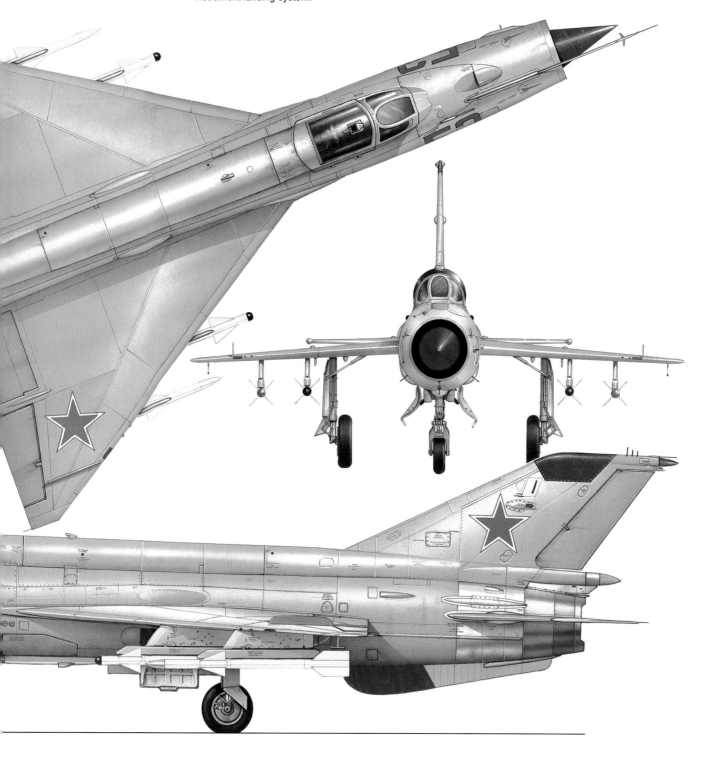

C-130 Hercules

The ubiquitous Lockheed Hercules is probably the best-known military transport aircraft in the world. Such is the inherent quality of the design that the aircraft has been little changed since it first flew in the 1950s. However, today's C-130J is a far more capable aircraft, with more powerful and efficient engines and state-of-the-art avionics.

Lockheed opened its Marietta, Georgia, factory in January 1951, and today it remains home to the world's longest continuously running military aircraft production line. Manufacture of the first two C-130 prototypes began at the facility in 1953, and the first production aircraft flew there on 7 April 1955. A first Hercules for the US Air Force was handed over in January 1956, and the production line has delivered more than 2500 aircraft to over 60 countries.

As the most ubiquitous Western military airlifter, the basic C-130 has proved to be a popular choice for adaptation for a range of roles over and above basic transport duties. The AC-130 covers gunship models, the first of which saw combat service during the Vietnam War.

SPECIFICATIONS (AC-130A)

Crew: 13

Length: 29.79m (97ft 9in)

Wingspan: 132 ft 7 in (40.4 m)

Loaded weight: 122,400 lb (55,520 kg)

Powerplant: 4 × Allison T56-A-15 turboprops, 4,910 shp (3,700 kW) each

Maximum cruising speed: 300 mph, 480 km/h)

Armament: 2 x 20mm (0.78in) Vulcan cannon, 2 x 7.62mm (0.3in) Miniguns, 2 x 40mm (1.57in) Bofors cannon

AC-130A 'NIGHT STALKER'

Named 'Night Stalker', this AC-130A saw combat service in Vietnam, before it joined the 711th Special Operations Squadron, an Air Force Reserve unit. Serial 55-0011 was retired from active service in 1994. The unit flew its gunships in combat in Panama and in Operation Desert Storm in 1991.

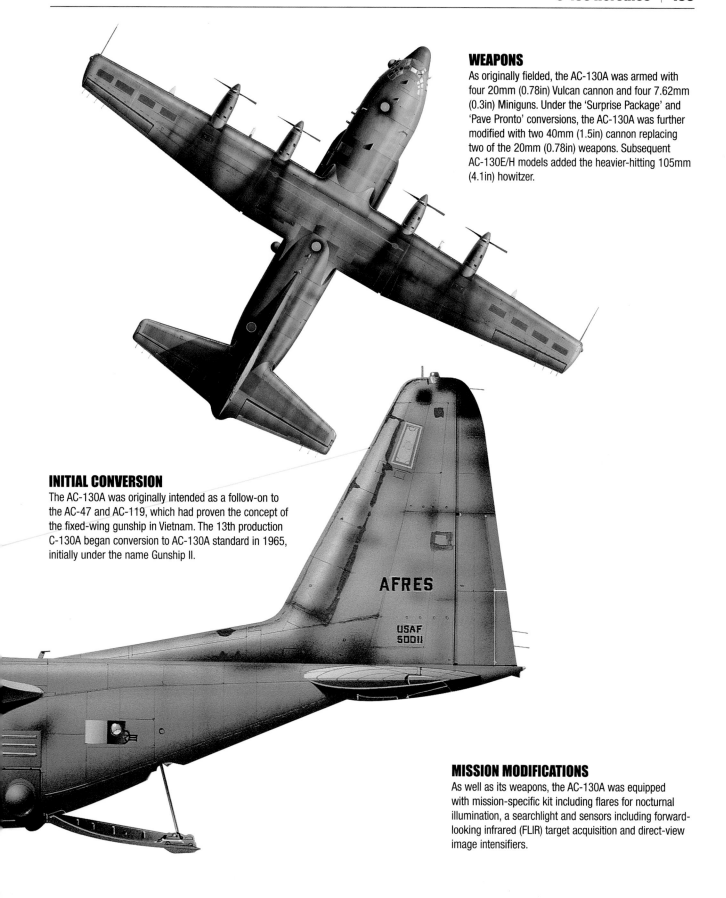

WEAPONS

As originally fielded, the AC-130A was armed with four 20mm (0.78in) Vulcan cannon and four 7.62mm (0.3in) Miniguns. Under the 'Surprise Package' and 'Pave Pronto' conversions, the AC-130A was further modified with two 40mm (1.5in) cannon replacing two of the 20mm (0.78in) weapons. Subsequent AC-130E/H models added the heavier-hitting 105mm (4.1in) howitzer.

INITIAL CONVERSION

The AC-130A was originally intended as a follow-on to the AC-47 and AC-119, which had proven the concept of the fixed-wing gunship in Vietnam. The 13th production C-130A began conversion to AC-130A standard in 1965, initially under the name Gunship II.

MISSION MODIFICATIONS

As well as its weapons, the AC-130A was equipped with mission-specific kit including flares for nocturnal illumination, a searchlight and sensors including forward-looking infrared (FLIR) target acquisition and direct-view image intensifiers.

A US Marine Corps KC-130 refuelling tanker in Somalia in support of Operation Restore Hope. The aircraft was from VMGR-352, normally based at Marine Corps Air Station El Toro, California. A US Marine Corps AH-1 Cobra attack helicopter overhead is preparing to land to refuel from the KC-130 on the ground.

The DC-130 designation covers drone control aircraft, the EC-130 covers electronic warfare aircraft, the HC-130 covers long-range search and rescue aircraft, the JC-130 covers temporary test aircraft, KC-130 covers inflight refuelling tankers, LC-130 covers aircraft with an Arctic capability, MC-130 covers special operations support aircraft, NC-130 covers permanent test aircraft, RC-130 covers reconnaissance aircraft, VC-130 covers staff and VIP transport aircraft, and WC-130 covers weather reconnaissance aircraft.

SUCCESSIVE IMPROVEMENTS

While the first two YC-130A prototypes were completed by Lockheed at its California 'Skunk Works', the subsequent aircraft were built at Marietta, starting with the C-130A model that began to be delivered to the USAF in December 1955. The initial production version was followed by the C-130B, which introduced improvements including four-bladed propellers and increased fuel capacity. In 1961, production switched to the improved C-130E. This was powered by T56-A-7 engines, each developing 3021kW (4050shp), and with maximum take-off weight increased to 79,379kg (175,000lb).

The definitive version of the first-generation Hercules was the C-130H, retaining T56 engines, but able to deliver a 19,686kg (43,400lb) payload over a range of 2298km (1428 miles). Although developed for the export market, the

MILITARY SURPLUS

As the USAF increasingly adds advanced C-130Js to its inventory, a number of first-generation C-130 transports have become available for transfer to US allies. Among these are the C-130Es transferred to the Iraqi Air Force. Iraq took delivery of three C-130Es, built between 1962 and 1963, but with relatively few flight hours accumulated.

C-130H began to be delivered to the USAF in April 1975. Major changes found in the C-130H include improved brakes and a strengthened wing centre-section. A specific derivative of the C-130H, the C-130K, was produced for the Royal Air Force, with British avionics and equipment. Two discrete C-130H/K models were made available: the basic H/K and the H-30/K-30, which featured a fuselage stretched by 4.57m (15ft) in order to increase the maximum capacity from 92 to 128 troops.

Beginning in the late 20th century, Lockheed Martin introduced the second-generation C-130J, which is known to the company as the Super Hercules. This is a much-

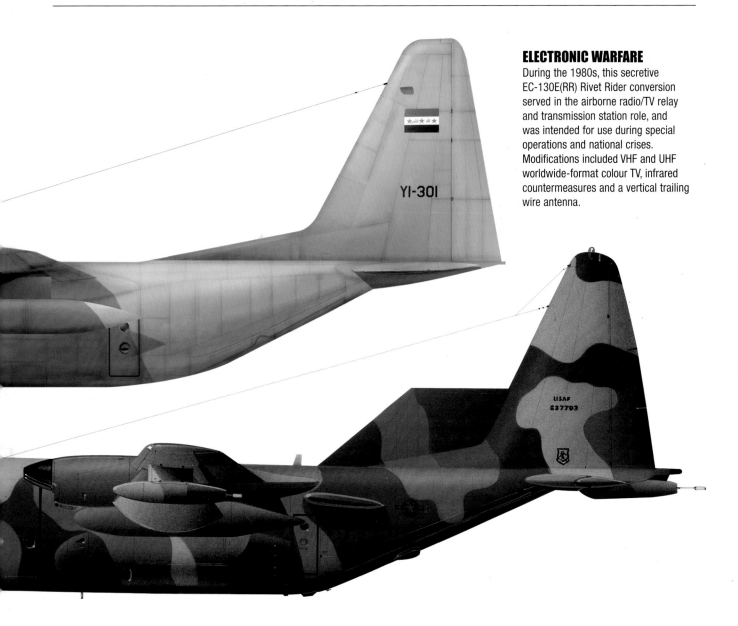

ELECTRONIC WARFARE
During the 1980s, this secretive EC-130E(RR) Rivet Rider conversion served in the airborne radio/TV relay and transmission station role, and was intended for use during special operations and national crises. Modifications included VHF and UHF worldwide-format colour TV, infrared countermeasures and a vertical trailing wire antenna.

improved development of the original aircraft, making full use of modern technology and avionics. The main difference is the powerplant, which now consists of four AE 2100 turboprops driving efficient Dowty propellers, each comprising six curved composite blades. Other major changes include a two-crew 'glass' cockpit with four flat-panel liquid-crystal displays. Like the previous model, the Super Hercules is available in standard-length and stretched C-130J-30 iterations.

The C-130J has proved to be as adaptable as the first-generation 'Hercs'. The current USAF inventory includes the basic C-130J/J-30 airlifter, as well as the AC-130J

gunship, or Ghostrider, which is armed with 30mm (1.1in) and 105mm (4.1in) cannon and precision-guided munitions to attack ground targets. The EC-130J Commando Solo is modified for Military Information Support Operations (MISO) and civil affairs broadcasts in FM radio, television and military communications bands. The MC-130J Commando II is the latest special operations version, used for missions including aerial refuelling of helicopters and tilt-rotor aircraft, infiltration, exfiltration and resupply of special forces by airdrop or airland. Finally, the WC-130J represents the current weather reconnaissance version, used for studying tropical storms, hurricanes and winter storms.

P-51 Mustang

The North American P-51 stakes its claim as the finest all-round single-seat fighter of World War II. With its superb balance of performance, agility and handling qualities, as well as an enviable combat record, it is perhaps the greatest fighter aircraft of all time.

The P-51 was originally designed in 1940 to meet a British requirement. This yielded the North American NA-73 design, a prototype of which was first flown in October 1940. In its initial form the fighter was powered by an Allison V-1710-F3F inline engine developing 820kW (1100hp). Two early aircraft were also trialled by the US Army Air Force as the XP-51, but no order was placed. Instead, the bulk of the initial production was delivered to the Royal Air Force, where the aircraft entered service as the Mustang Mk IA and Mk II. A total of 620 of these two models were supplied to the RAF. The early Mustangs were especially well suited to low-level operations, and possessed impressive range, which saw them assigned to the ground support (army cooperation) role.

The P-51 was finally adopted by the USAAF once the United States entered the war in December 1941. The initial order comprised 148 aircraft armed with four 20mm (0.78in) cannon and bomb shackles under the wing. In this configuration, the aircraft was designated A-36A and, once again, was intended for ground support work.

MERLIN POWER

In the UK, development of the Mustang continued, and the addition of the British Rolls-Royce Merlin engine would forever change the fortunes of the fighter. The first four aircraft so converted immediately impressed with their performance. In the meantime, however, the USAAF persevered with the Allison engine, and placed orders for 310 P-51As in 1942. The P-51A combined the 895kW (1200hp) Allison V-1710-81 engine with a reduced armament of four 12.7mm (0.5in) machine guns in the wings.

POWERPLANT

The P-51C model was powered by a Packard V-1650-7, a licence-built version of the Rolls-Royce Merlin 61. The P-51C featured a refined engine installation with a rectangular air inlet either side of the carburettor intake under the propeller.

ARMAMENT

The wing guns on the P-51B/C were restricted to four 12.7mm (0.5in) Browning MG53-2 machine guns. The inboard guns had 350 rounds, while the outboard guns had 280 rounds.

SPECIFICATIONS (P-51D)

Crew: 1

Length: 9.85m (32ft 3.75in)

Wingspan: 11.28m 37ft 0.25in ()

Empty weight: 3232kg (7125lb)

Powerplant: 1 × Packard Rolls-Royce Merlin V-1650-7

Maximum speed: 704km/h (437mph) at 7620m (25,000ft)

Armament: 6 x 12.7mm (0.5in) machine guns in the wings and provision for up to 2 x 454kg (1000lb) bombs or 6 x 127mm (5in) rocket projectiles

TUSKEGEE PILOT

'Ina the Macon Belle' was flown by Lee 'Buddy' Archer, the highest-scoring African-American pilot flying in a segregated Army Air Force. After training to fly at Tuskegee, Alabama, Archer was posted to the 332nd Fighter Group, part of the 15th Air Force in Italy. He was officially credited with four kills.

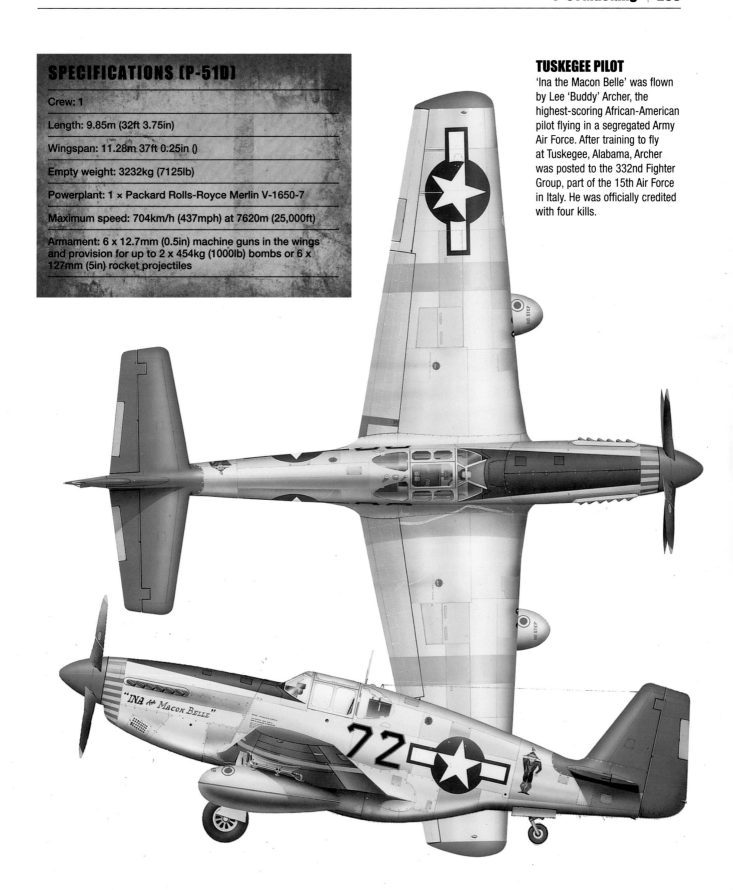

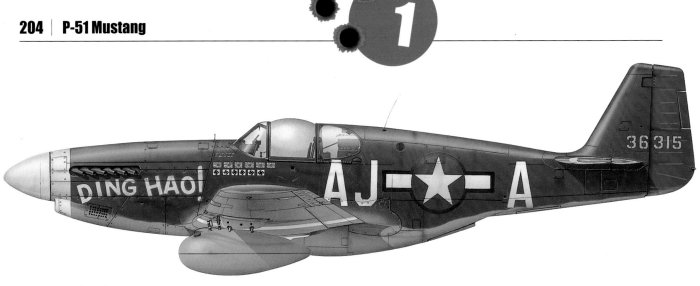

P-51B 'DING HAO!'

As a member of the American Volunteer Group in China, Major James Howard's Mustang featured both Japanese and German kill markings. This aircraft was the personal mount of Howard when he led the 356th Fighter Group, part of the US 9th Air Force.

F-6D 'LIL' MARGARET'

The F-6D was the reconnaissance version of the Mustang, modified by the addition of camera equipment in the rear fuselage. This example was flown by Captain Claude B. East, who served with the 15th Tactical Reconnaissance Squadron, 10th Photographic Group (Reconnaissance). East was the unit's leading ace, with 13 victories.

Such was the advantage offered by the Merlin engine that the powerplant began to be built by Packard in the US, to equip the P-51B model. Powered by a Packard-built Merlin V-1650, the P-51B was the first version to be built in significant quantities, with 1988 examples coming off the production line at Inglewood. Another 1750 of the similar P-51C were completed at Dallas, Texas. Later-production P-51B/Cs featured a revised armament of six guns and additional fuel capacity, allowing a range of 3347km (2080 miles) – sufficient to escort bombers flying missions from the UK to Berlin.

Further improvements were incorporated in the P-51D, distinguished by its cut-down rear fuselage and teardrop canopy for improved pilot vision. In RAF service, the P-51D was known as the Mustang Mk IV, which complemented the earlier Mustang Mk III (P-51B/C). While the P-51D had the endurance and the agility to accompany heavy bombers to Germany and then take on the Luftwaffe's best fighters, the P-51H offered another boost in performance. The H-model was the fastest wartime version, with a top speed of 784km/h (487mph) achieved through a reduction in airframe weight. A total of 555 were completed before the end of

Today the P-51 is an extremely popular performer on the warbird circuit and a frequent sight at airshows around the world. In the United States alone, more than 200 privately owned P-51s are on the FAA registry, most of them still flying. This example is P-51D 'Ferocious Frankie', a World War II veteran and star of Hollywood blockbusters that is operated by the Old Flying Machine Company in the United Kingdom.

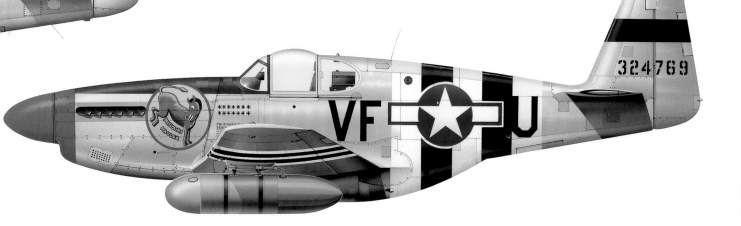

the war. Total production of the P-51 was 15,586, which included 7956 examples of the P-51D and 1337 of the similar P-51K, which featured an Aeroproducts propeller.

The Mustang remained in large-scale service after the war (known as the F-51 from June 1948), and also spawned the F-82 Twin Mustang, which allied two fuselages and power units on a common wing. The F-51 and F-82 saw service with the US Air Force and Royal Australian Air Force in Korea. Remarkably, the very last Mustangs in front-line service soldiered on with the air force of the Dominican Republic until 1984.

P-51B 'MISSOURI MAULER'

This aircraft was flown by Captain Willard 'Millie' Millikan, who accumulated 13 kills. Millikan's career followed an unusual path. After having initially been rejected by the US Army Air Corps he then had an unsuccessful period with the Royal Canadian Air Force, before becoming a successful ace with the US Army Air Force. He later led a jet fighter unit during the Korean War.

Index